TWINNIE'S TRUTH

PALMETTO
PUBLISHING
Charleston, SC
www.PalmettoPublishing.com

Copyright © 2024 Frank R Aliazzo, Esq.
All rights reserved First Edition

NEWMAN SPRINGS PUBLISHING
320 Broad Street Red Bank, NJ 07701

First originally published by Newman Springs Publishing 2024

Hardcover ISBN: 9798822958852
Paperback ISBN: 9798822958869
eBook ISBN: 9798822958876

TWINNIE'S TRUTH U.S. COPYRIGHT SERVICE NUMBER
1-2009875011 TWINNIE U.S. COPYRIGHT REGISTRATION NUMBER
TXu 2-349-208

Printed in the United States of America

TWINNIE'S TRUTH

A tough New York neighborhood
taught him lessons about life.

Then he became a lawyer.

Frank R. Aliazzo, Esq.

Dedicated to Ronnie and Bonnie

Contents

Introduction	i
Anthony Kiminski	1
Ralph Lucie	25
John Adams High School	69
George Guseman	84
The People of the State of New York versus Frank R Aliazzo, Esq.	133
Patrick Lucie	160
Bob Viccara	183
Frankie Cantone	236
Donald-Tommi-Stephen	296
A Week in the Life	351
About the Author	379

Introduction

I do not like introductions.
I like to get right into the book.
But after starting this one I realize they're necessary, so
I'll make it as short as possible.

My name is Frank R Aliazzo, but everyone calls me Bobby. I'm a lawyer. My twin brother is a criminal lawyer. My wife is a criminal lawyer. My older brother is a criminal and civil lawyer. My father-in-law is a Patent Lawyer. My brother-in-law is a civil trial lawyer. We are a family of lawyers and therefore Not Quite Right. This book is about people we have known. People who are friends, con men, relatives, homicide detectives, murderers, geniuses, small and big-time gangsters and ordinary people in anything but ordinary circumstances. We (Ron and I) grew up and started practicing law in Ozone Park, New York, home to many of the most infamous gangsters in the mid-1960's. Hard to believe that some of the most legendary movies were made about them (Goodfellas, Gotti.)

To me growing up they were just guys and kids in the neighborhood. The people you are about to read about are real, the stories are real, but circumstances, time lines, names, and locations on occasion have been changed to protect their identity, the attorney-client privilege and the continuation of my good my health. Conversations that happened decades ago were recreated from memory.

Anthony Kiminski

It's the day before Christmas Eve, 1971. It's quiet as it generally is this time of year. The courts are closed, and office parties are in full swing. I have no appointments and I'm trying to catch up on some cases when my secretary knocks and comes in.

"Bobby, there is an Anthony Kiminski here to see you. He was recommended by a former client whose divorce you handled. He has no appointment but looks distressed. Can you see him?"

I'm tired of doing paperwork and need a break, so I say, "Okay bring him in."

As he steps through the door, my first impression is that he looks very ordinary, like an everyman. He is wearing a gray coat, scarf, and gloves and looks to be in his late fifties. I point to a chair in front of my desk.

I introduce myself and ask how I could help him. He says he can't go home, and since tomorrow is Christmas Eve, he doesn't know what to do. His manner of speech appears to be slow but coherent.

I ask him where he lives, and he gives me his address, which is in Ozone Park, only a few blocks from my office. I tell him, "I'm sorry, but I don't handle landlord–tenant cases," assuming that's his problem.

He says, "No, that's not the problem." He explains his parents left him the house he lives in, but Henry is there now so he can't go home. I ask who Henry is. He tells me Henry is from Philadelphia and, he thinks, works for organized crime. He and his wife are very frightened of him as he has threatened them many times about consequences of telling anyone about him.

I ask, "What is Henry doing in your home?"

He says about three years ago, he and his wife decided to rent out an extra furnished bedroom they have in the house. They needed the money, and the room had its own bathroom and was on the first floor; all the other bedrooms were on the second floor. Henry found out about the room and called to ask if he could rent it for the weekend and, if he liked it, would rent it month to month, even though he would only be using it a couple of days a month, if that, since his home base was in Philadelphia.

They thought it was a great deal. He didn't recall how Henry found out about the room. Over time, Henry confided to them that he worked for wise guys in Philly, and most of what he had to do was in Queens County where their house was located (Belmont and Aqueduct race tracks were within fifteen minutes of the house), and they believed that he had something to do with placing large bets or paying off people for his Philadelphia bosses.

When he came to New York, he always had two bags. One had his clothes and stuff, and the other was a small leather duffel-type bag that he always kept locked and in the closet of his room, which he also kept locked. They surmised that the reason he rented the room, in addition to its location, was that it was safer to keep money in a private house when he went out than to leave it in a hotel room. He usually came to New York once a month and stayed for two or three days. At first, they were happy with the arrangement.

The problem was that over time, when he came to New York, he would get drunk and become violent and abusive to them. It went from being abusive to sexually assaulting his wife and later his sixteen-year-old daughter. He would get drunk and demand that Anthony sleep in the guest room because he was going to sleep with his wife, and sometimes, he would allow Anthony to sleep with his wife so he could sleep with his daughter.

They were all deathly afraid of him. He always had a gun on him; he carried a large amount of money, and when drunk, they felt he would shoot them in an instant if they didn't obey him. They were more than afraid of him, they were terrified.

They managed to get to this point because he wound up coming only four or five times a year, but strangely, always paid the rent in full, even for the months he was not there.

This was the first time Henry had appeared during the holidays and also the first time he threw Mr. Kiminski out of the house. He had nowhere to go.

I asked him why he had never called the police or asked his family or friends for help. He said that Henry told him that if he ever told anyone or called the police, he would kill them all and he believed him. He believed he was capable of doing it.

I'm sitting there with my mouth wide open, not believing what I was hearing. My first hunch that he was somehow impaired was proving to be correct. I'm thinking, *only someone mentally impaired would allow this to happen.* My mind is now racing. *How can I help this guy?* I had been in practice for several years and had done many divorces and had seen a lot, but never anything like this. This was a *Ripley's Believe It or Not.* What to do, what to do? Law school never prepared me for anything like this.

The courts were closed for the holidays, although I probably couldn't use them anyway and my client wouldn't permit me to go to the police. Then the solution hit me. If you walked out of the front door of my building and made a left turn and walked four blocks, you were at the Bergin Hunt and Fish club (John Gotti's club), and if you left my office and made a right and walked several blocks, you would be standing in front of the pizza place made famous by the movie *Goodfellas*.

I knew some of the guys who were members of both establishments and had represented or given legal advice to them over the years. The advice was always given to them on the QT as they never wanted anyone to know their business. My thought was to get in touch with one or two of them and have them pay Henry a visit.

Even if Henry was a Philadelphia-connected guy, they would be just as repulsed as I was with what he was doing and ask him to back off. It was a mob unwritten rule that you didn't mess with someone's family.

Whenever I had helped them out in the past, their parting words were always, "Bobby or Counselor (or Twinnie for those who knew Ronnie and me when we were really young and couldn't tell us apart), I owe you one. If you ever need anything and I can help, let me know."

Well, I thought now is the time, and I would even sweeten the pie with a couple of hundred apiece. Then I started thinking, *what happens if they go there, and Henry gives them a hard time or is disrespectful and things get out of hand?* These guys were capable of anything. As much as I despised Henry, I didn't want to be responsible for someone being killed.

Come to think of it, maybe this was not such a good idea. What to do, what to do?

Then a light bulb went off in my head. I got it. I tell him that I may be able to help him then buzzed my secretary and had her take Mr. Kaminski into the reception room while I made some calls.

I picked up the phone and called the District Attorney's office in Queens County. I ask the person who answered the phone to connect me to the Homicide Bureau.

Peggy answers the phone. I said, "Hi, Peg, it's Bobby. Is Ronnie around?" Peggy is Ronnie's secretary; Ronnie is my twin brother. He is an Assistant District Attorney who was presently trying a murder case that was in all the papers. It was not your normal case like two guys get into a fight in a bar and one kills the other in front of witnesses. These kinds of murder cases were frequent in South Jamaica, Queens County, a very tough neighborhood and were called "Jamaica Specials" by the District Attorney's office because they were easy to get convictions if the defendant refused to take a plea.,

The case Ronnie was trying involved a man killing his wife after taking out a $300,000 life insurance policy with a double indemnity clause which means he gets double that amount, $600,000, if she dies from anything other than natural causes. An accident or murder is not a natural cause, kicking in the double indemnity clause.

I knew the trial was put over until after the Christmas holidays and figured Ron would be in his office with the two detectives who caught the case. The way it generally works in murder cases is that the detective or detectives on duty, when the case is called in, "catches" the case, meaning it's his or hers or their case. When the case was called into 911, Tommy O' Connor and his partner, Joe Rizzi (the very two guys I was looking for), were on duty, caught the case and arrested the suspect after several months' investigation.

They then put all of the evidence together and submitted it to the District Attorney's Office where it was assigned to a specific ADA (Assistant District Attorney) who would put the case in proper order to present to the grand jury for an indictment. In this case, the indictment would be for murder in the first degree. Generally, the best trial lawyers in the DA's office try the murder cases. There were over a hundred ADAs, and the four or five best tried the murder cases.

Even though only the best were assigned murder cases, the detectives were anxious about who caught their case. Ronnie was a favorite among the detectives because he had only lost one case after he first started with the DA's office, and the detectives knew it.

The only case he lost was the first case he tried. It was a drunk driving case which was not a felony but a misdemeanor. In New York State, there are two classes of misdemeanors: a (B) misdemeanor (punishable by up to three months in jail and/or a fine, and an (A) misdemeanor (punishable by up to a year in jail and/or fine). The problem with the case was that the defendant was a city bus driver and would lose his job if he were found guilty. He hired a very young talented lawyer who was a little older than Ronnie and had already tried several felony cases as a defense lawyer and won them all.

Prior to becoming a defense lawyer, he had been an Assistant District Attorney in Manhattan and had won nearly all his cases there. Normally, he would not take a drunk driving case as it was beneath him. He only handled felony cases; however, because the defendant could lose his job, he took the case after receiving a substantial fee. His name was Danny O' Dwyer. He was a handsome, blond, blue-eyed Irishman who could charm the devil himself. He had a way about him that made you like him right away and knew all the jurors would be rooting for him, so you had better have a strong case.

I had a case that day in Queens Supreme Court and was meeting Ronnie for lunch. I finished early and went to where Ronnie would be trying his case to wait for him. It was about twelve so I took a seat in the back and watched, until the court adjourned for lunch at one.

Danny got up and started to address the jury. He introduced himself and his client as he calmly walked toward the jury box. He looked at the jurors who were already gazing at him admiringly and asked if any one of them had ever gotten into a car after having dinner and a couple of glasses of wine, even though they knew they probably shouldn't be driving home but did anyway.

He asked anyone who has ever done that to raise their hand. Silence in the courtroom. No one raises their hand. I'm thinking he screwed up this time. Then one hand goes up. Whose hand is it?

It's Danny's hand. There is a little laughter in the courtroom, and then suddenly, one of the juror's hands goes up, and then another juror's hand goes up, and before you know it, five of the six jurors' hands are in the air.

Ronnie jumps up and says he wants a new jury as five of the six jurors have admitted driving slightly intoxicated or drunk. Danny jumps up, and a yelling and shouting match starts with the judge banging his gavel for order. He dismisses the jury for lunch, telling them to be back at two. Ronnie and Danny are heading back to the judge's chambers.

I don't know how long they'll be, so I tell one of the court officers, who I know, to tell Ronnie I left and I'll speak to him tonight. Around seven-thirty that night, Ronnie calls. I ask him what happened. He said the judge refused to dismiss the jury, and after lunch, Ronnie put on his case which went very quickly.

To make a long story short, the jury was out for forty-five minutes and came back with a not-guilty verdict. This was the only case Ronnie ever lost. After that case, realizing what a special talent Danny was, I used him whenever I was lucky enough to get him. He and Ronnie became and remained close friends, although Danny never let Ronnie forget that the only case he ever lost was to him.

Getting back to Ronnie and the murder case at hand, most detectives wanted him to try their cases because, in addition to his winning record, he was a tireless worker, obsessive about getting everything right, great with a jury because he had a kind, easy way about him and a sense of fairness that became palatable in the courtroom. He would always tell the detectives that he was there to prosecute the defendants, not persecute them. In their way, even though they always wanted a conviction, they respected his sense of fairness.

He was an Ozone Park street guy who had common sense, unlike some of the other ADAs who they viewed as stiffs, with no sense of humor and no sense of the streets or criminals.

At the time, Ronnie was single and had a penthouse apartment (that I subsidized on occasion when he would inform me that while not broke, he was temporarily short of funds). He was six feet tall, in good shape, with dark hair that he gave a hundred strokes to each morning, good-looking (I know what you're thinking; since I am his twin brother…what can I tell you?), and had a never-ending string of beautiful girls visiting his penthouse. Of course, all of the detectives (most of whom were married and had children) who worked for him idolized him and lived vicariously through him, haunting him for details about his girlfriends.

He would tell them about how he met them, their backgrounds and so on, but never personal stuff, which drove them nuts. He had one beautiful blonde Scandinavian airline stewardess who was a guest at his penthouse apartment for the weekend. She had come to the office, and from there, they were going for dinner, so all of the detectives met her. Of course, when he came to work on Monday morning, they were all waiting to see if he would talk about her. When asked, he said he would not be seeing her again. Why? He said she truly was a sexual Disneyland, and he could not deal with her. Of course, they went nuts, wanting to know all the details; but he would say nothing further.

Peggy tells me Ronnie went to my mother's for lunch, with Tommy O' Conner and Joe Rizzi. She said they left ten minutes ago. Then I remembered that my mother called me earlier this morning and left a message with one of my secretaries to call her back. It must have been because she made lasagna and knew it was one of my favorites. I called her and told her I was on my way and to tell Ronnie and the guys not to start without me.

My mother's house is a brick two-family right down the street from the Forest Hills, West Side Tennis Club. My office in Ozone Park was a five-minute drive away. When I got there, Tommy O' Conner answered the door. He had a small white towel covering the front of his shirt with a couple of drops of red sauce on it. Before I could say anything, he said they couldn't wait.

The smell from inside the house was heavenly. I walked in through the living room and into the dining room where they were at the dining room table and had already begun eating. They had big napkins hanging in front of their shirts to protect them from sauce stains since they all had to go back to work. My mother had made lasagna, meatballs, and a salad. I heard her in the kitchen and called out, "Nancy, I'm here!" and went in to hug her.

She said, "Nice, you call your mother Nancy."

I said, "Ma, that's your name." I was just plain crazy about that lady. She loved to cook, and seeing her sons and their friends enjoying her food made her happy.

I went back into the dining room to start eating. I looked up at Tommy and Joe who were in a state of bliss, eating my mother's food, and said, "Would you guys take a break for a minute? I may need your help."

They stop eating for a second and look up. "What's up, Counselor?"

They normally call me Bobby, but when there was something criminal or legal involved, they call me Counselor. I said, "Sit back and take a five-minute break. I want to tell you about a client I just left and need your help with."

I tell them the story, and Ronnie says that it sounds like *Ripley's Believe It or Not*. I told them I had the same reaction when I heard it. Tommy says, "That's why you're twins. You think the same."

I told them I was contemplating calling in a couple of guys from the neighborhood but finally thought better of it. Joe says, "Good thing, you know most of those guys are nuts and could really hurt the guy or worse. And you don't need those kinds of problems."

I tell them my client is afraid to call the cops. "I don't think it would work anyway. If they came, Henry could say he has been living there for three years and they want to evict him and that none of what they say is true; in all probability, the cops would say this is a landlord–tenant matter. That's why I need you guys.

"Here's what I would like you to do. Go over there at about five this afternoon. He's almost always there at that time. I'm going back to my office where my client is waiting and will have him call his wife and daughter and have them come to my office so they will not be there when you show up. They will stay at my office until I hear from you. I will explain to them that you are not regular cops but detectives who will make sure Henry never comes to their house again."

"I want you to go over with a felony weight bag of white powder which I know you always have on hand. After explaining who you are and why you're there, show him the bag of white powder and tell him if he ever comes back, you will plant the powder on him, and since it's felony weight, he is going to do felony time. If he gives you a hard time, do what you have to do, but don't fuck him up too badly."

Tommy and Joe say, "You want us to threaten to plant him with drugs?"

As it happens, they were both famous in Ozone Park for doing just that, and as a result a lot of street drug dealers stayed out of Ozone Park. The felony weight bag of white powder they carried was actually baking soda put in a blender to make it look exactly like cocaine or heroin. They had tried talcum powder but figured someone might smell it and realize it was only talcum powder. Baking soda had hardly any smell.

Ronnie looks at me and says, "I can't believe you're asking them to do this shit in front of me."

I say, "Excuse me, Mr. Assistant District Attorney, when did you become the Virgin Mary? This guy is a lowlife scumbag, and I want to try to help these people. What do you suggest?"

As he's thinking, Joe says, "Bobby were working for him, so we can only do it if the boss says it okay." The boss was Ronnie, who they always referred to as the boss.

Ronnie looks at both of them and says, "Okay, but don't fuck this up, and don't hurt the guy." And then he pauses and says, "Too badly."

I tell them, "Now listen, if this goes well, there's a new hat in it for both of you."

Tommy was excited. "A new hat? What kind of a hat." I say, "Maybe a nice baseball hat."

Tommy replied, "I was hoping more like a fedora or Stetson." Ronnie looks at him. "See, right away you have to be greedy."

Tommy said, "You know we would do it for nothing for you or Bobby." Ronnie looks at them with affection. "Yeah, I know."

Tommy said, "Can we finish now before it gets cold?" Ronnie replied, "Didn't you guys eat enough?"

I tell Ron to leave them alone. They love Mom's food. He says that's the problem. She encourages them to eat more and more, and then they go back to the office and are so full they fall asleep at their desks.

Tommy looks at me. "See, Bobby, he's always picking on us."

I tell them to be at my office at four-thirty, and I'll give them the address of my client's house, and if they need any information from my clients, they can speak to them. Now they get serious. They don't want to meet the clients. If it goes well, they will never see Henry and that's all they need to know. "If he ever shows up again, they will call you, and you will get in touch with us, and this time we will plant the real thing." I feel better and can finally eat and better hurry before there's no more food left. You know, there's an old Polish saying. "You guys eat like two blind horses."

*****

Back at the office, I call Mr. Kiminski. I tell him I think I may be able to help him but I can't tell him how, and he has to trust me on that. After tonight, he will never see Henry again. First, he has to bring his wife and daughter here as I need to speak to them. I want to make sure what he is telling me is true. Second, I tell him my fee for doing this will be five hundred dollars. I, and the boys would do it for nothing. Of course, he doesn't know this, but if he does have the money, then Tommy and Joe are going to have a very Merry Christmas. That amount of money would buy five fedoras each. I want nothing. I consider this my attempt at pro bono work for Christmas, and I just feel too bad for the guy and his family.

He tells me he has the money and will go to the bank to get it and then get his wife and daughter and bring them back here. I ask for Henry's full name and address as the boys will want to look him up to see if he's got a criminal record. He tells me he doesn't know his last name or address but does have a phone number where he can leave messages. He thinks it's some kind of store. He asks for Henry. Sometimes he's there, and if not, he leaves a message for Henry and he calls back. They only called that number five or six times in three years and only when he is supposed to come and hasn't shown up. They found out the number is a Philadelphia area code. I ask him to describe Henry. He says he is about six feet tall and has dark hair. He guesses he is about thirty-five. It's now two-thirty and I tell him to be back at four.

As he leaves, Ronnie is on the phone. He asks me for Henry's name and address so his investigators at the DA's office will look him up before the boys go talk to him. I told him what my client told me. He's not happy not knowing more about Henry. I tell him that as soon as the boys get that info from him, they will call and let him know.

It's a little after four when Roe, my secretary, buzzes me that Mr. Kiminski is here with two women. I tell her to put them into the conference room and I'll be right there. Upon entering the conference room, Mr. Kiminski rises up to greet me. He introduces me to his wife, a very attractive blonde whom I would guess was in her mid-forties, and his daughter, also blonde and very attractive. They look normal. You would never guess the horror they were going through.

Mrs. Kiminski looks at me and then turns to Mr. Kiminski and starts speaking angrily to him in Polish. He responds in kind, also angrily, and they start to argue.

The daughter is looking at them, somewhat embarrassed, but says nothing. As they are arguing, I look over at the daughter and ask if she knows what's going on. She says yes and then in a loud voice speaks to them in Polish. They stop arguing and turn to me. Mr. Kiminski, looking embarrassed, cannot find the words to tell me what the problem is. I tell him I can't help them if I don't know what the problem is.

Finally, he starts to speak. It seems his wife is uncomfortable with me representing them because I look so young. At the time, I was thirty-one but looked several years younger. It had been a problem when I first started practicing.

I found that I lost several clients who were recommended to me when I first started, for the same reason. They came for a consultation and never came back. I asked one of my closest friends, Warren Capelan, who is a doctor and who recommended his cousin to me for a divorce, why she never returned. I met her, did not charge a consultation fee because she was Warren's cousin and spent time with her explaining the law. Her divorce would be simple because there were no children, and since they were not asking each other for anything and, would be uncontested. It went very well, I thought, and then I never heard from her again.

I called Warren and asked him why she didn't retain me. The fee I was charging her was less than I usually charged because she was Warren's cousin. He thought she had retained me. When he got back to me, he said that although she liked me, she thought

I looked too young, and because I was young and nice looking, her husband would think maybe we were having an affair. I told Warren, "That's ridiculous. Why would it matter anyway? They are getting a mutually agreed upon divorce."

He said, "Beats me."

At that time, the dress code was casual, slacks and a shirt or sweater. My secretaries also dressed casually in jeans and a blouse or sweater.

Having lost several clients from looking young, I changed the dress code. All attorneys in the office agreed to wear suits, shirts, and ties, including me, and all secretaries had to wear dresses or skirts and blouses or sweaters and heels to make everyone look older. It worked. I stopped losing clients.

I explained to Mrs. Kiminski that I was duly licensed to practice law in New York and had handled many matrimonial matters, although I did have to admit I had never handled a matter like this. Mr. Kiminski interrupted while we were chatting and said something to her in Polish. She turned and gave me a long look and then said in English, "Yes, yes, okay. We do whatever you tell us."

She then turned and started again speaking Polish to Mr. Kiminski.

I looked around and asked the daughter why the sudden change. She tells me her father forgot to tell her that I was the brother of the Assistant District Attorney who was in the papers all the time with a murder case. I guess in Poland, it's who you know. Come to think of it, it kind of applied here too. It's because of my brother and the detectives who worked for him, and he allowed them to help the Kiminski's that we were able to proceed. Yes, sometimes it comes down to who you know.

Now we sit down to discuss what Mr. Kiminski had told me. I ask her if she wants her daughter to leave the room. She says no, she was and is a part of this nightmare. The facts as told to me by Mrs.

Kiminski are basically the same as told to me by Mr. Kiminski. This is an attractive, tough, Polish lady who as she relays the story to me occasionally lapses into Polish and cries. She said they got used to the money since he paid them every month, even for the months he didn't come.

He didn't send them money every month, but when he came, he paid them for the months he wasn't there as well as for the months he used the room. It only started getting bad when he began drinking and talking about being connected and "taking care of people when he had to."

The sex started after a year and then not all the time he came. It happened when he was really drunk, and that's when he was the most violent and dangerous. Most of the time, he was so drunk he couldn't perform, but it was always horrible and humiliating and terrifying.

At first, the husband didn't know. She submitted because he was holding a gun and he threatened to kill her, then her daughter, and then himself. Her husband found out about it when in one of his drunken rages, he told him about it and threatened to harm him, his family and then himself, if he, the husband tried to interfere.

He said, "I believed him at that moment. I didn't know what to do, but I knew I could not risk my wife and child's life as well as my own. This man was in a depressed, drunken rage, and I felt he was capable of doing exactly what he said."

Mrs. Kiminski starts to cry and tries to explain the terror they felt. I ask about her daughter, and she starts to cry again. Her daughter comes over to comfort her. Mrs. Kiminski says she didn't know what was going on until he had sex with her when she happened to come home early, and there was no one home; he showed up unexpectedly and drunk. He would get up the next day and act like nothing happened. They were not even sure he remembered what he had done the night before.

Their daughter was frightened to tell them he was having sex with her, too. When they finally found out, it was too late. He had complete control over them. Mrs. Kiminski looked up at me and between tears asked, "Can you really help us?"

I wanted to tell her, "Yes, I can if I have to go over there and shoot the son of a bitch myself."

I told her I was sure I could. She looked at me again with a fierce intensity and said, "I think if you fail, he will come back and kill us."

At that moment, I got really frightened and thought, *what have I gotten myself into? I may be putting these people's lives at risk. Maybe I should back off.* But I knew in my heart that was really not an option.

I asked Mr. Kiminski to come into my office. I explained to him that although I was pretty sure I could permanently get rid of Henry, there was always a risk. He said he could no longer go on like this and that anything was better than living like this. I told him I wanted him to get new locks for his home and install them this evening. He said he was handy and could do that.

I told him that if Henry came back, he should not answer the door and call me immediately. I gave him my home number as he already had my office number. If he could not get me, I told him to call the numbers I would give him later, that would be Tommy and Joe's office number, assuming they would agree. If he could not get any of us, he should call 911 and tell them that someone was breaking into his house.

Under no circumstances was he to tell them anything more. As far as he was concerned, this was someone he didn't know trying to break into his house. The last couple of times Henry showed up at the house, he had been drunk, and if he did show up again, there was a possibility they would arrest him.

I asked him for the keys to his house. There was one to the front door and a different key for the side. He gave me the key to the front door and explained the layout. Upon opening the front door, there was a small foyer with a closet on the left. Walking out of the foyer, there was a stairway on the left that led to the bedrooms upstairs. The living room was to the right. Straight ahead was the kitchen, and to the right was the dining room. Behind the dining room was Henry's room which had been a shed that was enlarged and turned into a spare bedroom with its own bathroom. I asked if there was anything else I should know. He couldn't think of anything else.

I told him to take his daughter and wife with him, go get a lock, and then go out for dinner and be back at my office by six this evening. If they got back earlier, the door would be open, and one of my secretaries would be here. We would know by that time whether Henry was gone or not. He did not ask me how I intended to get rid of Henry. I think he was afraid to know.

Tommy and Joe showed up right after Mr. Kaminski left around four thirty. We all went into the lunchroom for some coffee and got down to business. I explained the layout of the house and everything Mr. Kaminski had told me. I asked them to be careful and not fuck this guy up too badly, just enough to get rid of him. As far as we knew, he was at the house now. They said, "Okay, Counselor, we're on our way."

I gave them the key to the front door. I told them I would be at the office until they came back. As they left, they had one last question. They were trying to decide where they were going for dinner after they finished with Henry. They wanted to know, should they plan on going to White Castle for hamburgers or to Peter Luger's Steakhouse?

I said, "Definitely Peter Luger's."

They start rubbing their hands together, saying, "Boy, Oh boy, oh boy."

*****

At five-forty-five, Roe buzzes me. They're back. They came in smiling. I look at them, and simply say "Well?"

Tommy says, "Like peeing off a pier, like peeing off a pier."

"Tell me what happened from the moment you walked in."

"We opened the front door quietly and saw him in the kitchen. We both had our shields hanging around our necks as we wanted him to know immediately that we were cops. He was having a beer and watching TV with his back to us, so he didn't hear us until we were almost on top of him."

"Tommy screamed, 'Police officers, don't move or we'll blow your head off!'

"Joe walked in front of him with his gun drawn, I grabbed him by the shoulders and stood him up, cuffed his hands, and sat him back down. He started to say something. We told him to shut the fuck up and only speak when spoken to. We asked him if he had a gun. He said yes, in his bedroom. Joe went to his room, searched it, and found the gun. He also saw the leather satchel was unlocked and empty.

"He found his wallet and took it back to the kitchen. Mr. Henry Esposito from Philadelphia, PA. I asked Tommy to make a call to see what kind of rap sheet he had, if any. Tommy calls the DA's office and speaks to Peggy, Ronnie's secretary; he gives her Henry's full name and address and tells her to contact Philadelphia and find out if Henry has a rap sheet. He gave her the phone number of the house and told her we were with the suspect and would wait for an answer. She said to give her ten minutes.

"Henry is listening to everything said and starts to look frightened. Finally, we both sit down and start to talk to him. We ask him if he knows why we're here. He says he has no idea. We tell him everything, we tell him the truth. For the first time, his frightened look is replaced with self-righteous indignation. He starts to raise his voice and stand up. 'Those motherfuckers,' and in a rage, he starts to tell us what he is going to do to them when he gets his hands on them.

"Tommy loses it and smacks him so hard he goes flying against the stove and falls down. By this time, he has me in a rage. The arrogance of this piece of shit. I kick him a couple of times when he's down, and Tommy had to pull me away. We lift him up and sit him in the chair, and Tommy says to me, 'Add resisting arrest to all the charges.' Now he looks frightened again."

"Joe tells him he is the most despicable human being he has ever met. We tell him he is going to jail for a long time for rape and for statutory rape. He doesn't know that the Kaminski's are too frightened and too embarrassed to ever press charges. We had two other cards to play, and now was the time to play them.

"Tommy goes into his pocket and takes out a plastic bag, the kind with the Ziploc top, with white powder inside. 'It's almost a pound. It's what is called felony weight, meaning if you get caught with that much heroin, the charges will be a felony which carries much more time in jail than a misdemeanor, which only carries up to a year.'

"Of course, if one has a criminal record, which we were waiting to find out, the amount of time could be substantially more. Joe looks at him and asks if he knows what's in the bag. Henry says no. Joe tosses him the bag and says, 'Take a look.'

"Henry, whose hands are cuffed in front, picks up the bag and starts to unzip it but is having difficulty because his hands are cuffed. Joe says, 'Let me help you' and takes the bag from Henry and puts it into another bag that is bigger. He then takes out a magic marker and starts to write something on it.

"Henry asks, 'What's going on?'

"Tommy tells him his fingerprints are all over the bag with the white powder which they found in his bag in his bedroom. The bag contains heroin which feels like it is more than a pound which is felony weight and that Henry is going away for a very long time.

"Henry is outraged and starts to stand up. Joe pushes him back down so forcefully he goes flying off the chair. They both pick him up and slam him back into the chair. Tommy now tells him to listen carefully. 'You are going to pack your bags and you are going to leave this house and New York and you are never going to return. You are never to contact the Kaminski's again. If you try to, the Kaminski's have been instructed to let us know immediately, and we will arrest you, plant this bag which has your fingerprints on it, and away you go for a very long time. Do you fucking understand?'

"Henry starts to protest. Joe says, 'Okay, let's go' and starts to lift Henry from the chair, telling Tommy to plant the bag in Henry's overcoat pocket and, 'Let's take this piece of shit in.'

"Joe starts to read Henry his Miranda rights. 'You have a right to remain silent, anything you say—'

"Just as this is happening, Peggy calls. Joe picks up the phone and puts his fingers to his lips to indicate silence. Peggy asks if he has a pen and a lot of paper because this guy has a rap sheet three pages long, almost all of it for petty crimes. Mostly, he's been busted for being a numbers runner for the Philadelphia boys, also for petty theft and grand theft auto. He has served a total of two and a half years in jail.

"Joe tells Prggy to hold on to the rap sheet and that he will pick it up later. He asks her to tell Ronnie we will be calling him shortly. Joe sits Henry back down and starts to talk to him again. 'That was the DA's office reading your rap sheet. You have been a pretty busy boy. With a rap sheet three pages long, you're going away for a long, long, time.

"'The boys in Philadelphia are going to be hearing about how you were terrorizing this family. They're not going to like it. You know the rules. When you finally get out, I'm sure they will be waiting for you. If not a bullet in the head, you will never work for them again.

"'You're lucky because we are going to give you a choice. Leave New York forever, never come back, and never, ever contact the Kaminski's or off to jail you go right now for a very long time.'

"Henry looks surprised and thankful that he has a choice and wants to go home. Tommy says, 'Smart choice.' Henry asks if he can get his stuff, and Tommy goes with him to grab it.

"As they are about to walk out, Joe asks for Henry's wallet which contains several hundred dollars. Joe takes out the money and puts back one hundred. 'For you to get home.' He takes the rest of the money and wraps it in a napkin and puts it on the table and looks at Henry and tells him, 'You can never repay them for what you did to them, but at least they will have a better Christmas.'

"Henry says nothing. He looks at them and asks if he can ask a question. He wants to know where we came from. We tell him that Mr. Kaminski has a friend who has a friend who is very high up in the DA's office and who has taken a special interest in Henry. We tell him once again, if we hear that he is in New York, there will be no talking to him. It's off to jail. He says he understands. We take the keys to the house away from him. We then walked him to his car with the cuffs on. No one is around. We remove the cuffs.

Tommy has one last thing to say to him. He tells him he has been on the job for over eighteen years and has seen all kinds of horrible things and people but tells him he is the most despicable, disgusting excuse for a human being he has ever seen and to get out of his sight before he changes his mind. Henry quickly goes around to the driver's side door, throws his bags in, and drives away.

"Tommy looks at Joe. 'What do you think?'

"He's a lowlife and a coward, and I don't think he has the balls to ever come back.' My assessment of him is that he is just some low-end runner for the Philly guys. If they knew what he was doing to the Kaminski's, he would never work for them again if he survived the beating he would get."

I tell them I love them for doing this for me and Ron and mostly for the Kaminski's. I get up and tell them I'll be right back. I go out and ask Roe where the Kaminski's are and she says they are in the lunchroom, having coffee. I go in and tell them that Henry is gone and that they can go home and that we think he will never come back. If they ever hear from him, even so much as a phone call, they are to call me.

Mrs. Kaminsky starts to cry, and she comes over and hugs me. I start to get emotional myself. I wish them a nice Christmas and tell them, "By the way, Henry left you a little going away present."

They look at me but don't understand. I tell them it's his way of saying he's sorry. Mr. Kaminski hands me an envelope with the five hundred in cash in it. I thank him. They hesitate as if they are afraid to leave. I tell them, "It's okay, Henry is really gone forever."

They thank me over and over again as they leave.

I go back to my office where Joe and Tommy are waiting. I open the envelope and give them two hundred and fifty each in cash. They look at the money and then at me. A really nice hat is maybe fifty bucks. They were not expecting this much. In today's dollars, that amount would be fifteen hundred dollars each.

Tommy jumps up and looks at Joe and says the, "Son of a bitch, we're rich!"

They both come over and give me big hugs. We settle back a little bit and chat about the whole thing. Their disgust for Henry is palpable. Tommy talks about dropping a dime with the Philadelphia boys. I look at him. "Tommy, don't start that."

"I wish I could have at least beaten the shit out of him."

I tell him, "I understand how you feel, but we just really did a good thing today and helped this poor family."

They ask me what would have happened to them if they went to a regular, legit lawyer. I say, "Gee, thanks."

They say, "You know what we mean."

I tell them since they would not call the cops, starting an action in court to remove him would in effect be calling the cops. A successful action would have involved a court order to remove him, and thus the police would have been involved, which is exactly what they wanted to avoid. It would have also taken a lot of time. Since the courts were closed until after the holiday, it would be weeks before we could get before a judge and cost a hell of a lot more than five hundred dollars.

They ask me, "By the way, how much did he actually pay?"

I tell them the truth, five hundred. They're upset because I didn't get paid and offer to split the five hundred three ways. I tell them, "No thanks. This is my pro bono good deed for the month and maybe for the following year, and I'm doing really good this year, so don't worry about me."

Tommy asks, "If we didn't help them, what would have happened to them?"

"I probably would have advised them to sell the house and move away and leave no forwarding address, and I could not have helped them this Christmas."

"Well," they say, "we did a really good thing."

I tell them I know that and thank them once again.

As we are walking out, a thought occurs to me. I tell them, "You know, of all the domestic relations cases and divorces I have ever done, this one is the most satisfying. What would have taken months in the legal system we accomplished in an hour or so. The sad part is that lowlife gets to walk away without paying for what he did. But I think it was more important to help these people than to punish him. Besides, what goes around comes around, and sooner or later, he will wind up dead or in jail. People like him always do. He is a typical criminal, thinks he's smarter than everyone else, will never get caught again, and that people who follow the rules are schmucks. Glad we did what we did."

As they are walking out, I wish them a Merry Christmas and tell them I will call Ronnie and tell him what went down. As they are leaving, they tell me, "If you ever need us again for anything like this, we will be there in a heartbeat."

Little did I know that after getting $500, they would call me once a month to ask if I needed them for anything. I would tell them no. This was a one-time thing. Boy, how I loved those guys.

I called Ronnie and told him it went well and that I would stop by on my way home since I didn't want to discuss it over the phone.

For the next twenty years or so, Mr. Kaminsky would stop by every Christmas with a bottle of twelve-year-old Scotch. They never heard from Henry again; they never even knew his last name.

Ralph Lucie

I'm trying to remember how this whole nightmare with Ralph started. I recall I was just finishing an arbitration in my office when my secretary popped her head in the door and asked if she could see me for a moment, it was urgent. I excused myself and went into the hallway, pissed off because the rule was never to come into my office while I was in arbitration, unless there was a crisis.

I was a member of the American Arbitration Association (AAA) and active as an arbitrator, who heard cases for the AAA. The courts were so backlogged at the time that many companies had clauses in their contracts that any disputes that arose out of said employment were to be settled by binding arbitration. It was much cheaper and quicker than going through civil litigation, which could take months and sometimes years. We heard all types of civil litigation. Any matter could be settled by binding arbitration as long as both parties agreed.

At arbitration, the parties involved could be represented by counsel or could represent themselves. In all the cases I presided over, the parties were always represented by counsel.

I did not set out to become an arbitrator but was roped into it by some of my fellow lawyers who I appeared before as a plaintiff's attorney. They wanted me to return the favor by becoming an arbitrator so they could appear before me. There was nothing improper about it. All of us just wanted to appear before someone who knew the law and would be fair, which was not always the case, at least in our opinions.

I learned a lot about lawyers being an arbitrator. There were some greats who appeared before me, always prepared. The ones who pissed me off the most were the ones who showed up totally unprepared. It was a very small percentage but they stand out in my mind. If, after starting, they were smart enough to realize they were not prepared and could not bluff their way through it, they would ask for an adjournment, which I was inclined to grant, even though it would inconvenience the other side. I would rather have that, than a plaintiff or a defendant screwed because of the unpreparedness of their attorney.

I wasn't doing it for the money and it was extremely time consuming. I thought, *how can I get out of this gracefully?* I figured out the answer. Instead of giving long decisions, which most arbitrators did (as witnessed by some of the arbitration decisions I received on my cases), I decided to give one-sentence decisions which I thought would piss off the AAA so they would not send me more cases.

The first case I heard; I wrote a decision that read "Fifty thousand dollars awarded to the plaintiff." A seven-word decision. I dictated that decision to Roe and told her to send it out so that they would receive it the next day. I did this while the matter was still fresh in my head. I thought that would be the last I heard from the American Arbitration Association. Well, I screwed myself; just the opposite occurred. Then I found out why. It turned out that a lot of the arbitrators took a long time to render a decision, and when they finally did, after repeated calls from the American Arbitration Association, their decisions were sometimes long-winded and confusing as if they didn't want to make one but had to. Long decisions that were confusing opened the door to other problems that caused more problems.

Now they get my decision the next day. It was "Oh my god." Not only did they get the decision super-fast but one that could hardly be challenged. I think they figured we finally got someone who can help us get rid of our backlog.

In the next couple of days, they inundated me with new cases. I went crazy, called them up, and asked them if they were nuts and why they were sending me so many cases. When they told me, I almost fell out of my chair. What the hell was I thinking? I tell them I'm sending back all the cases they sent me.

There is no way I can handle them and I was still maintaining a practice. I agreed to do two a month and see how it goes. If that was unsatisfactory, they could not send me any cases at all. They accepted.

Now getting back to the emergency with Ralphie. My secretary told me, "Ralphie is really upset." She never saw him like this before. I tell her to take him out of the waiting room, bring him back to the lunchroom, get him some coffee, and tell him I will be with him shortly. She says she already did that.

When I get back to the arbitration, the attorneys are gathering up their papers. I tell them they will be hearing from the American Arbitration Association with my decision in a week or so.

They thanked me as they left.

I go back to the lunchroom, and as soon as I see Ralphie, I know something is seriously wrong. He is sweating and looks like he is having a heart attack. I tell him to go into my office as I don't want people walking in on us. I get my coffee because I feel like I'm going to need some strong java for this.

He is sitting in a chair in front of my desk. I walk to the couch and tell him to come join me as I want this to be as informal as possible. He comes, sits down, and starts to tell me what happened.

Ralphie works for a trucking company at JFK airport. He picks up boxes and packages from one airline and delivers them wherever instructed. Lots of times, he would be asked to deliver an additional package to a place on the route where he is headed and would be given a ten or twenty-dollar cash tip for doing so. He made himself a few hundred extra dollars a week doing this. This morning, he was given a box to drop off in Jamaica, which is close to the airport.

Normally, he didn't leave the airport, but Jamaica was just a couple of minutes outside the premises, and he was given a fifty-dollar tip for his trouble. He made some stops first and then decided to drop off the package in Jamaica.

Just as he was making a right turn to leave the airport, a white van pulled up in front of him, causing him to stop quickly to avoid an accident; then two more white vans pulled up on both sides of him. As he was trying to figure out what was going on, men jumped out of the vans, pointing guns at him and screaming, "Hands up! And get out of the van!" Then he noticed they were all wearing blue jackets with the words FBI on them.

As he got out of his van, he put up his hands, frightened that some FBI agent might get nervous and shoot him. They put his hands behind his back, cuffed him, put him into one of the white vans, and drove away. The van he was driving was driven by an FBI agent.

They drove to a white nondescript building that he passed often. He thought it was some kind of storage facility. They took him to the back of his van, uncuffed him, and asked him to open the back doors. He did. They then asked him to open the box that was to be delivered to the Jamaica, Queens, address. They gave him a box cutter knife. He opened it. They asked him to show them what was in the box. The top of the box was filled with crumpled newspaper. As he removed the newspapers, he saw what looked like ten to fifteen handguns. He was shocked. When delivering boxes around the airport for a couple of bucks, which he had been doing since he started the job, he never asked what was in the box or boxes. Sometimes he knew because one of the boxes was slightly open and he could see different garments, like ladies' sweaters or scarves or gloves.

He knew some of the boxes contained airport swag (airport stolen stuff), but that was none of his business. He just dropped it off where he was told. He knew he would never be given drugs to deliver because there was too much money involved to take a chance on someone like him, who didn't know what he had and could lose it or misplace it as often happened at the airport.

They took him into the white building. The front room looked like a working/shipping area. They walked through a door into the rear of the building and entered a large room with bright neon lights in the ceiling and about fifteen desks with twenty or more people working at the desks. There were computers and phones on all the desks, and everyone seemed busy at work. At the back of the room were three or four offices with large glass windows.

They took him to one of the offices where two men were waiting for him. They directed him to a seat and asked if he wanted a coffee. They introduced themselves, telling him they were FBI agents and that this was an FBI field office that had been set up to investigate all the criminal activity that had been going on at the airport. They told him that they had been tracking the guns through several states and that the address he had been given was a junkyard in Jamaica that also had a car crusher and that business was a front for one of the five crime families. They suspected that the guns he was delivering would be sold at five to ten times their cost to bodegas throughout the city.

Ralph was speechless and scared to death. He knew the junkyard well and the people who ran it but didn't know the actual address, and that's why he was surprised when they told him it was the junkyard he knew. He pleaded that he delivered boxes all over the airport and didn't know what was in them. They said not to play innocent with them and that they knew all about him and his family, his mother and her criminal record and his famous Aunt Anna. He told them, "That's my mother and aunt, that's not me, and they have not been in trouble for years."

The fact that he didn't know what kind of swag he was delivering was irrelevant. He had committed several crimes, and they started to name them; but if he cooperated with them there was a way out for him and they would guarantee he would do no jail time. He asked what he would have to do. He was told he would have to get wired up and deliver the guns to the address he was given. He knew that one of the captains of a crime family worked out of there and was a childhood friend of his. He told them he wouldn't do it. They said, "Okay, it's off to jail for you for a long time" and started reading him his Miranda rights, which they had failed to do when they first arrested him. In reading him his rights, they tell him once they book him, there is no turning back.

They tell him that if he cooperates, he can go home tonight and that it will take weeks or even months before they will make arrests, and by that time, they may not even need him or his tapes. They leave the room and tell him to think it over.

He finally agrees to cooperate, talking himself into believing that maybe they will not have to use the tape he is about to make and no one will ever know. All he wants to do is go home.

They take off his shirt and tape a recorder to his chest. They tell him that before he is about to speak to the guy, he was delivering the box to, press a button on the recorder and do nothing; the recorder would run up to six hours. He was instructed to ask for Jimmy Luca, who was a captain in the Gambino crime family and tell him that when he got the box it was partially opened, and in trying to close the box, he saw what he thought were guns. He knew several guys who were looking to buy. They wanted Ralph to get Luca on tape saying they were his guns and were for sale. They tell him that he is to come right back after he delivers the guns and not to touch the tape recorder as they didn't want to take a chance of him screwing it up.

Ralph wants to know what happens if Luca is not there. Is he supposed to just drop them off or should he say he will only deliver the box to Jimmy Luca? They tell him to leave the guns as they have information that guns are arriving at JFK on a weekly basis and they will get another shot at dropping off guns at that location.

They tell him they will play the tape when he comes back, so they better hear him ask for Jimmy Luca. He is told not to speak to anyone or stop anywhere. He is to go directly there and come directly back. He tells them when they stopped him, a small crowd gathered around, and what if someone saw him get arrested and the news of his arrest spread around the airport? They assured him the chances of someone seeing him get arrested were small, but if someone saw what happened, he should say it must have been someone else. He asks why it was necessary for three vans full of FBI agents to stop and arrest him. "Why couldn't one van quietly stop him and then no one would have known what happened? You guys may have caused me some real problems now."

No one says anything. Ralphie, who by this time had calmed down a little, is starting to get angry and tells them what they did was just plain stupid. No one says anything.

They started to give him last-minute instructions, but by this time, he was angry and confused and frightened and didn't hear much. They told him his van was in the garage in the back of the building so no one could see it when he came back to pull into the garage. He told them it was a little late for keeping everything under the hat now. He asked them if someone was going to follow him. They said no, they could be spotted. He tells them, "Now you think of that." They walk through the building to the van, give him the keys, and tell him they will be waiting for him.

He gets into his van and drives away. If he's lucky, maybe they will not need to use the tapes and no one will ever know. He knows he's probably lying to himself but feels he has no choice.

He pulls up to Tony's junkyard, which is where Jimmy Luca has an office in the back. Ralph has been there before. Everyone in the neighborhood knows the place and what they do. They have a million-dollar crusher which is always busy. They are famous for doing insurance jobs. An insurance job is when someone wants to make a score by getting rid of his car and collecting the insurance. It works the following way:

One of Tony's guys goes to the home of the guy wanting to get rid of his car. The owner gives him the keys to the car together with the insurance and registration. The guy drives the car to Tony's. If he should get stopped for any reason, he can say he borrowed the car from his friend and present the registration and insurance card. If for some reason the cop should want to verify his story, he can call the car owner who will verify it.

Once the car is in Tony's yard, there are several guys waiting for it. It is brought indoors and totally dismantled. Within three hours, the car no longer exists. The car is then sold for parts. Nothing goes to waste. The doors, seats, tires, engine, transmission, etc. Everything that can be sold is put into its proper bin.

Tony gets to keep all the money from the sale of the parts which usually is in the thousands. The owner of the car reports it stolen the next day after the car no longer exists, and usually, after a short wait time to see if the car is recovered, the owner gets his insurance check.

They also do cars on order, meaning you order the car you want. Let's say you want a 2018 black Porsche 911 Turbo. Tony can find the car in minutes; he knows every 2018 black Porsche 911 Turbo sold in the northeast as well as when where and to whom it was sold to along with their present address.

He then sends his guy or guys out with a truck that has ramps that will roll out the back and a pulley mechanism installed by Tony that can pull the intended Porsche into the truck in about sixty seconds. The truck is small and can only take one car. Tony's guys generally will go to a certain area that has several black Porsche 911 Turbos available.

A favorite place is the Maryland and Washington DC area. Since they know where the car is located and the name of the person who owns it, it's pretty easy to track down the car and steal it. They know not to come back until they have the car.

Upon returning Tony does his thing with VIN numbers and titles. The paperwork is acquired through a source in Philadelphia who works for the Department of Motor Vehicles and it is very handsomely paid for providing a proper new title and registration. He has one or two other states with connections in the Department of Motor Vehicles who do the same thing for him. The car is then delivered to the customer who ordered the car. The customer will generally pay 50 percent of what he would pay if he bought the car from a legitimate dealer.

I knew a lot about this because Ron was assigned to the homicide bureau after he worked in the auto theft division for almost a year. I got to hear all the stories and there were lots of them. One involved Tony. It seems a young guy from Connecticut found out that Tony had a hard-to-find part for his red 1983 Porsche. He comes to Tony's and pulls up in his red Porsche right in front of Tony's office, parks, and goes into the office and asks where he could get the spare part he needed. Tony is there and tells him where to get the part but first asks him to move the Porsche since it was blocking the path to the crusher.

This guy in his excitement to get the part, leaves the car where it was, blocking the path to the crusher. Tony sees this and yells at him to move the car first. The guy yells back, "In a minute, I'll be right back," and off he goes. The yard was over two acres, and there was no way he was going to find the part, remove it from the car, and be back in a minute. Tony, pissed off at the audacity of the guy, called over his man who operated the crane that had a huge magnet that lifted up whole cars, and had him lift the red Porsche and put it into the crusher. Within a couple of minutes, the car no longer existed.

No one said a word to Tony when he was angry. He called over two of his office guys and a couple of men who work close to the office and told them if questioned, just say the guy walked into the yard looking for a part, and one of the yard guys sent him into the office and that's all they know.

The guy comes back twenty minutes later with the part in his hands and, as he is going into the office to pay for the part, notices the car isn't where he left it. He asks how much for the part and asks where his car is. Tony tells him the cost of the part and says, "What car?"

The guy says, "My red Porsche."

Tony tells him he doesn't know what he's talking about. To make a long story short, the guy calls the cops. The people in the office and in the yard all repeat the same story. The guy walked into the yard. The guy must be nuts. There is no red Porsche anywhere in the yard.

The thing about auto theft is that the cops see it as almost a victimless crime. Almost all cars have auto theft insurance, and in the end, the insurance companies take the loss which they eventually pass on to the customers.

Ralph pulls into the yard, parks his van, takes the box with the guns out, and brings them into the office. He tells one of the office workers that he's looking for Jimmy and then presses the button on the recorder as he walks toward the back office which has the door open and sees Jimmy and asks if he can talk to him.

Jimmy, who is on the phone waves, points to a chair and indicates he will be with him shortly.

When he gets off the phone, Ralph starts telling the story that he had rehearsed, some of which is true. He was asked to drop off this box by a guy at the airport and noticed that the box was slightly open and, in attempting to close it, thought he saw some guns. He didn't want to open it further because if they were guns, he knew lots of guys who would pay a fortune to get their hands on them. Jimmy tells Ralph to put the box on the desk and close the door, walks over to the box, opens it and starts to remove the guns.

He feels comfortable doing so in front of Ralph because they have known each other since they were kids.

Ralph grew up in Ozone Park. He came from a large family, three brothers and four sisters. His father owned a pizzeria/restaurant for as long as I can remember. It was a busy place with great food. He, of course, started working there after school and on all school vacations and in the summer. I think I met him when I was seven or eight, and he was already helping out at the restaurant. A lot of wise guys ate there, and by the time Ralph was twelve or thirteen, he was like a master chef.

He was fat at first, but by the time he hit his teens, he thinned out some, but was always chunky. Because he was fat early on, he got the nickname Fat Ralphie. As he got older and lost some weight, he was called Ralph or Ralphie. He was only Fat Ralph when someone wanted to distinguish him from another Ralph in the neighborhood. He was the kindest, most popular, most beloved guy in our crowd.

He was also a soft touch, could never say no to junkies. He had a special aura of goodness that one could almost feel, yet he was tough and could handle himself when he had to.

I remember walking with him one spring night on Liberty Avenue in Ozone Park around eight in the evening, heading to the Saint John's diner to meet some of the guys. A big caddy pulled up with the windows rolled down and in the car was Jimmy Luca and one of his guys.

He yells at Ralphie, "You fat fuck, get in the car." I say, "What does Jimmy want?"

He says, "I borrowed two hundred bucks from him and I haven't paid him back yet."

I say, "I'll meet you at the diner."

I start to walk toward the diner as Ralphie walks toward the car. Jim yells out, "Twinnie, you too."

I think, *Oh shit*. But what can I do? So, I go over with him. Jimmy is driving. As we walk toward the car, Jimmy says something to the guy sitting next to him; the guy opens the door and gets in the back. Jimmy motions to Ralphie to slide in next to him, and I get in and sit next to Ralph so all three of us are in the front seat.

Jimmy looks at Ralph. "So, where's my two hundred?"

Ralphie looks at him with disdain and says, "A man of my caliber being bothered for two hundred dollars?"

Jimmy looks at him. "You, fat fuck" he says with affection and starts to laugh.

He is about to say something more when Ralphie says, "I got it at the restaurant, you can stop by later or I'll drop it off tomorrow."

Jimmy says, "I'll knock off fifty bucks if you tell me how you make IT."

Ralphie tells him IT is a family secret and he can never reveal it. Actually, it's not a family secret, it's Ralphie's secret that was discovered by accident. I knew how he made IT only because I caught him making it, and even then, I didn't know the last two ingredients.

What are we talking about? Rigatoni pasta with broccoli. A simple dish that he made and everyone loved. It was one of his most popular dishes at the restaurant. So here is how the secret that he would not tell anyone about came to be.

One cold day in November, he was cooking at the restaurant and he was behind on his orders. On the stove was a big pot of hot chicken soup when he got an order for Rigatoni and Broccoli. Since he cooked all his pasta fresh, not precooked as some restaurants do, he had to start boiling water (which takes time to come to a boil before you can put in the pasta). In a stroke of genius, he figured he could save time by taking some of the boiling chicken soup out of the pot, put it into another pot with the heat on, and throw in the pasta and broccoli, saving five to six minutes cooking time.

The rest is Ozone Park history. He served a big family style order of his new discovery, and the people loved it. They told the waiter it was the best pasta and broccoli they ever had. Apparently, the chicken stock gave the pasta a very rich texture. It was served with the only cheese he allowed to be served with the dish, grated genuine Locatelli Pecorino Romano. I made it once or twice a month when I was home and got it 90 percent right. It wasn't until he gave me the last two minor ingredients that it became perfect. I promised him I would never reveal the last two ingredients, so sorry folks, take my word for it, at 90 percent, it's still great.

His mother, whom we called Aunt Linda, and her older sister, whom we called Aunt Anna, were shoplifters who had been caught in stores several times.

The last time they were caught, they were on the front page of the Long Island Press, a neighborhood newspaper. When I saw the pictures of them in handcuffs, I didn't understand. I was only eight or nine years old. I could read but didn't understand.

I loved these two women; in a way, they were like second mothers to me and Ronnie—loving and kind, always feeding us, hugging us and watching out for us. They looked flashy like gun molls but they spoke to us like we were adults. We simply loved them for it.

Ron and I never spoke to them or to Ralphie about the arrests. One day, a couple of months after the story in the paper, I went to Ralphie's for a stickball game. Aunt Linda didn't answer the door; Ralph did. He didn't say anything to me, but I later found out that she and Aunt Anna had been sent to prison for eighteen months. They actually did a little over a year, as I remember, and during that time, Ralphie's two oldest sisters, who were still very young, took over and helped run the business and the house.

When they got out of jail, things went back to normal. When I first saw Aunt Linda, I ran over to her and hugged her and asked if she was all right. The only time she ever spoke to me about it was many years later. She said that she had made a stupid mistake and that she and Aunt Anna would never do it again. They didn't for almost fifteen years.

Then they started again but were caught after only a short time. Fortunately, when they were busted, the value of the stolen items on them was only worth a couple of hundred dollars, which was under the amount of money that would classify it as a felony. They were charged with petit larceny, a misdemeanor. I asked Bonnie, (my wife, who is a criminal lawyer to represent them), which she did (no charge, of course). Fortunately, they got off with a small fine and a stern warning.

I have so many memories of them. She and Aunt Anna were such colorful characters that I could write a book just about them. Here is one standout Aunt Linda tale. We were, I think, sixteen years old, and Minna, one of the local prostitutes, was working in the neighborhood. She used an apartment that a friend rented out to her for the night. It was only half a block away from Ralphie's family Pizzeria and Restaurant. When she was "working," there would be guys milling around, waiting for her. She was popular because she was pretty, wore no makeup, and looked like a high school cheerleader.

I'm in front of the restaurant waiting for Ralphie to come out since we had plans to meet some of the guys to go to Chinatown to "rib it up," Ralphie's term for going to Chinatown and eating all the spareribs we possibly could.

Aunt Linda sees me and comes out of the restaurant. Knowing I'm waiting for Ralphie, she asked me where we were going. I tell her, "We're going to Chinatown to rib it up."

As we are chatting, she notices the guys milling around a half block away.

She asked me, "What's going on?" pointing to the guys milling around.

I tell her, "Minna is working tonight."

She knows Minna because sometimes she eats at the restaurant. She likes Minna. Worried that Ralphie is still heavy, doesn't have a girlfriend, and may never get laid, she asks me (before we go to Chinatown) to make sure Ralphie gets in line for Minna. Then she asks, "How much does Minna charge?"

I tell her, "I'm not sure as I have never used her services."

She says, "Sure, you good-looking fuck, you don't have to pay for it." I say, "I think she charges twenty or twenty-five bucks."

She hands me thirty, telling me to make sure Ralphie gives her a five-dollar tip and says once more, "Make sure he gets in line. Tell him you're treating him; you had a good day at the track." As crazy as it seems, how could you not love this woman, especially when you're sixteen?

Jimmy opens the box of guns and looks them over. Ralphie says, once again, he knows guys who would pay good money if Jimmy hasn't sold them all. Jimmy says he's got them all sold and has a waiting list of people who want them. He is paying on average two hundred apiece and selling them for a little over a thousand each.

Jimmy goes on to tell Ralphie where he gets them from, how he has the serial numbers removed so that they are untraceable, and on and on. Ralphie knows he has more than enough and is getting ready to leave when Jimmy tells him to relax for five minutes; he has a new espresso machine and makes espresso for them. Ralphie stays for the espresso.

Ralphie and Jimmy go back a long way, Jimmy was a few years older than Ralphie. He was always very bright but a drug addict with a bad heroin problem. He was strung out a lot, always looking for handouts for drugs. I knew him well as just a regular neighborhood junkie, but I liked him; even at his worst, he had a great sense of humor, was self-deprecating and extremely funny.

Whenever I had a couple of spare bucks from working one of my part-time jobs, I would help him out. I never judged him, just helped him if I could. He was about six feet tall and, at his worst, still very good-looking. He had several beautiful girlfriends, but they all gave up on him after a while. Of all the people who helped him out, no one came as close as Ralphie. He would see him nodding out near his restaurant, go get him, bring him in, ask how he was doing, and ask when was the last time he ate. Then he would feed him and give him what he could afford and usually more. Some of the guys would get on Ralph, asking him why he was wasting his time and money on Jimmy. He was only going to be found dead from an overdose sooner or later.

They were all wrong. He finally got caught stealing a car and pleaded to an E felony. He was sentenced to three to six years in jail. He got out in a little over two years and was a changed guy. He was no longer a drug addict, having been clean for the time spent in jail, and decided being a junkie was not worth what he had been through.

He was a very proud guy and knew that people, especially the wise guys in the neighborhood, looked down on him, and so he decided to change his life. Not that he wanted to get a nine-to-five job. No, he decided he wanted to become a soldier in the local crime family and work his way up, which is exactly what he did. As I said, he was very bright, good with numbers, tough, fearless, funny, good-looking, and everyone liked him.

He was Sicilian, with a typically long Sicilian memory, and there were several people who he really cared for, people who didn't look down on him when he was a drug addict, people who helped him, and Ralphie was at the top of that list with me and Ron not far behind. When he had no place to sleep, we would let him stay in my older brother Vin's office. Vin did not know about it; he would go in the evening after everyone left and would leave before anyone came the next morning. Ron or I would let him in. There was always coffee and some food lying around in the kitchen. Those times when he slept in the office, never once was anything missing.

He eventually rose to become a captain in the local crime family in Ozone Park, and through all those years, we remained friends. He never took advantage and never asked me for anything (except every once in a while, he would ask me if I could talk to Ron about one of the guys in his crew who was in trouble.) He knew that I wouldn't and couldn't do it, but he asked me anyway. I didn't blame him for trying. I liked him a lot and did not judge him.

On the other hand, on a couple of occasions I asked him for a favor; he never turned me down. Here's an example: I walked into my office one morning, and I noticed that all the trash cans were full. I asked one of my secretaries, "Why are all the trash cans full?"

She tells me A&G Carting has not been to the office in over three months to pick up trash. I ask why. She doesn't know.

"Have we not paid the bill?"

She says, "Yes, we have, we have paid for the last three months, though they are not coming to pick up the trash."

I asked who had been taking the trash. She says all the secretaries have been throwing out the trash in plastic bags on the side of the building.

"That's for the tenants. We are supposed to pay for our own trash pickup, and the Department of Sanitation is supposed to pick up only the tenants' trash."

She says the Department of Sanitation has not noticed. I can't believe it. I'm up to my eyeballs with cases, and now I have to worry about trash collection. I dictate a letter to A&G Carting, telling them I no longer require their services. I tell them the reason why and that I want money we paid for services refunded since the trash was not collected. I told my secretary to find another carting service.

Several days later, I asked my secretary if she got another carting service and when they will start. She tells me no other carting service will come into this area, that this area is only serviced by A&G Carting. "Bobby, she says, "don't you know this whole carting business is controlled by wise guys? And by the way, two of A&G Carting guys got your letter, and they want to see you."

I tell her to make an appointment with them sometime when I'm not in court and in the meantime to keep on looking for another carting company.

The next morning, as I come to the office, one of the local numbers guys is taking numbers from my secretaries who all played. I once tried to stop it, but all the girls got pissed off at me as did the numbers guy, and they snuck outside to bet anyway. I figured what the hell, they might as well do it inside as long as they didn't do it in front of clients and did it quickly.

Some Law Office with all my secretaries breaking the law. When I told them, "What you're doing is illegal," most didn't know and asked if I was sure, it was illegal. On occasion, Ronnie would come by with a couple of detectives who worked for him since one of the girls was being paid off. It was funny. The detectives knew what was going on and would shake their heads, laugh, and go back with Ronnie for coffee.

All of my secretaries were pretty with great figures. It was hard enough practicing law, which is mostly an adversarial profession so at least I deserved beautiful surroundings. Don't forget this was the early sixties and seventies before the world went crazy. The problem was the numbers guys felt the same way and wanted to hang out with the girls as they took the numbers. I had to put a stop to it, so I told one of my secretaries she had to take all the numbers for all the girls the night before and bring them over to Café Gio where the numbers guys hung out. That at least ended things going down in my office for a while.

As I walked into my office, I find a message that two A&G Carting guys had made an appointment to see me the next morning at 11:00 a.m. I call Jimmy to tell him what's going on, and he says he will be there.

Next morning at 11:00 a.m., sure enough, the two A&G Carting guys show up wearing blue suits, shirts, and ties. I got to the office at ten-thirty and was in the lunch room with Jimmy, having coffee and a Kaiser roll with butter, one of Jimmy's favorites. I ask Jimmy what to tell these guys. Jimmy says, "I will be in the room with you. Let's see what happens."

Into my office we go, get comfortable, Jimmy sitting in a chair on the side facing the two chairs in front of my desk. I buzz my secretary and tell her to show the two A&G guys in.

They both come in, chatting away, and I direct them to be seated in the chairs in front of my desk. When they see Jimmy, their whole attitude changes from being cocky to looking fearful. Before I could say anything, they said, "Mr. Aliazzo, there's been a mistake. We want to apologize for not picking up your trash. We will refund the money paid by you for the months we didn't do so, and of course, you can use any carting company you choose." I'm in shock, and before I can say anything, they get up, shake my hand, say, "Sorry for the mix-up" and leave.

I look at Jimmy who has not said one word. I say, "Jimmy, what the fuck just happened here?"

He says, "You got me."

I go over to him and say, "Fucking Jimmy" and give him a hug. This is the same Jimmy who is Ronnie and my and Ralphie's childhood friend who Ralphie just taped.

Getting back to Ralph. After getting Jimmy on tape, he comes to my office and tells me everything. I immediately tell him to take his shirt off; I help him remove the recorder taped to his chest. It's not a transmitter but a recorder, so the only info the feds will get is on the recorder. As we remove it, he is frightened, afraid the feds will be upset. He does as I tell him and I get on the phone to Ronnie. I get him and tell him it's an emergency, I need his help now. Luckily, he is preparing for trial but is not actually on trial and says, "I'll be right there."

I get the tape and the recorder, call in one of my secretaries, and tell her to carefully pull the tape out of the recorder, then cut it into little pieces and when it's all cut up, flush it down the toilet. Ralph is upset and asks me, "Are you sure this is what we should do?" He tells me he is supposed to meet the feds who are waiting for him.

I tell him to listen to me very carefully. "Are you listening?" He looks at me like I'm crazy.

"Fuck the feds. They have just put your life in danger. What do you think Jimmy will do when the feds arrest him? We all go back as kids together, but a rat is a rat as far as Jimmy and his crew are concerned."

"But they told me he may never know about the tape. They will only use it as a last resort."

Just then, Ronnie comes in. He sees Ralphie without a shirt but with some tape still attached to him. "What the fuck is going on?"

Ralphie looks at Ronnie as if Lord Jesus had just arrived. He thinks because Ronnie is an Assistant District Attorney in the homicide bureau and has all the detectives working for him, he can fix anything. I motioned Ronnie to leave the room, and I followed him. I tell Ralphie to put on his shirt. "I'll be back in a few minutes."

Ronnie and I go into the conference room and I fill him in. I tell him the tape is gone. He says, "Good." He wants to go in to speak to Ralph.

I say, "Ronnie, you can't." If it ever gets out that an ADA in the Queens Homicide Bureau came in and spoke to Ralph while the feds were waiting for him, he could lose his job and his law license. He knows I'm right. I tell him, "I just called you because I need your advice. I'm too close to this and I'm not sure what I'm doing is right."

He tells me I have no other choice. I tell him what I plan to do is give Ralph a letter on my stationery, stating that he has retained me and that I have advised him that pursuant to his Miranda rights, he has decided to retain counsel. I am that counsel and have advised him not to answer any further questions. Ron thinks this is the only option we have.

Together, we compose a letter with my secretary and ask her to type it up right away and make two copies and to address it to the Federal Bureau of Investigation, Kennedy Airport, envelope addressed the same. We discuss where we think he will be arraigned and when. We're sure this will hit the news. Once it hits the news and Jimmy finds out, what do we do? How do we protect Ralph? He says he will be back around six and we'll try to figure out what to do next. I tell Ron that Ralphie thinks some people saw him get busted, and if that's true, it will be all over the airport before it hits the papers, which means Jimmy will know about it soon if he doesn't already.

It's a little before twelve, and we agreed to meet back at the office between five-thirty and six. I go back to my office where Ralphie is waiting. He looks like he's about to have a heart attack. He is looking for Ronnie. I explained why Ronnie cannot be part of this. He understands. I tell him to relax, that I'm going to represent him for the present. He is to do exactly what I tell him to do. He says, "Bobby, my life and my family's life are in your hands, just tell me what to do."

Nothing like a little pressure. I tell him the tape has been destroyed. I show him the letter and tell him he should go back and meet the FBI agents at the arranged meeting place, and he is to hand them the letter and not to say another word.

"I want you to read this letter very carefully," I say clearly," and then you can ask me all the questions you want."

After reading the letter a second time, he looks up at me, confused. I say, "Okay, ask all the questions you want."

"What happens when they want to know where the tape recorder and the tape is?", he says.

I explain to him that any questions asked after handing them this letter are to be answered with the following sentence: "You have my attorney's letter and I have nothing further to say."

I tell my secretary to type a letter with the following sentence: "You have my attorney's Letter; I have nothing further to say." I tell her to write it as many times as will fit on one page.

Ralph has a lot more questions. I tell him I will answer them shortly. I ask where his wife, Anna, is. He says, "Probably home unless she went shopping."

I ask him whose name his house is in. He says his name and his wife's. It's worth about $250,000, and they have a mortgage of about ninety thousand. I tell him I need this information because bail will probably be set tomorrow, and I have to contact a bail bondsman so we can post bail when you're arraigned.

Now I tell him, "Let's talk about when you return to the FBI. The following is likely to happen. They will be angry. They will threaten you with additional charges. They will be especially pissed off about the tape. Getting Jimmy on tape is a big deal to them. Getting mafia captains on charges that can get a conviction on is a big deal." As I am talking, my secretary comes in with the page I asked her to type.

I tell him I want him to read the whole page out loud. He asks why. I tell him because I have given this letter to many clients over the years, and at least half of them started talking, ignoring the letter after a couple of minutes of being harassed. I tell him, "If you ignore this letter and start talking whatever time you're facing, which I think will be short, will be tripled. They want you to talk to hurt you, not to help you. Always remember that. Right now, they have you for having guns in your van. You have a clean record. You went in the army and served two years and got out with an honorable discharge. They think you're connected because you have so many friends who are wise guys."

He says, "They're your friends, too. You grew up with them, and so did Ronnie."

I tell him, "I know, but Ronnie and I were not caught with guns in a van, and we're both lawyers (and Ronnie is an ADA). So, I will tell you once again, if you don't want to be in real trouble, don't ignore the letter."

He says, "Okay, okay. I got it."

I tell him again to read the letter out loud. He doesn't want to, but he does. I then get one of my lawyers who was a former Assistant District Attorney for several years and tell him to take Ralphie into his office and try to get him to talk. He does. After fifteen minutes, he returns with Ralphie and says, "He almost slipped once or twice, but I think he's ready."

I tell him, "They will want you to explain what happened. Remember, in the army, if you are a prisoner of war, all you have to give is your name, rank, and serial number. Here, all you have to do is give them the letter. Eventually, they will take you downtown to book you, and you'll be arraigned tomorrow. You will have to spend the night in jail, probably at the Metropolitan Correctional Facility.

"We will get an attorney to represent you at the arraignment. He will be there with a bail bondsman."

Ralph says, "What do you mean? You won't be there?"

I tell him, "Ronnie and I have more pressing things to do, like trying to talk to Jimmy or your chances for a long happy life will be somewhat limited."

He turns white. He hasn't even thought about Jimmy. He said, "You know I didn't want to rat on Jimmy. They told me they probably wouldn't use the tape."

I tell him, "You're a street kid from Ozone Park, what the fuck are you talking about? You believed them?"

He says, "I was so scared I wanted to believe them."

"Okay, you did the right thing. You came here and didn't go back with the recorded tape." I tell him, "I'm sure you'll make bail. When you do, you leave with the lawyer we sent you, and go to a diner. Not in Ozone Park. And call me. If we can't straighten things out with Jimmy, then you're not going home, and we'll try to think what to do next." Now it's time to go. "Remember, the only person who can fuck this up is you, so remember to hand them the letter and shut the fuck up. Not a word out of your mouth."

I walk him out, telling Ralph it might be one night in jail. As Tommy DeVito used to say, "It's like peeing off a pier." I give him a hug, and off he goes. I have clients to see and a lot to do. Before I know it, my secretary comes in and tells me Ronnie just called and was on his way.

I looked at my watch, and it's already five-thirty. She knows Ralphie and, like everyone else, likes him. I tell her, "Ralphie's in trouble, I need you to stay late."

She says, "As late as you want me."

I thanked her and asked her to order some dinner from Don Pepe for me, her, and Ronnie. I tell her, "Get what you want for yourself, and for me and Ronnie, baked clams and linguine with white clam sauce."

She says, "Ronnie wants that?"

And I tell her, "We're twins, and whatever I like, he likes. Except ice cream.

Since we were kids, I always liked vanilla and he always liked chocolate." She says, "I'll order it now and go pick it up."

As she leaves, I start making phone calls and in the middle of one, Ronnie shows up. I wave and tell him to hold on. I'm on the phone with John Riga, a former client and a security guard at the airport. As I'm asking him how he's doing, he cuts me off. "Counselor, is this about Ralphie?"

I say, "Yes."

He tells me, "It's all over the airport. Everyone is asking about it. Are you going to represent him?"

I say, "I don't know yet." I asked him what he heard; he told me one of the airport truck drivers saw the whole thing. Says there must have been three or four white vans. "What did he do, kill somebody?" I tell him it's a bullshit thing, but I can't discuss it. I asked him if he heard anything else to call me.

Ron sat down and asked, "How bad?"

I tell him, "It's all over the airport, so by this time, Jimmy knows." "How much does he know?"

"He knows that Ralph got arrested by the feds this morning and then came over to see him and brought him guns. Since they spoke about the guns, Jimmy probably has figured out that Ralph was wired. He must be sick to his stomach. I'm sure he can't believe that Ralph would do that to him."

"Well, he sure is going to be happy to see us. No tape. Ralphie is represented by me and is not talking to anyone."

Ron tells me I should not represent him. I'm too close to him and can't be dispassionate and objective. I think he's right. I was not looking forward to representing him. I was nervous and afraid for him, and if there is one thing a lawyer should be, it's cool and clear-minded.

He tells me he is thinking of Steve Lynch. I love the idea right away. Steve is like an Irish bulldog, tough as nails, but has a way about him that makes everyone around him like him. He's a former Legal Aid lawyer who went on to the District Attorney's Office, trying and winning almost all his cases. He decided to go into private practice several years ago, and now there is a waiting list for him to try cases. A lot of his clients are referred to him by other criminal lawyers who have cases they don't feel qualified to try and give them to Steve. At least the good lawyers do.

I've been in court and saw lawyers trying felony cases who in my judgment were incompetent and shouldn't even be trying misdemeanor cases, let alone felony cases. Why do they take felony cases that they are not qualified to handle? For the money. They talk tough and confident in their office, but when they get before a judge and jury, they fall apart. It makes me sick every time I see it.

I don't mind them taking the cases that are unwinnable. In that case, they just plead out their clients, and that's it. It's the cases that are clearly winnable that they screw up and plead out that make me sick.

Ron tells me he'll call Steve later; he has his home phone number. We think Jimmy is probably seeing a lawyer right now. Ron says, "Let me call Jimmy."

I say, "Are you crazy? An ADA in the homicide bureau calling Jimmy? I don't think so."

He says, "You're right. See, this is what happens when you're too close to the problem. You become careless."

I picked up the phone to call Jimmy and started to dial when it hit me. I must be crazy. I got baked clams coming along with linguine and white clam sauce. I tell Ron, and a look of contentment comes over him as he says, "Best news I've heard all day."

We go back to the lunchroom and are setting up plates and cups when my secretary comes back. The aroma of the baked clams precedes her. She ordered veal parmesan for herself. She has family size orders as that's the only way they serve it. When we're finished with the clams and linguine, we'll help her polish off the veal parmesan. But, of course, our eyes are bigger than our stomachs, and after the baked clams, we could only get through half the linguine.

She leaves to make coffee for us as we discuss where we can meet Jimmy, assuming we can find him. It gets quiet as we drink our coffee, and I look over at Ron who's falling asleep. "Ron, wake up!"

He says, "Sorry, sorry. You know I was just thinking when you woke me up. I was thinking for all those people who can't sleep at night, we should promote pasta and call it Sleepy Time Pasta. Have a bowl of our pasta with our own special sauce, and we guarantee you'll be sleeping in half an hour."

I tell him I will put that on my list of future projects to make us rich.

I say, "Okay, I'm going to make the call." I called the junkyard, and after a couple of rings, Tony (Heart Attack) answers. How did he get the nickname? He had three heart attacks over the last couple of years and survived them all, thus the nickname. I tell him it's me (who he knows), and he says, "How are you doing, Counselor?"

I say, "Okay. I have to speak to Jimmy, is he around?" He says, "He's in his office talking to his lawyer."

I tell him to interrupt him and tell him it's me.

He says, "Okay." A moment later, Jimmy is on the phone. I tell him we have good news and have to see him now.

He says, "I'll send Heart Attack to pick you up" as he knows I don't want to have me or Ronnie or our car seen at his place.

Twenty minutes later, Heart Attack pulls up to the office in a big Cadillac. We see him. He must weigh ninety pounds, pale as a ghost and looks like he passed away but they forgot to bury him (he would go on to live another fifteen or so years). We go out to the car and get in the back seat. I ask, "Are you alone?"

He says, "Yeah, I went by a circuitous route." I asked how he learned that word.

He says, "What do you think, I'm a dummy? I happen to know a lot of big words. I'm also good at crossword puzzles, and when I get a new word, I write it down and try to remember it."

I say, "Good for you, Tony."

He says, "Jimmy told me to go the back way, so when you go through the gates, you go right into the garage and then close the garage doors after you. That way, no one can see anyone get out of the car."

As a lawyer, I can go see my clients anytime I want and anywhere I want. But with Ronnie, that's another matter. He's not breaking any laws by going to see an old friend, but under the circumstances, with what's going on with Ralph and the feds, it will not look good for Ronnie going to see Jimmy at this particular time.

The assistant head DA knows Ronnie well. In fact, they are good friends, and he knows that Ronnie can make between two and three times more if he came to join our law practice. So, it's not about money (or anything like that).

We follow Tony to a small room just off Jimmy's office. What is Jimmy doing? Making espresso. He must drink twenty cups a day. I say, "Brother Jim," a nickname I greeted him with since we were kids.

"Counselor," he says as he turns and then sees Ronnie. "Mr. ADA, you, handsome fuck" and goes over and gives Ronnie a big hug. "Bobby, you brought out the big guns, I see."

"Jimmy, we came here to talk about Ralphie."

He looks at us seriously for the first time. "You told me you had some good news. I can sure use some after Ralphie fucked me the way he did. In a million years, I would never have ever picked him to be a rat. We know each other since we were seven or eight. In fact, I don't remember when we didn't know each other, and you know how much I loved that fat fuck."

I tell him, "Jimmy, for the next ten minutes, don't talk, have your espresso.

I think I'll have some too." I look at Ronnie, and he nods yes.

Jimmy says, "It's fresh. I just made it."

I look at Ronnie, indicating, "Should I start or do you want to?" Ron says, "You go first. You were with Ralphie most of the day."

Jimmy turns from making us espresso, saying, "What the fuck is going on?

You were with Ralphie most of the day?"

I say, "That's right. After he left you, he did not go back to meet the feds but came to see me. Now relax, Jimmy, and I'm going to lay out what went down. Before I start, I want to give you the good news. There is no tape of you and Ralphie, so when we're finished here, you can call your lawyer and tell him you will not be giving him that fucking ridiculous retainer I'm sure he asked you for."

He looks at me, not quite believing.

"Okay, so here's what went down." I lay out the whole story from when Ralphie was arrested by the feds to where he is now, in the Metropolitan Correctional Facility. I tell him we got Steve Lynch, who Jimmy knows, and that I will not be representing him because I am too close; besides, there will be no trial. Ralphie is going to take a plea. We already told him he could do twenty-four to thirty-six months. He agreed. Since he has no criminal record, bail will be low."

"So, Jimmy, we are here for two reasons. One is to give you the good news, and two, to ask you when Ralphie makes bail tomorrow morning, we want him left alone. He lost his job at the airport, but I'm sure there is a waiting list for him as a cook." Something he did not want to do anymore because he says he's all cooked out. Well, now he will have no choice, although he will probably make twice as much money.

Jimmy looks at me, and I have a feeling I know what is to come. "I don't have any say as to what happens to Ralphie, it's out of my hands. It's all over, everyone knows what Ralphie did. No one is going to be able to save his ass now."

Ronnie asks him to put out the word about Ralphie. Jimmy is thinking. Ronnie sees it; before Jimmy answers, Ronnie says, "Jimmy, please don't lie to us. We've known each other for too long. We understand what went down. Ralphie came in wired by the feds and was about to ruin your life and your family's life.

"Now you know the truth. Instead of going back to the feds, he went to Bobby's office, and Bobby cut the tape into little pieces and flushed it down the toilet. Don't you believe Bobby?"

Jimmy looks at us both. "Yeah, of course. I knew when Bobby wanted to see me, I was going to have a problem, and then he brought you." He's looking at Ronnie.

Ronnie says, "Have a problem? Bobby just saved you twenty years in the can! A problem? What's the problem? You have to call off a hit on an old friend who made a mistake and correct it before any harm is done except to himself because now, he has to do the time?"

I look at Jimmy and tell him, "Before I flushed the tape down the toilet, I thought about this meeting and thought about keeping it. You know why? As insurance that Ralph wouldn't be whacked. Then I thought that when Jimmy finds out what went down, he would call it off. Anyway, I couldn't hold on to the tape. It's not my style, and it made me sick to listen to it."

Jimmy says, "This is above me now. New York wants it done after I told them what happened."

Ronnie says, "Call them back and tell them the truth. Tell them exactly what went down. You can use Bobby's name if anyone wants to speak to him. It's going to be on the news anyway."

Jimmy says, "You know how they are in New York. It looks bad if you let a rat go. It looks weak."

Ronnie says, "Here is what I suggest you tell New York: one, he is not a rat. It will be all over the news (including Ralphie not turning over the tape), about going to his lawyer and the tapes disappearing. Two, Bobby told me that he got Steve Lynch because he's too close to Ralphie, and Ralphie is going to take a plea. There will be no trial. Three—"

I interrupt Ronnie, "If New York still wants to proceed after hearing everything, Ronnie and the DA's office, not only in Queens County but New York County and Kings County, are going to come down on you any way they can, and you know Ronnie does not make empty threats. He has the manpower and connections to do it. So, we are asking, please give Ralphie a pass. He's not connected to you guys. He's just a civilian who is trying to make a few extra bucks and now will do several years in jail for getting an extra fifty bucks to move a box from one place to the other.

"Jimmy, for old time's sake, please do your best. We are going back to the office and not leaving until we hear from you one way or the other."

Jimmy says, "Okay, I'll make the call in a little while." He calls in Heart Attack and says, "Give the boys a ride to their office."

I say, "Wait, can we have a cup of the espresso you just made?"

We finish our espresso. We get up and follow Heart Attack. There are no goodbyes or hugs or handshakes. This is serious business. A man's life is on the line, and the funny thing about it is the man is someone everyone in that room loves, even Heart Attack.

When we get back to the office, Helen is still there. She wants to know if she can leave. We tell her we're waiting for a call and ask if she could stay until we get that call because we may still need her. Truthfully, we didn't want to be alone and just wanted some company. The three of us are sitting in the lunchroom, just talking and hanging out for about an hour or so when the front doorbell to the office rings. It's about eight o'clock. Helen jumps up. "I'll get it." She goes to the front door and opens it, and I hear her speaking to someone.

She comes walking back into the lunchroom followed by Jimmy who is alone and holding a white box from Artie's Italian Pastry Shop. We all looked at each other; it's a very emotional moment, and even Jimmy had a slight tear in his eye. Ronnie and I go over to Jimmy and hug him as he puts down the pastry. We know it's over and Ralphie got a pass. I asked Helen to make some fresh coffee, both espresso for Jimmy and regular for Ronnie and me as we would have heartburn and be up all night if we drank more espresso. Before she goes to make the coffee, she takes the pastry box and puts the pastry on a large plate. I look over. Fresh pastry—I'm in heaven.

We start to talk about how he convinced New York to give Ralphie a pass. He said, "To tell you the truth, it was a little of what Ronnie told me to tell them. When I told them he never turned over the tapes but instead went to Bobby's office; the tapes disappeared, he was going to be represented by Steve Lynch, he was going to take a plea and they were leaning on giving him a pass. When I told them Ronnie intended on really breaking balls if they whacked Ralphie, that was the straw that broke the camel's back. They didn't need all the problems that would come, and they knew that giving Ralphie a pass was the right thing to do anyway."

Helen brings the coffee, and we are suddenly hungry and dig in. We all finally relax. Before you know it, we are laughing and talking about old times. It was really a nerve-racking day, and after two pastries and two coffees, I'm starting to feel really tired. I tell the guys I'm ready to call it a night. I have to be up early tomorrow morning. Ronnie tells Jimmy how everything will play out with Ralphie and if he has any questions, to speak to me.

I tell Jimmy, "No phone calls, let's only speak in person." He says, "No problem."

I tell Helen to leave a note for the cleaning crew not to touch the pastries. As Jimmy is leaving, we go over to him, give him a hug, and thank him once again.

After Jimmy leaves, I tell Ronnie that Ralphie is all set for tomorrow. The bail bondsman and Steve will be there for the arraignment.

*****

The next morning, I got to my office around nine-thirty and asked my secretary if she had heard anything from Steve. She says no. I tell her that as soon as Steve calls to put him through to me. When not in court, my regular routine in the mornings is not to take any calls or see any clients.

I had my desk fixed so that there were two buttons installed right next to where the top of my right knee is, and on the outside doorjamb, two small round lights. One is red when lit up and the other is green. When the red light is lit, that means no one can enter my office, with one exception, if the building is on fire and entering when the light was on for any other reason would result in death (okay, so maybe I'm being a little overdramatic, but you get my drift).

Why the red lights? There are times when I cannot be disturbed; when I'm listening to a case as an arbitrator for the American Arbitration Association or if I'm with clients and things are heating up or for one hundred other reasons. I don't want one of my secretaries to come in and say, "What would you like for lunch?" or "Louie wants to know what time to meet him at the track." After trying to have my secretaries and lawyers use their judgment as to what's important, I gave up and installed the red and green lights.

Why the green light? It's a call for help. There is also a green light on my secretary's desk. When I have a client in my office and they are going on and on and on. Or, they came in to see me for a case we have coming up for trial and we went over everything we needed to go over; now they decide that as long as they are with me, they would like to discuss their grandmother's estate or their brother's divorce. Rather than being impolite and telling them the truth, which is not what I have been retained for, or giving them the bum's rush, I simply hit the green button under my desk and my secretary comes into my office to say something like, "Mr. Aliazzo, your next appointment is getting a little antsy and they have been waiting a while," which thankfully gives me a proper reason for ending the present meeting with my client.

Now getting back to the quiet time. That's when I catch up with cases that need attending to and also catching up with the lawyers that are part of our firm. Do they have any questions that I can help them with? Because sometimes it's good to get a second pair of eyes looking at a case. Most of the time, they do not need my help because they are for the most part smarter than me. Well, I'm certainly not going to hire lawyers that I'm smarter than. But lots of times, there was something missing, either they were bad with clients or shy or just didn't connect with them.

There was one law student who was dating one of my secretaries. He was in an ivy league law school, going into his senior year, looking for a summer job at a law firm as an intern. My secretary asked me if I would consider hiring him for the summer. I told her to let me meet him to see if I liked him and if he had a brain. She said, "Bobby, he's very smart, and it's just for the summer."

I told her to make an appointment for him to come in. She did. He had just come home from law school, which was out of state. The next day, she came in with his resume. I browsed through it. One of the things that jumped out to me was he liked to sing light opera. I thought, *this guy is definitely not for me.* I had two cousins who were opera singers. One became pretty famous in opera circles and became the lead soprano at La Scala opera house in Milan. Her stage name was Franca Duval.

My mother made me and Ronnie go see operas when we were young. We both hated them but had no choice. We especially hated the Saturday matinees because we belonged to the Nativity Crusaders football team, which was part of the Pop Warner football league, and the games were played on Saturday afternoons.

Anyway, getting back to the young law student who wanted to intern, my secretary had already made the appointment, and there was no way I could back out. So, on the next day in the afternoon, she brought him to my office. He was about six feet tall and handsome (this could have presented a problem because I don't like to hire anyone better looking than me). As soon as I saw him, I liked him. There was something about him, a kind of warmth and honesty that I felt. I could tell he was a little nervous after hearing about our office and how unconventional we were. I told him to sit down, relax, and let's chat. He had a folder with him which I believe had his school records, the courses he took, and his class ranking which, if I recall correctly, showed him in the top half of his class. I put all this info aside, and the first question I asked him was, "So what's the deal with the light opera?"

My secretary jumps in, "Bobby, you said you were going to be nice." I tell her, "All right, Annie, get out."

She gives me a "Please be nice" look, turns to Michael, smiles, and leaves.

I repeat my question.

He looks at me and starts to realize I'm somewhat nuts. "Well, I started singing in the church choir. I kind of liked it and then I was in the glee club in high school. I don't remember how I got into light opera, but I really liked it."

I asked him if he knew what a Bill of Particulars is. He said he did. "If you are going to be sued, you are served with a summons which in effect summons you to court and a complaint, which tells you why you are being summoned to court. The party receiving the summons and the complaint puts in an answer denying the charges made in the summons and complaint and requests a Bill of Particulars, so named because you are asking the person who served you with the summons and complaint particular questions."

I have three cases on my desk that are all waiting for Bills of Particulars. I gave them to him with a yellow legal pad and pen and asked him to do the Bills of Particulars. I bring him to a back room and tell him to do them, and when he's finished, return them back to me.

He follows me into the room, sits down, and I leave. About an hour and a half later, there was a knock on my door. It's Michael with the three Bills of Particulars. I read them; they are perfect.

I tell him, "You're hired. When can you start?" He says, "How about tomorrow?"

I say, "Okay, generally, the hours are nine to five."

He says, "Great." Though interns are typically not paid because it takes more time to teach them then they're worth, I can see Michael is special and doesn't really have to be taught much. Therefore, I tell him he will be getting a salary and tell him the amount which is pretty generous; he is surprised and thanks me.

He worked for me the entire summer, was exceptional legally, and liked by everyone. When the summer ended, I told him that after law school, he had a job with me if he wanted it.

I have always signed payroll checks. The last week before Michael was going back to school, I was signing payroll checks quickly, as usual, rarely bothering to examine them; but one check I was about to sign had the name Michael Rodriguez. I say, "Who the hell is Michael Rodriguez?" I called my secretary and asked her who Michael Rodriguez is. She tells me it's Michael. I say, "Michael who?"

She says, "Michael, our Michael." I ask if Michael is Spanish.

She says yes.

I say, "I thought he was Italian. He likes light Italian opera."

She says, "Bobby, you know you're really crazy, you didn't know he was Puerto Rican?"

I told her, "No, I didn't. I thought he was Italian."

She gives me a look of pity and affection. I say, "What the hell do you know?" I can't believe it. It dawned on me, and I asked, "Does he speak Spanish?"

She says, "Of course."

I say, "Son of a bitch." I have so much difficulty understanding Spanish clients, and Michael is here the whole summer and nobody tells me! I asked her to bring Michael to my office.

I say, "Michael, you're Puerto Rican and can speak Spanish, and you didn't tell me."

He says, "Bobby, I can't believe you didn't know."

I said, "How was I supposed to know; you like Italian light opera."

He says, "Wait until I go back to law school, no one will believe what happens here."

I laugh, get up, give him a big hug, and tell him how much I'm going to miss him.

Getting back to Ralphie, my secretary buzzes me. Steve is on the phone. I picked up the phone. "Steve, how did it go?"

"Nice and easy, bail was set at fifty grand which was covered by the bail bondsman. I'm at a dinner on Queens Boulevard with Ralphie and his wife. How did it go last night?"

"I spoke with Jimmy, and everything is cool, Ralphie can go home." "Boy, will he be happy to hear that."

"I'll be in the whole day tomorrow and we can straighten things out." "No problem, Bobby, see you tomorrow."

"Steve, thank you again for your help. One last thing, tell Ralphie to come by later on today."

"You got it."

Ralphie comes in about five that night. My secretary brings him back to my office. He looks good. I ask him, "How did it go last night?"

"After searching me, they gave me an orange jumpsuit and put me in a cell by myself. I couldn't sleep because some guy was screaming all night. First thing this morning, they gave me my clothes back, and I'm in court before you know it. Steve was there with a bail bond guy, and I was out of there in an hour. Bobby, thank you."

We both have questions to ask each other. I go first. "How did it go when you went back to the feds?"

"Well, when I went in and gave them your letter, it was like the end of a New Year's Eve party. They were excited to see me, but when I showed them your letter, it was like someone put a pin into a balloon. They were at first pissed off and started to yell at me. I did what you told me. I just stood there and looked them straight in the eye and didn't say a word. One of them said, 'It's fucking Aliazzo.'

"Then another one said, 'Isn't that the guy whose brother is an ADA?' After that, they didn't ask me any other questions and didn't threaten me with more charges. They cuffed me and took me to jail. It wasn't as bad as I thought it would be. Before I start asking you what happens next, I want to know what happened with Jimmy. I assume it went okay because Steve said I could go home."

I tell him about Ronnie and me meeting with Jimmy last night and that New York and the local boys have decided to give him a pass on condition that he talks to no one and takes a plea. "I told them you had already agreed to that. One last thing, Jimmy wants the recipe for the pasta and broccoli."

He looks at me. "All right, as long as he doesn't start giving it out to everyone."

Now I tell him, "Here's what is going to happen. Since you have already been arraigned, the next thing that will happen is Steve will meet with the feds to work out a plea deal. They're going to want you to plead to a higher felony so that you get more time. If you're lucky, and we get a good judge with a brain, I think you will get between two and three years. Generally, you do two thirds of the short time. Here, the short time is twenty-four months, and you should do two-thirds of that, which would be sixteen months or so. This is a guess that is pretty close to what should happen. More importantly, we are going to fight like hell to get you into a minimum-security prison. We'll try for Allenwood. It's in Pennsylvania where the Watergate guys were sent. It's basically white-collar criminals, so you should be okay. I know this is a lot to take in, but the time will go fast. In the meantime, what are you going to do for work?"

He said, "I'll go back to cooking. I already got an offer this morning. I think I can take my pick of two or three places. I'll be making almost twice what I was making driving, but the hours suck. Generally, from four to twelve, so I go back to not being able to have dinner with the family." He asks, "Bobby, how long until I have to leave for jail?"

"Probably two to three months. I'll be at the sentencing and will write a letter to the judge on your behalf and so will Ronnie."

At his sentencing, Ronnie showed up to speak on his behalf. When he showed up, the judge, who knew Ronnie and knew he was an ADA, asked what he was doing there. Ronnie said he was there to speak on behalf of Ralph.

The judge was about to say something, I guess something like, "You're an ADA, you should not be here."

Before he could say anything, Ron said, "I'm here as a private citizen who has known the defendant since I was eight years old and would like to speak on his behalf."

The judge said, "Go ahead."

Ron then proceeded to give the most eloquent speech about Ralphie and all his wonderful qualities. It was quite moving. Word was the judge had intended to give Ralphie three to six years, but after Ronnie's speech, he gave him two to three years, as I had hoped. That's just a guess, but that's what I think. The best part of this whole thing is that we were able to get him into Allenwood Penitentiary.

Ronnie had managed through the Department of Corrections to make arrangements to have Ralphie surrender himself at the prison. Ronnie decided to take him there himself to calm him down as he was still frightened to death. The night before, Ralph stayed at Ronnie's apartment. Ron went to bed and, in the middle of the night, found Ralphie sleeping on the floor in his room—he was too frightened to sleep alone. This is the same dangerous criminal the feds wanted to put in jail for twenty years.

They leave in the early afternoon, Ronnie thinking we'll get there before dinner, so Ron can take Ralph for dinner in a restaurant and then surrender him at Allenwood. They get to Allentown around five in the evening. They went to a nice restaurant that Ron heard about and had a lovely dinner (polishing off two bottles of wine.) It's now after eight, and Ronnie is about to surrender Ralphie.

They started driving, then stopped at a gas station to ask how far to Allenwood Penitentiary. They are told it's about 120 miles. Ron says, "How can that be? We're in Allentown already."

The station attendant tells him, "That's right, but Allenwood Penitentiary is not in Allentown, it's over a hundred miles away."

Ron thinks, *there is no way I'm going to drive over a hundred miles in the dark while I'm half drunk.* He calls Allenwood, tells them, "This is ADA Ronald Aliazzo, and there has been a delay in surrendering prisoner Ralph Lucie. He will be arriving tomorrow morning before noon." And then he finds a motel for the night.

As they are driving to the motel, Ralphie turns to Ronnie, saying, "Boy, you're some lawyer, you can't even get me into jail."

A week or so after Ralph went to Allenwood, I called to see how he was doing. As one of his attorneys, I get him on the phone with no problem. I tell Ralphie, "I'm joining a book club and I will pick out the books and have them sent directly to you. The reason for a book club is the prison does not allow me to send them directly to you, but you can receive books directly from a book club. I want to educate you, I don't want you to come out the same dummy you were when you went in, and I'm going to discuss the books with you after you read them because all the books I send you I have already read."

There's silence on the phone for a moment, then I hear, "Bobby, I fucking love you."

The first book I sent him was *The Pope of Greenwich Village* because I knew he could relate to it and would like it.

"So how has your first week been?"

He has a lot of news. He tells me they put him into a room with some Chinese guy who prays all the time, cannot speak English, but is really a nice, quiet guy. I ask, "What's he in for?"

He says from what he can make out, income tax evasion. He says, "I think he used to be some kind of minister or something."

I ask, "Are you sure he's not Korean?"

He says, "Maybe. I can't tell the difference between Korean and Chinese." He later found out that it was not Reverend Moon, who served his time in Danbury Correctional Facility, but he was Korean and a minister.

He said, "It's really not that bad. Everyone minds their own business. If you screw up here, they send you to Lewisburg Prison which is for hardcore criminals, so everyone is pretty cool here." They found out he was a cook and assigned him to the kitchen. He said the quality of the food is okay, but how they tell him to prepare it is terrible and has no taste.

He said the other day, chicken was on the menu. He prepared it the way they told him to; he said it was tasteless and he couldn't eat it. There was a lot of leftover uncooked chicken, so he made for himself and one of his helpers some chicken parmesan and pasta. One of the guards came over and asked what that was. Ralph told him and asked if the guard would like to try some, which the guard did. The rest is history. Within a couple of weeks, Ralphie was making gourmet meals for all the guards, including the sergeants and higher-ups.

He was supposed to serve sixteen months which is two-thirds of the short time of his sentence; this reduction is conditioned on good behavior. He got out in earlier because the guards, on their own, wrote a letter to the parole board recommending his early release. He didn't know they did that for him since he never would think to ask them to do it. You see, the guards, like everyone else, once they got to know Ralphie, couldn't help but care for him.

Once he found out what they did for him, he went to thank them. They told him they would like to ask him for a favor in return. Would he teach his two helpers all the meals he had been making for them? He said they already knew most of them, but he agreed to write them all down. They asked Ralph if it would it be okay for them to call him from time to time if they had any questions. He said, "Sure, I'll give them my number before I leave." He still had a week and a half before his release date to make sure they knew how to make all of Ralphie's dishes. Ralphie is the only prisoner I know of who became an adviser to a prison on its culinary affairs.

After his release, he almost became an intellectual. All the reading he did while in prison just whetted his curiosity. I sent him books on politics, including Ronald Reagan's autobiography. After reading it, he became a staunch Republican and conservative. We used to debate politics because I tend to be a fiscal conservative but a social liberal. I have voted Republican and Democratic, depending on the candidate. I think with Ralphie, I created a monster who became very conservative in his thinking.

Eventually, he made up with Jimmy. How did it happen? Ralphie, on occasion, would cook for some of the local wise guys at their club for parties and special occasions. They all knew what had happened, but that was over a year ago, and they knew that Ralph had kept quiet and did the time; so as far as they were concerned, it was history. If he knew Jimmy would be there, he would just say he couldn't make it, he was busy. This one time, they asked him to cook, knowing that Jimmy was not in town. He was wrong. Jimmy came into the club while Ralphie was setting up. They looked at each other. Everyone stopped dead in their tracks. Jimmy looked at Ralph, came over to him, looked him dead in the eye, and said, "You, fat fuck" and gave him a big hug.

John Adams High School

Ron and I went to grammar school at the Nativity of the Blessed Virgin Mary in Ozone Park between Ninety-first and Ninetieth Streets. We lived on Ninety first Street right across the street from the school and the church which was next door. There were fifty-nine kids in our class, thirty-six girls and twenty-three boys. We all started in kindergarten and went straight through to eighth grade.

So, all of us kids were together for eight years. Everyone knew everyone. There were no Black or Spanish kids in our class. It was 100 percent white; the ethnic make-up was Italian, Irish, and German. Our teachers were all nuns who were very strict. It seemed everything we did was a sin—cursing was a sin, missing mass on Sunday was a sin, fighting was a sin, eating meat on Friday was a sin, looking at girls with impure thoughts was a sin and nearly anything else we did. We spent a lot of time in church and there always seemed to be another religious holiday where mass was required.

It was an environment that was very strict. As a result, we were all pretty repressed in our social life. Even though we boys and girls were together for all those years, we were shy around each other. In all the years that I was in that school, I never heard a boy curse in front of a girl. We had homework every day, and if you didn't do it, you stayed after school for detention to complete your homework. From what I could see from my friends from PS 63, a public school, we were light years ahead of them academically.

After graduation, we all went to different high schools. Most of the kids went to Catholic high schools. Those who didn't went to public high schools, and if you lived in Ozone Park, the high school you went to was John Adams High School. It was a fifteen-minute walk from my house, and that's where Ron and I went. After graduation from Nativity in June, we had the summer off and then in September, we started John Adams. We were warned before starting by a friend, Louie San Botti (who had graduated from Nativity and was in his second year at John Adams), what to expect and how to handle ourselves along with the dos and don'ts to get along. Among the don'ts were, "Do not ever give money to the Black kids, because if you did, they would take you for a mark and would want money from you every day. Most of them think because you're White, you're rich, so if they ask, just say no. Don't lie to them because if they see you buying lunch, which we intended to do, they will accuse you of lying and cause you problems. What kind of problems? They will harass you, make fun of you, or challenge you to a fight; and if you refuse to fight and report them, then you would really have problems. It's like what you see in the movies, no one squeals to the guards."

September comes, and it's off to high school. A couple of weeks before school started, we received cards telling us what homeroom to report to so we could be given our different class assignments. At Nativity, we stayed in the same classroom all day long. Now, every forty minutes, we would leave the class we were in and go to another room with different people, which was all new to us. The worst part was that Ron and I had different homerooms and didn't know when we would see each other.

September 6, the first day of high school, we get up and get dressed, have breakfast, say goodbye to our parents, and it's off to John Adams.

We arrived at school fifteen minutes early, and a crowd that looked like more than 100 people is waiting by the closed doors which open at eight-thirty. More than a third of the students waiting are Black, both boys and girls. We're kind of in shock and a little intimidated. We had never been around that many Black people in our lives. I see a Black guy with a huge comb with a large handle in his hair. As I had never seen anything like this before, I went over to him, thinking that he forgot to take the comb out of his hair.

Trying to be cool, I say, "Hey, bro, you forgot to take the comb out of your hair."

He looks at me. "Are you trying to fuck with me?" I say, "No."

He says, "Boy, you don't know shit, that's the style, man."

I say, "I'm sorry, I didn't mean to fuck with you, I didn't know." He looks at me, knows I'm sincere, and says, "No problem, man."

I go over to Ronnie. He asks, "What was that all about?" I told him. He says, "That's the latest style among Black people."

I say, "How do you know?"

He says, "Last week, I took the Q8 bus to Jamaica to see Big Mike who worked at the department store Montgomery Ward." He needed some clothes for school. Ron says on the bus going into Jamaica, which had a large Black population, he saw lots of guys with big afros with large combs in their hair. As we are talking, the doors open, and everyone starts walking in. There are signs with classroom numbers and arrows pointing us in the direction of our assigned homeroom. My classroom number is to the right, and Ron's number is to the left. Ron says, "If we don't run into each other all day, I'll meet you at the doors we came in."

I say, "Okay, see you later."

As I am walking, looking for my homeroom number, I see three Black guys talking and looking at me. I attempt to make believe I don't see them and try to walk by. One of the three, the tallest one, over six feet, comes up to me. He says, "Yo, bro, you new here?"

I tell him, "Yes, it's my first day." He says, "Let me hold a quarter."

Hearing Louie's voice in my head, I say, "No." He says, "What do you mean no?"

I say no again.

He says, "Let me hold a quarter or meet me after school at the radiators."

I say, "Where are the radiators?"

He says, "In the end of the boy's locker room." I say, "What for?"

He says, "So we can settle our differences without being disturbed. Make sure you show up or I'll see you tomorrow before school starts and fuck you up in front of everybody."

I look him in the eye. "Fuck you, I'll be there, count on it." And I walked away.

Growing up in Ozone Park, I had been challenged to fights many times and I learned really quickly that if you backed down, you would be bullied and harassed and be looked upon as weak, and even your friends would avoid you. Better to get a black eye or a bloody nose or both than be looked upon as a coward by your friends. So, I had some experience and had been in my share of fights, but this guy was taller than me and weighed more than me.

The thing I was concerned about was Ronnie not being there. He had always been there when I had a fight, and if I was getting beat up, Ronnie would stop the fight or more often jump in, so it got around if you fought one, you had better be prepared to fight both. That was a good thing since a lot of fights were avoided because people were aware of that. Although I had been in my fair share of fights and won more than I lost, I hated fighting and tried to avoid it if at all possible. As Mike Tyson once said, "Everyone is brave until they get punched in the face."

I had been punched in the face, and I can tell you it's a very unpleasant experience. Well, I knew one thing for sure, I was going to show up, as I said before. Better a bloody nose or a black eye than to be someone's patsy in the future. The thing was, how do I find Ronnie or Louie? There were over 2,500 kids in the school.

I found my homeroom. The class was almost full with four seats empty. It was mostly Black kids. I found a seat near a window in the back. There was a Black girl sitting behind me. She tapped me on the shoulder. I turned around, and she said, "You good looking, you "EYE'-talian"?"

I'm a little shocked and embarrassed. None of the girls at Nativity had ever said that to me. Sure, there were crushes, but everyone was too shy to ever say anything.

This was a new world to me. Over the course of my years at John Adams, this happened several times. These Black girls thought nothing of coming up to you and asking you if you wanted to hang out, today's equivalent of, "Do you want to hook up?"

I was thirteen and still a little timid around girls. Most of these girls at thirteen and fourteen were not virgins. I was. I would hear them talk about their sexual experiences out loud and they didn't seem to care who heard them.

The teacher came into the room. Believe it or not, her name was Mrs. Jones. She had a purse, some books, and a newspaper. She turned and wrote her name on the blackboard. She was around fifty, White, and while looking at the class, appeared bored. She said, "Welcome, everyone. My name is Mrs. Jones, and I will be your homeroom teacher." She told everyone how the school operates and how every forty minutes, we would go from classroom to classroom, and each class would have a different teacher and a different subject. A couple more kids came in, and now the class was full.

She picked up a stack of papers, gave them to the people in front and asked to pass them back. She announced, "This is a test to determine where you are academically," and instructed anyone who didn't have a pen or pencil to come up to the front and get one. She said the test should take about thirty minutes. "If you finish early," she concluded," start on one of the books you've been given."

"Okay, everyone, start," she firmly announced.

I looked at the test and the questions. These questions would be for sixth-graders at Nativity. I couldn't believe it. I went through the exam in less than five minutes. The Black kid sitting across from me whispered, "You know the answers?"

I said, "Yes."

He asks if he can see them. I say, "Sure." As I look up at Mrs. Jones, who is reading the newspaper and has it in front of her face and can't see what's going on, I slip him the test, and he quickly fills in the answers and then passes his test to his friend who copies the answers, and before you know, it is passed around to the whole classroom. I can't believe these kids don't know the answers. Up until today, I never realized what a good education we received at Nativity.

With about ten minutes left, Mrs. Jones finally looks up from her newspaper, looks around the class, and asks, "Has anyone finished the test?"

Everyone raises their hand. She says, "Only those who have finished the test, raise their hand."

Everyone proudly keeps their hand up. She looks shocked. She says, "Okay, pass the papers to the front."

She starts to go over them. She calls the student whose test she just went over and says, "Very good, you have a perfect score." She reads the second and third test, and then the fourth and fifth, and all are perfect scores. Now she is suspicious. She quickly goes over a few more tests, all perfect scores. She looks around, wondering what's going on. No one says anything.

She gets up from her desk, walks in front of it, and asks one of the students who had a perfect score one of the questions on the test. He doesn't know the answer. She asks him a few more test questions, and he doesn't know any of the answers. She does the same with a couple of other students, none of whom know the answers. She says, "What's going on here?"

A couple of the kids look over at me as if I'm smart, like I'll know what to do. I don't know what to do. She sees them looking over at me. "You, what's your name?"

I told her.

"Did you give everyone the answers?"

I say, "No." She looks for my test, perfect like everyone else's. She looks at the grammar school I attended (which was requested at the top of the test paper). She says, "You graduated from Nativity?"

Apparently, Nativity had a good reputation, and the students from Nativity were always way ahead of the students from the public schools.

The bell rings, all the kids get up to go to their next class. I get up to leave. She says, "You, Mr. Aliazzo, come up here." She asks again if I gave the answers out. I deny it again. She says, "I don't believe you, and I'm reporting this cheating to Mr. Clark." He was the principal. "You will be hearing from him." She says, "You can go now."

I'm confused and frightened. In my first twenty-five minutes of high school, I had a fight at three and now I'm being reported to the principal for cheating. I walk out, looking for my next class, hoping Ronnie is in one of the classes.

The rest of the day goes quickly as it is all new to me. I keep to myself, hoping to at least see one of my former Nativity classmates. I don't run into a single one. The classes are all the same, mostly things I learned in sixth or seventh grade.

I get back to my homeroom at the end of the day. Mrs. Jones asks if anyone has any questions. Most of the questions are about finding the way around a school which is very big. I didn't have gym today, so I asked her where the gym is. She tells me, and also that Mr. Clark will be wanting to see me tomorrow.

The bell rings, class is dismissed, and everyone is heading for the door. The school is so big I don't know what door I came in. There is no way I'm going to find Ronnie. I think, *okay, bite the bullet, go down to the gym, and if I can't talk my way out of the fight, the worst thing is I get a black eye or bloody nose or both.* I find my way to the gym, then through the gym to the locker room.

Standing in front of the lockers is the guy I'm going to fight, and with him is a small Black kid. The small kid says to the guy I'm about to fight, "Is this the guy, Ken?"

Now I know the guy's name is Ken. He looks at me, and I think he is a little surprised that I showed up. He says, "Follow me" and starts walking between the lockers to the back of the gym where I assume the radiators are. The lockers are a couple of feet apart with a bench between them. Trying to be cool, I get up on the bench and start walking on the bench, following Ken to the radiators. The little Black kid is behind me.

As we get to the end, I can see the radiators ahead. I'm right behind Ken, still up on the bench. I don't think he is going to want to talk. As he turns to face me, I see his hand go into his pocket. My heart stops. Everything in that split second has changed. This is no longer a black eye or bloody nose. If he is reaching for a knife,

I could be seriously hurt or even killed. My heart is racing out of my chest.

Just then, as if God had put it there, I see an empty six-ounce thick Coke bottle laying on its side. I grab the bottle, and I'm on him before he even gets his hand out of his pocket. I hit him square on the top of his head, and down we both went. Blood is already flying all over the place. I'm on top of him and hit him again with the bottle. I can see he is out of it, bleeding and no longer able to defend himself. I stop, then I jump up quickly. Where's his friend? His friend with his eyes wide open is staring at me. As I quickly stand to face his friend, he runs away.

I look to see what Ken had in his hand, which is now laying on the floor beside him. It's a roll of pennies. Not a knife, but if he had hit me with that roll of pennies in his hand, I would have probably parted with a bunch of my teeth. I go over to the sinks and start to wash the blood off of my hands and face. The Coke bottle never broke, and I have no cuts on my hand. My shirt and parts of my pants are covered in blood. I clean up as best I can and start to leave.

I look over at Ken. He is up on one elbow, bleeding and still groggy. I grab two towels and I wet one and go over to him and give him both towels. He puts the wet one on his head and starts to clean himself up. I look at him square in the eye. He looks back. No words are spoken. I leave.

I finally found my way to an exit out of the school. There are still a lot of kids hanging out. As I start to walk my way through the crowd, everyone is staring at me. With blood all over me, I know why. I walk as quickly as I can, but I don't run. I keep my head down.

When I get home, I look for Ronnie. He's in the kitchen having a snack.

He looks at me. I say, "Where the fuck were you?"

He says, "Waiting for you, where were you? And what happened?"

I tell him everything. He asks if I'm all right. I tell him, "Yes, but I don't know what's going to happen tomorrow. Is Ken going to have his friends looking for me? I don't know how badly he was hurt. Will the cops come and arrest me? Will I be expelled from school. What's going to happen when Mom and Dad find out?"

He says, "First things first, get out of those clothes and put them in the washer and dryer before they get home." They both worked and didn't get home until after six.

That night, we talked about our first day of high school and how we liked it. We told them it was okay, but it would take some time getting used to.

After dinner, we go out and go over to Louie, who lives up the street from us and tell him what happened and our concern that there may be a bunch of Ken's friends waiting for me tomorrow. He says once a fight is over, it's over, but just to be safe, he will walk to school with us and tell a bunch of his friends to meet him there just in case. I feel a lot better. When I went to bed that night, I was feeling better still because no cops had come to arrest me and that maybe Ken was okay.

The next morning, we meet Louie and walk to school together. When we get there, the doors are about to open. There is no Ken around, but everyone is staring at me and Ron. As the doors open and I start to walk toward the doors, it's like the parting of the Red Sea. Everyone moves aside and lets us pass, again staring at us. I think it must be about the fight. But how could anyone know? It happened after school, and there were not that many people who saw me with the blood on me, yet it seemed like the whole school knew. I was to learn that things like a fight spread around the school like wildfire. I think they weren't sure which one of us was in the fight.

We now figure out which door we came in and again agree to meet after school. However, we exchanged our class schedules with the room numbers the night before so we knew where each one would be during the day in case of an emergency.

I find my way to my homeroom and go to my seat. Mrs. Jones comes in, puts her things down, and starts to read a note on her desk. The Black kid to my right who I had given the test to the day before leans over and whispers, "Was it you or your twin brother who fucked up Kenny Williams?"

I say, "How do you know I have a twin brother?"

He says everyone knows. I say neither one of us was in a fight. He starts to say something else but is interrupted by Mrs. Jones who has just finished reading the note and turns to look at me and says, "Frank Aliazzo, you are to go to the principal's office right now."

I think, *Here I go again.* I asked her where the principal's office is. She tells me. I think she thinks this is about the cheating that went on yesterday. I'm prepared to deny it again.

I find my way to the office and walk in. There's a secretary in the front office sitting at a desk. She asks me what I want. I told her I was sent to the office by Mrs. Jones, my homeroom teacher. She asks me my name as she is looking over some papers on her desk. I tell her. She stops and looks up and stares at me. I think even she knows about the cheating. She gets up and goes over to the closed door of the principal's office, knocks, opens the door, and says, "Frank Aliazzo is here." I don't hear what the principal says, but she waves me in.

As I walk in, I see Mr. Clark the principal sitting at his desk, and right in front of the desk, standing there, is Kenny Williams. His head is all bandaged, his forehead is swollen. I look at him. I'm in shock. Mr. Clark asks, "Is this him?"

He says, "No, I never saw this kid before."

Mr. Clark asks me to show him my hands. I do. There are no marks on my hands because the Coke bottle never broke, and I only hit him with the coke bottle. I have no marks on my face to indicate that I was ever in a fight.

He looks at me and asks, "Did you do this to him?" I say, "No, sir."

He looks up at Kenny who is much bigger and heavier than me. I think I know what he's thinking. *How could these two be in a fight when the big guy is all bandaged up and the little guy doesn't have a mark on him?* He looks at us both for a long moment and then says, "You can both leave."

I'm out the door first and head back to my homeroom, not believing what just happened. There's about five minutes before classes start. As I sit down, a student aide opens the door with a note which she gives to Mrs. Jones. She looks up at me and says, "Frank Aliazzo, go to the principal's office."

I say, "I was just there."

She says, "Well, I guess he wants to see you again."

I head back. I know the way now. As I walk in, his secretary says, "Go in, Mr. Clark wants to see you again."

I knock, open the door, and walk in. Mr. Clark looks up and motions me to have a seat right in front of his desk. He then picks up what looks like a note and starts reading it. He looks up. "This is a note from Mrs. Jones regarding your cheating on the test she gave out yesterday. What's going on with you? First the fight and now this. Did you cheat on the test?"

I say, "No, sir."

He says, "I am prepared to call everyone in your class one by one, and if you're lying to me, I will find out, and the consequence for you will be much worse than if you tell the truth. I will ask you one last time, "did you cheat?"

I say, "Yes and no."

He says, "What do you mean by that?"

I just can't lie anymore, so I tell him the truth. I say, "I always thought cheating was when you didn't know the answers to a test and got them from someone else. What happened yesterday was that I knew all the answers to the test and finished it in about five minutes. I was going to start reading the book we were told to do if we finished early, when the kid next to me asked if I knew the answers. I said yes. He asked if I would give him my test with the answers. It was my first ten minutes in high school. I didn't know what to do, so I slipped him my test. He copied the answers and gave me back my test. I didn't know he would pass the test around to everyone else."

He asks what grammar school I attended. I told him. He looks at me and asks, "Were you the smartest student in your class?"

I say, "No, sir, there were a lot of kids smarter than me."

He looks at me for what seems like forever then says, "I will let this matter go if you promise you will never give answers to anyone again."

I am so happy I'm not going to get into any more trouble. I immediately said yes. I kept that promise for quite a while and only broke it to help out close friends who needed help, and then only to them. They knew not to give the answers to anyone else.

I ran into Ken Williams a couple of days later. He was hanging out with some friends. I walked over and asked him if I could talk to him. We walked far enough away so we wouldn't be heard, and I thanked him for not ratting me out. He told me, "No problem." We were on the school football team a while later for a short time and actually became friends.

The end of this little story was that three years later, my father pulled us out of John Adams and shipped us off to Mount Assumption Institute in Plattsburgh, New York, a private Catholic boarding school. Why? We failed all our courses in our third year at John Adams. Why? We never went to class. My father didn't know the reason for us failing all of our classes. He asked our brother, Vin, who was already an attorney, to go speak to our grade adviser. I remember him telling Vin, "If they're not college material, then we'll find them a nice trade so that they will be able to support themselves."

My father made us go with Vin to speak to the grade adviser who advised Vin that we were college material. In fact, very bright, and that the reason that we flunked out was because we did not attend the required number of classes, and therefore, we automatically failed. He said when we did occasionally show up for a final, we mostly received As and some Bs, but without the required number of hours, they could not pass us. Vin thanked him. When we left, we begged Vin not to tell the old man.

He had always protected us from my father when he was on the warpath with us for one of our screwups. He told us, "Not this time, this is too important." He told our father everything. We were expecting to get our asses kicked, but no, my father was very calm. I think he was happy to know he didn't have two sons who were dummies.

He said, "I know you have your summer jobs all lined up, and we'll talk about school in September."

In September, on a Sunday morning, a few days before school started, we came down for breakfast and saw a few suitcases all packed. We asked, "What's going on?"

My father looked at us and said, "You're leaving for Mount Assumption in a couple of hours."

We knew about Mount Assumption because Vin and my cousin Anthony Urso, who also were the same age and both lawyers, had attended Mount Assumption but for different reasons, although I don't remember what those reasons were. I remember them telling us that the Brothers of Christian Instruction ran the school, and if you got out of line there, they would beat the shit out of you. That coupled with the fact that Plattsburg was almost on the Canadian border and freezing cold made us, shall I say, not happy being sent there. My father looked at us and calmly said, "I'm trying to save your lives." That's when we knew there was no talking him out of it. We had too much love and respect for him, and so off we went, but that's another whole other story.

George Guseman

Ronnie and Bobby

It was, I believe, February third at around 6:00 p.m. I'm in my office waiting for Ronnie who had called me in the afternoon to say he wanted to go to Don Pepe's for dinner. He said he had been dreaming of Linguine and Clam Sauce for a week. He also wanted to discuss something important with me. I called Bonnie and asked her to join us as Ronnie usually confided in her more than me. One of the joys of my life was that Ronnie and Bonnie cared for and confided in each other so much. She was the sister he never had. But that day, she had just gotten home from court, was exhausted, and passed on dinner.

Both Ronnie and Bonnie had previously worked as Legal Aid criminal lawyers at the Queens County Supreme Court and were actually, on occasion, in the same court room representing criminal defendants; this was a bad idea, since the two of them often found almost any and everything funny. Sometimes in social situations or, believe it or not, at funerals they were unable to control the humor they saw in the same, very inappropriate things. It's usually not a good idea to have the lawyer representing you in what you believe is a serious matter that could result in you going to jail, laughing, sometimes uncontrollably. Bon and Ronnie were in the misdemeanor part at the time, and the charges, for the most part, were not serious, but nevertheless, the defendants and the judges were not happy. Eventually, the bosses at Legal Aid finally agreed to keep them in separate court rooms.

Finally, Ron shows up when I'm engrossed in a case I was preparing for an EBT (Examination Before Trial). I ask him, "What's going on?"

He says, "Let's talk at dinner." He hasn't eaten all day. He asks if Bon's coming.

I tell him, "No, she just got home a few minutes ago and is tired." He says, "Okay, let's go."

We get to Don Pepe's in a few minutes and the place is crowded as usual, but there are a couple of tables still open. George one of the owners I know and represented, sees me and comes over and says, "Avvocato"—the Italian word for lawyer, "Welcome, how have you been?"

I say, "Good, George"

He looks at Ronnie and says, "I see you brought the law with you" and gives Ronnie a big hug.

Ronnie and I have known George for as long as I can remember. We were neighborhood kids, and occasionally, when we were hanging out and he saw us, he would ask us to do small chores for him. We never said no for two reasons: (1) because he always gave us big tips and (2) because it would have been disrespectful.

He brings us over to a table and tells the waiter, who must have been new because I knew all the waiters, "This is my lawyer, take good care of him."

We look around—still the same old Don Pepe's; nothing has changed. The kitchen was totally open, and you could see all the cooking going on. All the chefs were male, all the waiters were male and that's the way it has always been since I could remember. The food was indescribably delicious. George bought only the very best of everything.

Don Pepe's was very close to Aqueduct Race Track, so a lot of jockeys and trainers ate there. Then the horse owners found out about it through the jockeys and trainers and started eating there too. Most of the owners were wealthy and from all over the country; it became an "in" place to eat. On any given night, there would be limousines parked in front with chauffeurs waiting for their rich employers. The neighborhood was not fancy, but the place was immaculately clean.

The great and unusual thing about it at the time, was that the kitchen was open. As soon as you entered, the overwhelming aroma of delicious food hit you and you became immediately hungry. The waiters treated everyone the same except for the gangsters who got preferential treatment.

On any given night they were there; from John Gotti on down, they were there. They were huge tippers and knew all the waiters by name. There was one guy who was always there who I knew only as Tony the Sheik, nicknamed because he was always immaculately dressed, always with a suit and tie. He had a special table just for him. I never found out who he was or what he did, and growing up in Ozone Park, you learned not to ask questions and to mind your own business.

I once had an incident with George, the owner, which left me embarrassed, and whenever I went to eat there, I always checked to see how crowded the place was. I went there one night with some doctor friends who had heard about the place but were told it was hard to get in. They took no reservations, and if it was crowded, you simply had to wait. My friends said they were okay with that and when we arrived it was indeed packed and we had to wait. As I was giving my name to be put on the list, George sees me and yells, "Avvocato!" He comes through the crowd and says "Counselor, what are you doing?"

I told him to put my name on the waiting list. He tells me if I ever come there again and there's a waiting list, go around the back where the kitchen is and ask for me, or if I'm not here, Frank, and you'll get the next available table. "You can wait in the kitchen and have a drink while waiting." He asks, "How many people are with you?"

I say, "Three."

He says, "Follow me, a table just opened."

My friends and several other people who have been waiting have heard this whole conversation. I say, "It's okay, George, we'll wait our turn."

He looks at me. "What? Follow me."

One of the patrons who has been waiting starts to complain. George leans over and whispers in his ear loud enough for several people to hear, "If you don't like it, you can leave."

I'm embarrassed, but to avoid creating a bigger scene, I follow him. It turns out he only did this for the top wise guys, so now Ron and I are in the same class as the top wise guys—what an honor

We sit down after passing a couple of tables where wise guys we know are eating and say a quick hello. George knows this is being respectful and waits for us. Normally, an Assistant District Attorney would ignore a known wise guy, but not Ronnie. To him, most of them were just guys from the neighborhood whom he has known his whole life.

We finally sat down. There are no menus. An enormous board lists everything Don Pepe's serves. We order and ask for a bottle of the house red which arrives in a bottle with no name on it. We don't know what kind of wine it is, but it is delicious. As we are waiting for our food and are enjoying the house red we begin to chat. "So," I ask, "What's going on? What do you want to talk about?"

Ron starts by telling me he has decided to leave the DA's office. He loves it, but lately, he has been under a lot of pressure. As soon as he finishes one trial, there are five more waiting, and he seems to be getting all the tough cases, the ones that require a lot of time and are tough to win. "They know that I am a neurotic and compulsive worker. It's not that I like to win so much, it's more that I hate, just hate to lose, and they know it. It's also a little about the money. I'm always a day late and a dollar short when it comes to money. It's a struggle, and I'm tired of always living from paycheck to paycheck."

I say, "What are you worried about? I always have you covered."

He says, "Yeah, but you make three to ten times what I make, and you were always better with money than me. Besides, I don't want to have to depend on you all the time."

I tell him, "If you didn't spend money like a drunken sailor, maybe you wouldn't be broke all the time."

He says, "What do you mean?"

I say, "Take for instance, Huck Finn Day. You probably blew a thousand dollars in just that one day."

He says, "How can you mention that? That's only a couple of times a year, and it's Ali."

Now you may wonder what Huck Finn day is and who is Ali. Well, Alison, Ali, is my daughter who is at that time in grammar school and has quite a special relationship with Uncle Ronnie. He is her hero. She simply adores him and him her. If he is coming to visit and we tell her, she is looking out of the window every ten minutes until he comes, then runs out to his car, yelling, "Uncle Ronnie, Uncle Ronnie!"

Huck Finn is a character in Mark Twain's book, *Tom Sawyer*, and in its sequel, *Huckleberry Finn*. He is a character who plays hooky from school to go on adventures. He told her about Huck Finn and says, "Someday, we have to play hooky and go on an adventure."

She never forgot it, although Bonnie and I did.

The first time it happened, we were surprised. He simply called one morning around seven and asked to speak to Ali. I think she was five or six when he said, "Okay, Ali, it's Huck Finn Day."

We heard her scream and come running down the stairs, yelling, "It's Huck Finn Day, it's Huck Finn Day!"

Now how the hell do you tell her she can't go on Huck Finn Day because she has school? Simply put, you don't. Bonnie and I always felt one day with Uncle Ronnie was worth ten days of school. I ask him, "What the hell are you going to do with her all day?"

He says, "I will be picking her up around eleven-thirty. Al Grosso is driving us." So, wherever he was taking her, he was taking her in a limousine. He was taking her to a Broadway matinee (we loved Broadway musicals, and as a result, Ali did also), then to the Russian Tea Room for dinner, then to a New York special dessert place called Serendipity. Bonnie helped her into a new dress and she looked beautiful. He showed up dressed in a suit and tie, and off they went. This was a typical Huck Finn Day. The cost, I don't know, between the limousine, the tickets (he only would get the first five rows because she was small and he wanted her to see everything and be close to the action), The Russian Tea Room followed by Serendipity probably cost close to a thousand bucks. Of course, he was insulted when I offered to chip in.

As our food comes, he tells me he has not officially quit his job but has asked for a year's break, a kind of sabbatical. They agreed and told him he could come back anytime he wanted as long as the present DA was still in office. I asked him, "How are you going to support yourself for a year?"

He says he was thinking he could try some civil cases for me, if I wanted. He said with me, he could try a case then take some time off before the next case; it wouldn't be the kind of job where he had to report to work every day. I knew he had lots of offers but I knew other than the DA's office, he would never work with anyone but me.

I had told him that when he gets tired of playing cops and robbers, come back to the office, and he would be my partner immediately. "It's one thing to be young and poor," I said "but quite another thing to be old and poor." As we were talking, I had another thought. I ran it by him. I told him that I was thinking of opening a small satellite branch office in Jackson Heights, Queens. We were getting a lot of cases from that area, and I anticipated a small branch office would be a winner. I explained it would be a very small office with space for one attorney's office, a secretary and a waiting room.

I had already found just the right office and furnished it. It was on the second floor of a building right on Roosevelt Boulevard above a Travel Agency that had just opened up. Though small and not particularly elegant, if we signed up just a couple of good cases a year, it would pay for itself several times over. I told him I planned to put a paralegal and a secretary in to sign up and work cases before sending them over to us.

The problem was I was having a hard time finding a paralegal that I felt confident in. I said to Ron, "I want you to consider taking over the office for a short time until we can find a paralegal. I'm sure we'll find one we like within a month or two. We'll pay you the salary you were presently getting as an ADA and since the office is going to be slow getting started, you can begin writing your book (he wanted to write a book about the murder case he had just finished). So, it would be like getting paid to write your book."

His eyes lit up. "Getting paid to write my book. Seems too good to be true." Now the thing about Ronnie was that he was a trusting, easy mark. People would take advantage of him all the time. An example: It's Christmas time and Ronnie is in Manhattan Christmas shopping. He stops by a guy who has a stand and is selling beautiful men's cashmere sweaters. He stops to look. They're beautiful. He asks, "How much?"

The guy, a Rastafarian with long dreadlocks, tells him, "Forty dollars each." Ron asks, "How can they be so cheap?"

The Rastafarian tells him he got a great deal on them. Ron asks, "Are these legit?"

Guy appears hurt by the question. Ron asks, "Do I get a receipt?"

The guy says, "Of course." They're long sleeved, V-neck sweaters. He opens up a couple of boxes with sweaters in them, all in the size Ronnie wants.

Ron says, "I'll take five," thinking what great Christmas gifts they will be for me and our brother Vin, and he will have a couple of extra sweaters that he will decide what he will do with. The guy wraps the boxes up, and Ron gives him two hundred bucks for five sweaters. As Ron is leaving, he stops, turns to the guy, and says, "Where are my receipts?"

The guy says, "Coming right up."

Ron says, "I want five in case someone wants to return one." He then says, "Wait a minute, how do I know you will still be here after Christmas?"

The guy says, "Man, I'm here all year-round selling winter stuff, and in the summer, summer stuff. Just ask the guys next to me." There are two other stands next to the Rastafarian selling cashmere scarves and hats and a stand next to that stand selling pocket books. The other sellers are not Rastafarian and seem to be legit and tell Ron that the Rastafarian, Max, has been in that spot for over a year. Ron is satisfied, and the deal is done.

Fast-forward to Christmas eve. We are opening our presents. Ron gives me a box, Vin a box, and has one for himself and says, "Let's open them together because they are all the same."

We open them. The sweaters have no backs or sleeves, just a front. I fall over laughing. Vin asks, "Ronnie, where did you buy them?"

Ronnie, who still is in shock, tells him. Vin looks at him in amazement and then with affection. He can't believe his brother who works with criminals and con artists every day could be such an easy mark.

So now getting back to Ronnie, that trusting soul; I tell him he can also hire a secretary who can help him with the book when things are slow at the beginning. He says, "I don't even have to think about it, it's a done deal." We get up, hug, and shake hands. "Let me give Tommy (the head assistant DA) a few weeks' notice." He says, "I can't believe it, the same money with no trial pressure and the time to write my book."

I remind him, "Don't forget, in a couple of months, when we get a good paralegal, you're coming back to the office as my partner to try cases." He says trying civil cases after trying felony cases is a mere bag of shells.

He's right. With civil cases, money or property are at stake. With criminal cases, a person's liberty, his or her freedom, are at stake. Did you ever wonder why people, for the most part and with lots of exceptions, respect doctors and lawyers? Most people think because if you're one or the other, you have a chance of making good money and therefore having a good life. But why a doctor or a lawyer?

Here's what I figured out. The most important asset anyone has is their health and if you're too sick to enjoy life, support your family, etc. or you're dead, nothing else matters. Doctors are the ones who take care of our ailments and basically save our most important asset—our health.

Why, lawyers? Because after your health, most people think their most important asset is their property. They're wrong. It's their liberty. Without their liberty and freedom, their property, money and possessions are meaningless. Therefore, after your health, the two most important assets people have is their liberty first and their property second; and lawyers are the ones who protect your liberty and your property.

So, it appears I now have Ronnie on board. I didn't tell him that Roosevelt Boulevard has an elevated train right next to his new office window, so as a train goes by, especially at night when the trains are lit, you can see the passengers sitting, reading the newspapers or holding on to the poles. When I rented the place, I hadn't envisioned Ronnie working there, even for only a couple of months. I justified renting the place, thinking a paralegal wouldn't mind the trains, because I would pay him or her well and they would learn a lot.

The lease was month to month, and if the office did well, I would find a nice, larger place away from Roosevelt Avenue. Besides, I figured the train lights go on in the evening, and by that time, the office is closed, and lastly, I was told by the landlord that during the day, the trains did not run that often. It was the morning and evening rush hours that were a problem. In the morning, the rush hour was mostly over by 9:00 a.m., when office hours started, and in the evening, when the offices closed after 5:00 p.m.

While I was talking to the landlord in the office, I noticed a big problem when a train went by. It was incredibly loud. We had to stop talking until the train completely passed. I thought, *how is this going to work if you're talking to a client and a train goes by?*

I expressed my concern to the landlord who said, "It's no big deal, the people here are used to it."

I thought, *Is this a mistake?* Then I figured *I've made so many mistakes.*

What's one more?

As this goes through my mind, my wonderful trusting brother is happily eating Don Pepe's famous baked clams. I can't do it; I have to tell him the truth. I tell him about the train problem, hoping the meal he is happily eating would lessen the blow. He stops eating, looks at me, and says, "I knew it, I knew it, I knew it was too good to be true."

I act hurt, like he is not trusting me. I tell him to stop acting like a pussy. "It's only for a couple of months. You've become so delicate; a little noise is going to bother you."

He says it's not the noise, it's the whole atmosphere. I know he's right, but I push on. "Ronnie, it wasn't meant to be your office, you will be coming back to our offices in several weeks. Look at the positive side, you will get paid your same salary as an ADA for sitting in an office, writing your book with the help of a secretary."

He thinks about it. He doesn't want to think about it too long as he wants to get back to his baked clams before they get cold. He finally says, "Okay, but I get to pick and hire the secretary."

I had no idea what a big mistake I just made allowing him to pick and hire the secretary.

I tell him, "Now that the issues of the new office are settled, I'll get the place ready to open in two weeks." I told him that I met a guy who works in the travel agency downstairs. I had stopped by and introduced myself figuring it would be nice to get to know people in the neighborhood. "They seem to be a very busy travel agency, and some of their prices for airline tickets are unbelievable. They have only been open a month or so and seem to be doing great. They are mostly Spanish speaking. Anyway, the guy's name is George Guseman. I think he's Jewish, but he has a gold medal of the Virgin Mary around his neck."

Ron asks, "If he's Jewish, why does he have a medal of the Virgin Mary around his neck?"

I say, "You got me, but he's some character. He speaks Spanish and perfect English. I think his family comes from Chile or Columbia and they are in the jewelry business. When I told him we were going to be his upstairs neighbors and that we were opening a branch law office; he said 'Welcome' and asked if anyone in our office spoke Spanish because he might from time to time, be able to send us clients.

"I told him we were looking for a secretary who was bilingual and spoke Spanish as well as English. She didn't need to have any legal experience. We would train her, but she had to be able to type. He told me he thinks he might be able to help and gave me his card and told me to call him in a couple of days." I give Ron his card and tell him to be sure to call him. "You can hire anyone you like. If George can't recommend someone, we'll call some agencies, but you'll have to interview them since you want to pick your own secretary."

He says, "Okay, sounds good."

Lastly, I tell him, "You're going to like George, there's something special about him. He's bright, good-looking, and very funny. He offered to put some of our law cards in his office. He has a lot of traffic coming and going and thought maybe he could send us a client or two. I asked him, how come all the women who worked in the agency were so good-looking? He said just by accident. He thinks a lot of them want to travel, and one of the perks of working there is that they get free airline tickets to anywhere they want to go on their vacations."

We finish dinner and Ron says he will tell Tommy, his boss at the DA's office, that he is leaving in two weeks. Before putting the finishing touches on the new office, I ask Ron to meet me tomorrow after work to take a look at the office. I don't want him to back out after seeing the office.

*****

The following night, at about 5:00 p.m., Ron comes by to pick me up. I told him that I had called George and he would be meeting us at the office. I think it is a good idea to get the lay of the land, and George can show him around and tell him where the good restaurants and stores are… When we get there, the travel agency is still buzzing. It seems that after working hours, the agency gets busy with people stopping by who are planning vacations.

We walked up the stairs to the second floor. I had the hallway painted and installed new carpet and new lights. I hung a nice painting of three judges in robes, looking down at the courtroom. I also added an umbrella stand and a coat rack because I was trying to give the place a little class and make sure Ron wouldn't get depressed when entering the hallway. Actually, the hallway looked pretty good. I also had the office painted, freshly carpeted and fully furnished. I thought the place looked pretty decent. It felt clean and new, and to my surprise, Ron liked it. In fact, I thought he liked it better than I did (despite my spending several thousand bucks getting it in decent shape.)

As I'm showing Ron around there is a knock on the door, I yell, "Come in!" and it's George. I introduce him to Ron, and they start chatting.

He tells Ron, "I can't believe what your brother has done to the place." He had also been following the murder case Ron had been trying, since it had been reported in a number of newspapers; I could tell George liked and was impressed with Ron. I thought this was a match made in heaven because I could tell Ron liked him, too.

It was hard not to like George Guseman. I thought it was great that Ron had a friend in the neighborhood. They were about the same age. Little did we know that George Guseman was not only one of the greatest con artists of all time but a brilliant one, a kind, lovable one, a gentle soul and fiercely loyal friend. To be around him was a sheer delight. He was very smart, had an incredible sense of humor and was always smiling and happy. To know him was to love him; that's why he was the ultimate con man. He was like a modern-day Robin Hood, taking from the rich and giving to the poor. However, the split between the poor and George was not quite equal. The split, I would guess, was something like 90 percent for him and 10 percent for the poor. Still, 10 percent for the poor when you're making over a million dollars a year is still a lot of money to give away.

Why did he give away so much money? Well, it turns out he had a wife. Her name was Maria. She was a very religious Catholic who went to Mass at least three times a week. She was beautiful, kind, and from Columbia. She had a very slight Spanish accent and spent her time looking after Georgie (as she called him) and doing charitable work in her Spanish Catholic parish. She was by far the largest donor to the church and was well respected. They had no children.

We were to find out later that she did not know the true nature of what George really did. As far as she knew, he bought failing travel agencies, turned them around very quickly into big money-makers, then sold them. They had moved around quite a lot, but they seemed to have settled at last in New York. George still traveled out of state on his travel businesses, but New York was now their home base and she was happy here because she had family close by, as did George. His father owned a very successful jewelry store in Corona, Queens County, one of the five boroughs of New York City. His customers were mostly Spanish, and he conducted business semi-legitimately. That's a whole other story which I'll explain later on.

When you walked into George's house, there was a very large foyer, and against one wall on a stand about four feet high was a statue of the Virgin Mary. On the stand, there was always a lit candle. I once asked Ron, "What's the deal with the statue? George is Jewish."

He said, "George is crazy about his wife and will do anything for her. He's not religious, but he's superstitious and really believes that her praying at that statue has brought him good luck, so he's not going to do anything to mess that up. That's why he wears that gold medal around his neck."

All of the above we didn't know when we first met him. Little did we know, Ron would eventually represent him in a major, seemingly unwinnable criminal case; win the case, and save him many years behind bars. I will come back to this later, but let me talk about that first meeting.

So, as we were chatting that first night, George tells Ron and me that he thinks he found a secretary for the office. She types, takes shorthand, and is finishing her last year of college attending evening classes. She was born right here in Queens County. Her mother and her family come from Spain, and her father is Italian, and she speaks both Spanish and Italian fluently. She's in her twenties and is prelaw in college and wants to eventually go to law school.

We say, "She sounds great. When we can meet her? We intend to open in two weeks."

He says, "Whenever you want."

I tell Ron, "If you like her and want to hire her, it's okay with me. I don't have to be there when you interview her." Another big mistake on my part.

George says, "Why don't you meet her tomorrow or the next day? I think you're really going to like her. And if so, why go through the bother of interviewing other people?"

Ron and I both think it's a good idea, and Ron agrees to meet her the next day after work, if she is available. We chat a little more, and I thank George for all his help and make plans to see him again before the office officially opens. Ron will be seeing more of him, and they make plans to meet the following night so that George can officially introduce him to Lisa, the potential new secretary.

A couple of days later, I called Ron at the DA's office. It's officially his last few days there. I asked him if he interviewed the girl George recommended. He says, "Yeah, I did."

I ask, "Well, how did it go?"

He says, "Great. She's everything George says she is." I ask, "What's her name again?"

He says, "Lisa."

I asked if she agreed on the starting salary we discussed. He says, "Yes, she was happy with it."

"Did you test her shorthand and typing speed?"

"No, I didn't have to. She is really smart, on the ball and I didn't want to offend her by testing her."

I say, "Ron, suppose she can't type."

He says, "She wouldn't lie to me; she's not that type of person. She's very elegant and classy." Turns out he was right. She could type and take shorthand as well as any of my secretaries.

I ask, "What does she look like?" He says, "She's okay."

"Married, divorced, boyfriends?" He says, "No, as far as I could tell."

"Are you officially going to start next Monday?" He says, "Yes."

"Normal hours, nine to five."

"Great, I'll see you over the weekend." We were having a Bocce tournament on Sunday, and Ron and I were the Bocce champs.

I live in Lloyd Harbor, a little incorporated village north of Huntington and have over two acres of land, so I built a Bocce court. When I lived in Ozone Park, our next-door neighbor Giovanni had the most beautiful Bocce court in the neighborhood. It was under a huge grapevine, and he had tournaments all the time. He was an older Italian man from Italy and hardly spoke any English. He had ten kids, one boy and nine girls. His daughters were all older than us by at least ten years. They were almost like older sisters to us and babysat for us all the time. We were close to them, shared a backyard, and were in their house more than our own.

Their mother, Mary, a little gray-haired Italian lady, was like a second mother to us, always calling us in to eat something. Our mother worked, so after school, we played in our shared backyard. Giovanni taught us how to play Bocce, and we could use the court anytime it wasn't being used, so we became really good.

I built my own Bocce court for a couple of reasons. I loved playing Bocce because anyone could play. We would have tournaments where my mother and aunts could play because there was no age where you couldn't play; so, everyone got involved. The other reason was because I was finally able to beat Bonnie (at least sometimes at a game.) She had been a ranked tennis player, played in the US Open when it was held at Forest Hills; and the only reason she didn't turn pro was it was still an amateur sport at the time. Although she came from a reasonably affluent family, she wanted to be independent and earn her own living. Eventually, she became a lawyer.

She taught me how to play tennis. I'm a pretty good athlete, but after all these years of playing, I still have not won a set from her, came close once or twice, close but no cigar, as they say. I used to play with her tennis friends once in a while, and of course, got crushed by them too; but they were also teaching pros. It wasn't until I played with regular people and won sometimes that I realized how much Bonnie and her friends had taught me.

So come Monday evening, after our Bocce tournament on Sunday, I get a call from Ron, telling me he would meet me at our new office. He had been there all day and had settled in, and the train had not been so bad after all. I asked how the new girl was, and he said, "Great."

I said, "To keep you and her busy, I am going to bring a couple of dozen files that need work and explain what has to be done."

As I pull up a short time later, I see the travel agency in full swing, busy as ever.

I lug the files up the stairs, and as I'm opening the door, I hear Ron on the

phone. I walk in and see a girl sitting at the typewriter, typing away at a really good speed. I'm happy. I think this girl can really type. She hears me and gets up and turns around, and my heart sinks. I know this is going to be trouble. She is tall, thin, and absolutely beautiful with an incredible figure to match. I'm speechless. She looks at me and smiles—what a warm, beautiful smile. I'm in love with her already, and I don't have to work with her all day, every day.

She says, "Oh my god, you look just like Ronnie. I'm sorry, I'm Lisa. You must be Bobby. Ronnie has told me all about you." And with that, she comes over and gives me a big hug. There is such a genuine sweetness about her I know Ron or her or both of them are in trouble. How is this going to be just a working relationship?

I tell her, "It's nice to meet you. George has told us so much about you."

Ron is off the phone and comes out of his office. Lisa turns to look at him, and I can see love in her eyes; and Ronnie, who has had so many girlfriends, looks at her with a look I have never seen before that tells me this is definitely going to be a problem. Then he looks at me with guilt in his eyes.

I look at him and say, "So what's shaking?"

He says, "So far, things are falling right into place."

I tell him, "Here are the files I talked about, and I have some more in the car. I'll be right back, and we can go over them."

Lisa says, "Let me help you."

I tell her, "It's not that many, I'll be right back." I get the rest of the files, and as I'm walking back, I see George coming out of the office. He sees me, and as I walk up to him, he smiles, all excited.

"I was just coming up to see you or Ronnie. I have a case I want to recommend to you guys." It's a medical malpractice case, and I know from the permanent injuries George describes and the type of malpractice that occurred, the case is worth several hundred thousand dollars. He says, "He's in the hospital, and if you want, I'll go with you tomorrow to sign the case up."

I ask, "How do you know this guy?"

He says, "Maria hears about these types of things all the time at her church and told me about it. Most of the time, nothing is done about it because the people are too frightened to do anything. They don't speak English, are happy to get medical treatment since they don't have insurance, and if someone screws up, they think there's nothing they can do about it since they have not paid for the care they received."

He says, "I hear about these cases all the time, and the people need someone like you and Ronnie to protect them."

I'm thinking with this one case, our fee will be enough to pay for the office and Ronnie and Lisa for the next year with a substantial amount left over as profit. George is talking about more to come, and he thinks we're doing him a favor. Boy, did I just hit the jackpot, and in addition, we would be helping people. My whole attitude about Ron and Lisa just changed. They could fall in love and walk off into the sunset as long as they signed up the cases when they came in. I thank George and tell him either Ronnie or I would meet him tomorrow morning to sign up the case and thank him for the referral.

I then ask George, "What's the deal with Lisa. You expect Ronnie to have a strictly legal relationship with her?"

He laughs.

"It might be different if there were a lot of people in the office, but the two of them in the office alone all day is asking for trouble. I just met her and saw the way she looked at Ronnie and Ronnie at her."

He laughs again.

"How well do you know her, George? And what's the story with her?"

He says, "Let's go into my office for a minute and I'll tell you all about her."

We go into his office, and he asks one of the people working there to get us two Cuban coffees. She brings them back as George and I start to chat. They are small delicious cups of coffee with a little cream and sugar in them.

George starts to tell me about Lisa. He met her through his wife, Maria, at the church Maria works at and gives money to. She volunteers there and helps Maria out, and they became friends. She lives with her parents and is religious; she doesn't date much as her parents are very particular about who she dates and they control a lot of what she does.

After meeting Ronnie, she told Maria she met the man of her dreams. He is smart, handsome, kind, and on and on.

I tell George, you know Ronnie has had lots of girlfriends; I just don't want her to get her heart broken. I'm going to have a heart to heart with him before they get involved.

Oh, back to the case George has referred. I tell him, I'm going to ask Ronnie to sign it up and tell him you're going with him since you know the client and speak Spanish. George agrees. I go back upstairs and tell Ronnie the good news about the new case and that in my judgment, the fees on just this one alone should cover all expenses for the office for more than a year, including both his and Lisa's salary or whoever replaces her in a couple of months.

He says, "You know, I feel comfortable here, maybe I'll stay longer."

Bells and whistles go off in my head. *Lisa, Lisa, Lisa.* I tell him, "Ronnie, George tells me Lisa is really a great girl. Be careful, don't break her heart."

We discuss it for a while, and Ron tells me he would never do that.

"I know you would never do that intentionally, but stuff happens." I ask Ron to sign up the case with George tomorrow. "He's expecting you at about two, and you'll go to the hospital together. I suggest you take Lisa as she can take down a lot of the info, and she makes a really good impression." I ask him to call me after the case is ours and let me know how it went. Little did I know I would not see Ronnie or Lisa for over a week.

The next day, Ronnie calls me around five to tell me he signed up the case and it looks better than we thought. I tell him I'll have one of my investigators pick up the case tomorrow morning and he asks me, "Did you hear there's a snowstorm coming?"

I say, "Yeah, hopefully, it won't be too bad."

The next morning, it snowed really badly. I call Ronnie and say, "Maybe you shouldn't try going to the office until you see how bad it gets."

He says he's going to give it a shot and see how it goes. After not hearing from him all day, I call George and got him at the agency. I asked him if spoke to Ronnie.

He says, "Yes, he was with Lisa, and they were leaving to get home before it got really bad. I assume he was going to drop her off and then go home."

I think, *oh no, please no*. I don't say anything to George and hope for the best.

For the next three days, no one can get in touch with Ronnie. No answer when I call. I call George, asking if he has seen Ronnie. He says no and that he has called him a couple of times but has not been able to get through. I ask if Lisa has been coming in. He says no, she has not been in either.

That night, I called Ron once again. No answer. I call the building he lives in and get the doorman, Charles, who I know well. I ask Charles if he has seen Ronnie. He says, "Yes, Mr. Aliazzo came home at the beginning of the snowstorm with a beautiful young lady, and as far as I know, he hasn't left the penthouse since."

I ask Charles to do me a favor and go up to the penthouse and speak to Ronnie and tell him I have been trying to reach him since the storm started three days ago; if he doesn't call me within the next hour, I'm coming over in my wife's four-wheel drive Jeep. I thank him and hang up, pissed off. Thank God we got that malpractice case or I would be paying for his early honeymoon.

Forty-five minutes later, my phone rings. It's Ronnie. Before he can say anything, I say, "So that's why you were going to give it a shot and try to make it in, to pick up Lisa. And here, the schmuck that I am, I thought you were really being conscientious."

Before I could go on, he says, "Bobby, stop, why are you so upset? They are going to drop the bomb anyway."

I say, "Don't give me that shit about dropping the bomb. Until they drop it, we have to behave responsibly.

Whenever things were going bad for Ron, he would always say, "What's the difference, they're going to drop the bomb anyway?"

I calm down. I ask him, "Okay, what's going on? I know Lisa's there and has been there for three days. What about her parents?"

He tells me indeed she is there and has been for the last couple of days. "It has been a sheer delight, absolutely wonderful. She has told her parents she is at her girlfriend's house and has been calling every day to check in. She is twenty-six and can do as she pleases but is respectful to her parents. They are religious and think you should only be with a man if you're married."

I say, "I thought she was religious also." He says, "She is."

I say, "Religious, like Miss New York."

Now as a quick aside, Miss New York was a runner up in the Miss New York beauty pageant. Somehow, one of the detectives he was working with was a born-again Christian and had talked Ronnie into atoning for his sinful ways and come with him to a born-again Christian meeting. Ronnie agreed, thinking in case they "drop the bomb," he'd be ready to meet his maker.

At the meeting, he sees her, the Miss New York runner up. She's a born again Christian and absolutely stunning. Prayers start, and while everyone is praying to the Lord for forgiveness for their sins, Ronnie is thanking God for making such a beautiful woman. He nudges Steve the detective. "Who's that?"

Steve looks over, then looks back at Ronnie. "I can't believe it." Ronnie looks over at Steve. "Maybe the Lord guided her to this meeting so I could meet her. It's about time I met someone with good Christian principles."

Steve thinks it over. Maybe if he met someone like Lilly, she could really change him. Ron asks, "She's not married or anything?"

Steve says, "No, she's waiting for the right one, and God will let her know when the right one comes along."

Ron asks Steve to introduce him after the meeting. Steve agrees but asks Ronnie, "You're not doing this just to try to get laid?"

Ronnie looks at him and sincerely says to Steve, "Of course not." And he means it. At the meeting, they have prayers, songs, and then the head guy gives a sermon, following which people line up to have "hands put on them," meaning

people go up to him, and he puts his hands on their heads and says a prayer; sometimes the people fall backward so, they actually have people behind them called "catchers," who catch them before they hit the floor. Ronnie has never seen anything like it.

Steve explains what's going on. Ronnie tells Steve he can't understand some of what the guy is saying. Steve explains, "The pastor is speaking in tongues," which is a practice in which people utter words or speech-like sounds often thought by believers to be a language unknown to the speaker. Ron thinks, *I want to believe, but this is getting weirder by the minute.*

Finally, the meeting is over, and people are having coffee and donuts. Steve leads Ronnie over to Lilly and introduces him. Up real close, she is even prettier. She asks, "Are you a detective too?"

Steve says, "No, Ronnie is actually my boss. He's an assistant district attorney."

They start chatting, and Ron asks if she would like to meet for coffee sometime. She says, "How about we meet here for coffee next Sunday after service?"

He agrees, and to make a long story short, they start dating.

They were dating for a short while, but Ron's feelings seem to be cooling off. I ask him what's going on with Lilly. He finally tells me he's no longer seeing her. I ask what happened. He says he started to have doubts that next Sunday after first meeting her, but he tried to ignore them. I ask what happened.

He says, "The meeting was going well. I was into the feeling of being at peace with God. After the meeting, instead of having coffee and donuts at the meeting, she invited me to her place for coffee and some homemade apple pie."

I said, "Sure."

"We get to her place, she puts on the coffee, and while it's brewing, she comes over to me and wants to start making out. I tell her, 'Lilly, this is wrong, we just came from a religious service.' And she tells me, 'The Lord will forgive us, he forgives all sinners.' Well, the Lord has a lot of forgiving to do because all she wanted to do was screw. The worst part was that she liked to have sex right after religious services on Sunday, always saying the Lord forgives us sinners. Instead of finding the Lord, I felt like a horrible sinner. That was it, I called it quits. When I told her, she was very upset but then said, 'I guess the Lord has other plans for us.'"

Ronnie tells me things are different with Lisa and they will be back at the office on Monday morning (this was Friday night.) I say,

"Okay, but don't screw this whole thing up because this office looks like a moneymaker."

The following Monday morning, they're back at work, and the office is really doing well. We're getting a boat load of new cases, most of which are really good ones. George was right, these people were underserved and needed us. Lisa turned out to be everything George said she would be. Ronnie and George became great friends. He and Maria had been to my mother's house for dinner many times, and my mother loved them both. Then the bomb went off.

One night after our office had been open a few months, Ron calls and says he wants to speak to me. I ask him what's up. He says, "Let's meet at my place this evening after work."

I say, "Okay, you are not going to tell me I'm about to become an uncle?" He says, "No kidding around, this is serious."

I say, "All right, I'll be there around six."

When I get to his apartment, he's on the phone. I ask, "Do you have anything to eat?" as he is always watching his weight and only ever has tuna fish.

He says, "Yeah, I stopped off and got over a dozen White Castle hamburgers, French fries and three large cups of White Castle coffee," which we both agreed was the best coffee money could buy. He says, "Don't start without me, I'll be right there. George should be here any minute."

"Why is George coming?"

"He's in trouble, criminal law trouble, and has asked me to represent him.

He's going to be indicted here in Queens County, so that's the good news."

"George is being indicted? What for?"

He says, "It's a long story, I only heard some of it. It's complicated, so I told him to come here as I didn't want to discuss it at the office with people coming and going. And, I wanted your take and advice on how to proceed."

As we are talking, the doorman rings and tells Ronnie, "Mr. George Guseman is here to see you."

Ronnie tells the doorman to send him up. I start heating up the White Castle burgers and French fries.

George comes in. He looks like he doesn't have a care in the world. He smells the burgers and asks if we have White Castle hamburgers. He says, "I can't believe you guys like those" and then starts to name five Spanish fast-foods that are better.

I say, "George, as an American, White Castle is part of our heritage. Have you ever tried one?"

He says, "No, I don't eat hamburgers."

Ron says, "Try one with some French fries."

He tries one, his eyes open wide, and George becomes a White Castle junkie. We polish off all the burgers and fries and go into the living room with some coffee.

We sit down and relax, and Ron says, "Okay, start from the beginning."

I say, "Before you start, give us twenty dollars each as a retainer, officially hiring us. That makes you our client, and the attorney-client relationship starts; now anything you tell us is privileged."

He looks at Ronnie, who says, "Now you know why I want him here, I can't think of everything."

George gives us the money; we sit back, and George begins.

He calls what he does and has been doing for over ten years his "travel agency business." His first job out of school was with a travel agency. He worked there for over a year and noticed that as the travel agency became bigger and more successful, the airlines extended them more and more credit, meaning instead of having to pay for the airline tickets they sold in thirty days, they could pay in forty-five days and then two months, then three months, and then four months and so on. As long as you kept on paying, they extended you the credit. If they stopped extending your credit, you would no longer use them and use another airline instead.

Some airlines were famous for doing this to their independent truckers. I know because I represented several trucking companies who got fed up waiting to get paid and slowly got new business to replace their airline business.

When the truckers told the airlines, they would no longer deliver for them unless they were paid in full for work already done, then the airline would stop giving them work and find another trucking company who was willing to wait for payment. The problem was that some of the airlines just ignored the request for payment from a trucker who no longer worked for them. Unless it was a large amount, some truckers just gave up because it would cost more to hire a lawyer and go through the whole legal process, then what it was worth.

That's where I came in. For those truckers who were owed too much money to walk away, they retained attorneys to represent them. The first company I represented was owed over fifty thousand dollars. I got the money for them without starting a lawsuit. Just one letter did it. I had one of my lawyers do some research, and the letter advised them that in addition to starting a lawsuit for payment of money owed, we would look into a class action and ask for millions of dollars. Since not all but some airlines worked the same way, holding back payment from truckers, the money held back got into the hundreds of thousands of dollars of which the airlines could get interest on or invest in any way they saw fit. The attorneys for the airlines apparently figured it was easier to just pay what they really owed than take a chance of some crazy lawyer putting together a possible class action that could literally cost them millions.

George, very aware of how things worked with airlines and travel agencies, came up with his new travel agency business model, and here's how it worked. First, and before he even started, he went to his father and told him what he planned to do. His father, who owned a large jewelry store and was a wheeler dealer himself, approved. George needed at least a hundred thousand to start.

His father agreed to lend him the money at 8.5 percent interest because he thought the chances of George getting caught were small. Otherwise, the interest rate would be much higher. The fact that George was about to start a business that was totally illegal and could land George in jail for a long time didn't seem to bother him. So, here's how George's plan would work. He would hire a front man, usually someone from Chile or Columbia who also spoke English. He would pay for him to come here and get him fake IDs. He would get him a place to live for six to eight months because by the end of that time, if all went well, he would be on his way back home with his real passport and more money than he could make in his native country in half a lifetime.

He would have the new guy come work in the travel agency he was presently operating. He then gave him a one-, or two-week crash course (depending on how fast they caught on) on how to run a travel agency. Not that they would be running it; George would run it behind the scenes and be in control of all finances. As far as anyone knew, he was a lowly travel salesman who also did accounting for the agency.

Buying a new agency was a lot trickier. He would find the agency he wanted to buy which was the easy part because there were business brokers who dealt with the sale of travel agencies (and a few who dealt exclusively with the sale of travel agencies.) He would have his new guy call the business broker he wanted to use and tell him he was interested in buying the travel agency George had picked out.

George had his own business model of the type of agency he wanted to buy. It had to be the right size. It had to have a good reputation, do at least a million dollars' worth of business a year, be in business for at least five years, have a large Spanish following and if possible, and most importantly, have a great credit line with the airlines. Without that credit line, he would not consider buying the business.

He would then have his front man (and on occasion woman) negotiate to buy the business. No one ever met George. His front man would call the broker, meet with him or her, discuss the business, and provide financials which George had arranged with different banks by simply having the front man deposit checks into new bank accounts, which of course George provided the funds for. The front man was 90 percent successful in purchasing the agency, simply because the price he was willing to pay for the agency was always higher than anyone else. The reason the price was always higher was because George never intended to pay all of it.

The deal the front man proposed, pursuant to George's instructions, was as follows: 10 percent of the purchase price in cash on the signing of the contract, 5 percent each month for the next five months. At the end of the sixth month, if everything was as represented by the seller, the balance of the purchase price would become due and payable. Since George was, in fact, buying the business and more importantly its good name and reputation, all the checking accounts of the business were turned over to the front man after the seller got his initial payment. The signer of the checks was now the front man.

Of course, the seller had to pay off all of the outstanding debt prior to George taking over. He had a clean slate to start. Usually, the seller was happy to pay off the debt he owed the airlines since the amount he sold the business for was far more than he ever expected.

George then put up his own money which showed it came from the front man, and they were off and running. As far as the airlines knew, there was no change of ownership, although most airlines didn't really know who the owner was. They just knew they had been dealing with this travel agency for years, and though they were late payers, they had always gotten paid.

George kept most of the staff, but part of the deal was that the seller had to leave as George or the front man had his own way of doing business and didn't want the seller interfering. Then slowly, at first, he started lowering the price of the airline tickets, and the rush to buy tickets slowly started. People bought tickets three months before they planned to travel, and George was keeping all the money. His specialty was selling first-class tickets at steeply discounted prices. Let's say a first-class ticket to Europe was $5,000 round trip. He would charge maybe $2,900. That's a profit to him of $2,100, and when he really got going, he was selling ten to twenty first-class tickets a day.

You do that for four to six months until the airlines start shutting you down, and you've made a lot of money. Remember, at that point, you're just a late or bad payer. As far as they know, you're not committing a crime.

When at last no airline will extend you credit and you are inundated with lawsuits from the airlines, you simply close the office down. The front man has gone back to his real identity and is on a plane back home. Since the front man didn't really exist and the employees have lost their jobs, including George, the airlines, for the most part, accept their losses and move on. That's the best way I could describe it. I'm sure I left out a lot and maybe made some mistakes in how he operated it.

Now, you may wonder how George got caught. Here is how it happened. The front man he had hired while working at the business became friendly with a pretty woman who worked for one of the airlines. They started seeing each other, and apparently, he promised to walk off into the sunset with her and instead flew off into the sunset back home. Unfortunately, in the more intimate moments they spent together, he told her everything, including his real name, where he lived in Columbia, and that George was his partner (because he believed this would make him seem more important). He neglected to tell her he was married and had two children.

When she finally realized he had abandoned her, she was heartbroken, then angry, then very angry, then vindictive and out for blood. She went to the airlines and told them everything she knew. Why hadn't she reported it sooner? She was afraid he would harm her.

They brought George in for questioning. Fortunately, he was smart and did what Ronnie told him. He told them whatever they thought he did, he didn't, and he would be happy to cooperate as long as his attorney was present, and he would do whatever his attorney advised. Who's your attorney? Ron Aliazzo. All hell breaks loose. "Ron Aliazzo is your attorney?"

"Well, yes and no. I mean, I never needed an attorney, but Ronnie and Bobby are friends, and I guess if you think I did something illegal, which I didn't, I'm going to need an attorney, and I know that Ronnie has been a criminal lawyer for a long time, so I guess I'll ask him."

They ask, "How do you know him?"

George, being well coached, thinks he probably said more than he should have already and answers, "If you want to know that or anything else, please call him as I intend to do as soon as I leave."

As soon as he leaves, he calls Ronnie and tells him what just happened. Ronnie tells him to meet him first thing in the morning and to speak to no one until they meet. As they are talking, the other line is ringing, and it's one of the ADAs. Ron doesn't answer it. He wants to wait until he sees George in the morning and George signs a retainer, then he can tell the ADA, he can't discuss the case because George just retained him. How strong of a case do they have against him and what are Ronnie's chances of winning?

We'll get to that in a moment, because something had happened before that night. Ronnie had called me, not knowing that George would be called in for questioning. He and George had made plans to go to Atlantic City on Friday for an overnight stay. George was a high roller and a big gambler, and the casino comped everything. Rooms, food, drinks—everything was on the house. I said I couldn't go. I had made plans with Bonnie and Alison and broken them so many times I couldn't do it again.

I told him, "I have an idea." I had just gotten off the phone with Dr. Joe, one of my and Ronnie's closest friends in the world. Dr. Joe, besides being tall, thin and handsome, was a genius in the true sense of the word. Alison and Bonnie adored him as did most people, especially women. I should know. I was the best man at all of his weddings, and I represented him in all of his divorces. To be fair, there were only two divorces and three weddings. The third was the charm, and he has been married for over twenty years.

The thing about Dr. Joe was that you could ask him almost anything, and he knew the answer. I once told that to Alison. She said I could ask him anything—well, just about anything. She went over to Dr Joe. and asked if she could ask him a question. Dr. Joe said, "Sure, Ali."

The question was, "Why is the sky blue?" He thought about it for a minute or two. I asked, "Joe, you don't know?"

He said, "Certainly, my good man." He annunciated his words so perfectly that he almost appeared to have a British accent (he called some of his close friends "my good man" and got the nickname of MGM). "But I'm thinking how to explain it so a five-year-old can understand it, which is somewhat difficult." He had or was going for PhDs in things I can't even pronounce. I could write a book just about him, and someday, I might. I told Ronnie I had a great idea.

Here's the idea. Since Dr. Joe, or MGM or Joe the Genius or simply Joe, which was the name he preferred, knew everything, let's ask him if he could figure out a way to beat the casinos. Ronnie thought that was a great idea and said he was going to call Joe. I asked him to call me back after he spoke to Joe.

Half an hour later, Ron calls me back, excited. He spoke to Joe and, after carefully considering Ronnie's question, said, "Yes, possibly." He said, "Card counting at Blackjack, even though it isn't technically illegal, is too easy to spot, and once spotted, the casino will not allow you to continue to play; they will get your picture and send it to all the other casinos. However, there is a possibility with Roulette. It seems that some Roulette tables, not many, but a few, are not balanced correctly, and if one could find the one or ones that are incorrectly balanced, even by a millimeter or two, you will have a winning advantage as the numbers will tend to show up more often in one sector of the table. The advantage is small, but if you play long enough, you should win."

He explained the reason why the casinos won was because they had that 1 or 2 percent advantage over the player in some games and even a bigger percent advantage in other games. That percentage was accurate if the player played correctly, but if the player played incorrectly or didn't really know the odds and how to play or was slightly drunk or really bombed, the winning percentage for the casino went up.

The obvious question? How do you know which table is incorrectly balanced?

Joe thought and said that during the day, some of the Roulette tables were closed and one could walk by and stop next to the table to tie one's shoelaces and put your wallet and cigarettes and small level (the one he had in mind was very small and looked like a cigarette lighter) on the table to judge if the table was slightly off and therefore fit our criteria. He said one could probably also go to a table that was open and active and place a bunch of casino chips on the table with the level which looked like a lighter next to it. But that was the more daring way. Joe told him where he could buy the level.

Ronnie was excited. He said, "Bobby, our ship may have finally come in." I said, "I hope it's not a rowboat."

He asked Joe as a personal favor to come with them to advise them, and if his theory worked, he would get part of the profit, plus rooms and food and drinks were all on the house as the casino always comped George and his guests.

Joe agreed, and so that Friday afternoon, off they went to Atlantic City. It was George, Ron, Dr. Joe, and George's younger brother, Pablo, who would be driving in George's new BMW. Now Ronnie had told George about Joe. George was impressed. "The smartest man you ever met. That's something, given the fact you must know a lot of really smart people." He was excited to try out Joe's system.

Now one of the things Ron had not told George was that Dr. Joe had some idiosyncrasies. He was not into sports. He liked guns. He owned over fifty. He liked cops and robbers and "shoot em ups". He also had a slight case of OCD (obsessive compulsive disorder) which manifested itself in unusual ways. Sometimes, out of the clear blue (while he was in his own world), he would make believe he was shooting at the enemy, hold up his arms as if he were holding a rifle and simulate vocally the sound of a gun being fired. As they were driving to Atlantic City—Pablo, driving with Joe sitting next to him in the front as Joe always wanted to sit up front, and Ronnie and George sitting in the back—apparently, Joe (who was in his own world, daydreaming) spotted the enemy and started shooting.

Pablo and George jumped up, startled. Ron, who was used to Joe, told them, "Relax, relax, sometimes when he's in his own world, he spots the enemy and starts shooting. Don't worry, he's harmless."

George looks at Ronnie. He can't believe what just happened. George whispers, "Ronnie, are you sure about him?"

Ronnie says, "You know, George, all geniuses are a little eccentric." George shakes his head, agreeing with Ronnie.

They finally arrive at the casino. Ronnie says, "I'm hungry, let's get coffee and a snack and go over everything one more time."

Over coffee and snacks, as Joe starts to explain how this is going to work, George gives Pablo the level which really looks like a cigarette lighter and tells him to try it out on a couple of tables to see if he could find one that was not completely level. "But do it carefully so you don't get caught."

Joe starts to object, saying, "We should go over everything in the room carefully before attempting to use the level." Ronnie later told me this was the beginning of what turned out to be a disastrous evening but one he would never forget.

George says, "Let's try to go over everything one more time."

Pablo leaves, and Joe seems a little frustrated that George didn't listen to him but pushes on. "Once we know which way the table is leaning, if we can in fact find one, the bets are only to be made on the numbers where the table is leaning, meaning if the table is leaning slightly to the left, even though the tilt is invisible to the naked eye, then we will play several numbers to the left, and I'll show you which numbers. Now, as I said before, we will only risk up to a thousand dollars as we try to perfect the system. So, George, did you bring a thousand dollars?"

George takes out a big bill folded out of his sports jacket pocket and says, "Let's see" and starts counting the money, all in hundred-dollar bills, counting in Spanish.

Joe says, "George, that seems like more than a thousand dollars." Ron asks, "George, how much is that?"

George, as he finishes counting, says, "Around $10,220." Ronnie asks, "Why did you bring so much money?" George says, "I always like to have extra just in case."

As they finish up coffee and snacks, Pablo comes back, holding a stack of chips. Joe says that it was quick for him to get a chance to use the level on some of the tables. Pablo says, "I tried it out on six tables. Four were level, one was off by a millimeter and a half, and the other was off by almost three millimeters, although to the naked eye, they all look level. I think that's the one we should play on."

Ronnie asks, "How did you do it and do it so quickly?"

Pablo says he bought a hundred dollars' worth of five-dollar chips and put them in front of me with cigarettes and the level, which really does look like a lighter behind the cigarettes. Then he dropped a chip on the floor and bent down to pick it up and looked at the level. No one paid attention to me. They were all watching the ball spinning around. It was easy. After I looked at the level, I left and went to the next table and did it again, no problem."

Joe felt relieved. For a while, he was worried that all the tables would be level. Joe says, "Okay, the next step is for us to check the table once more to make sure Pablo is right. Then, depending on which way the table is leaning, I'll give you the numbers to play."

Now George only bet a dollar on each number on each spin until we see how accurate we are. "We will be betting two boxes or eight numbers, so each spin will cost us eight dollars. Each number pays thirty-seven to one, so we'll see what happens and may have to adjust our numbers."

George looks at Joe incredulously. "Are you kidding me? If I start betting eight dollars a bet, they will remove all my comps. They're giving us free rooms, free meals, free drinks, everything for free. I'll never be able to come back here and be comped, and I love this place."

Joe thinks for a moment and says, "Okay, let's go to another casino."

George looks at Joe for a moment, then calmly explains, "I can't do that. They will find out, and I will never be comped here again." George says, "Look, instead of betting eight dollars a spin, I'll bet eighty dollars a spin. I've got ten thousand, so that should cover our plan to see whether it will work or not."

Joe says he is not comfortable betting that much money without testing the system. George says, "Don't worry, I can handle it."

Ron says, "Okay, let's go."

Joe says, "Remember, George, I'll give you the numbers."

They go to the table Pablo tested, and Pablo once again tests the table as the wheel is spinning. He nods at Joe. Almost three millimeters. Joe leans over to George and gives him the numbers to bet, and so the betting starts.

George plays the numbers Joe had given him and only those numbers, and after an hour or so, they are up over a hundred dollars. Joe, Ronnie, and Pablo are excited as it looked like the system was going to work. George, however, became bored and started to bet other numbers in addition to the numbers Joe had given him. Joe got upset and told George he couldn't do that as that would upset his whole system. George went back to betting the numbers Joe had given him for a while, then got bored once again and started betting other numbers, placing the table limits of hundreds of dollars on other numbers.

Ron tells George, "You're not playing Joe's numbers."

George tells Ron, "If I play the way Joe wants, what are we going to make?

Fifty or a hundred dollars an hour? That's like having an hourly paying job."

To make a long story short, within a couple of hours, George was back to betting the way he always bet and, of course, lost all his money. Pablo went to the craps tables and also lost the $150 he had with him.

George is not discouraged. He asks Ronnie and Joe how much money they have with them. Between the two of them, they had about $320. George asks to borrow it as he feels a hot streak coming on, and if he loses, he will pay them back tomorrow.

Ron says, "George, let's call it night."

George gives Ronnie a hurtful look. Ron and Joe give him the last of their money. Within twenty minutes, George loses it all. Pablo comes back to the table to tell them he lost all of his money. George acts like he hasn't lost a penny and asks how much money we have left. Turns out Ron and Joe gave George all their money. Pablo had lost all his money, and so between all four of them with change, they had $7.56.

"Well," George says, "we can't stay here, even if everything is comped." Ron says, "Why not?"

George says, "Because we can't tip the waiters or anyone else, and if we can't play, what's the point?"

They all agree. No one brought credit cards to limit losses as per George's instructions, a very smart move on his part. So, they decide to leave.

Now the problem is, do they have enough money to get home? Luckily, they bought gas when they arrived because they were running on fumes, so they had a full tank of gas. The tolls were two dollars. Since they had $7.56, they figured they had enough money to get home.

On the way home, everyone is quiet and depressed. George, sitting in the back with Ronnie, leans over and says, "Ronnie, it's so quiet. Ask Dr. Joe to start shooting his gun."

That breaks the sad mood, and they all start laughing and talking altogether. They arrive in Brooklyn at about 11:30 to drop Dr. Joe off, and as they are driving and are a couple of blocks from Joe's house, they see a Burger King. Pablo says let's stop and get something. Since he's driving, he's holding the $5.56 they have left. He pulls into the Burger King, and they all get out and go in. Pablo is first in line and orders a Big Whopper. George steps up and angrily tells Pablo, "Are you crazy? we only have $5.56! We should all order the dollar special burgers, then we can all have one and some coffee."

Pablo is angry that George yelled at him and angrily yells back, "I'm tired and wasn't thinking!"

And George yells back, "That's the problem! You never think!"

Pablo then yells back at George, but in Spanish, and in the next moment, George has Pablo in a headlock, and they're rolling around on the floor. Ron and Joe jump in and break them up and calm them down.

They go into the restroom one at a time to wash up and calm down. When they come back, Ron has gotten four 1dollar burgers, an order of French fries, and two Cokes, which they will share and still have some change left over. They all sit down, calm down, start eating, and in a minute, they are chatting away as if nothing happened. That, however, was the end of their trying to beat the casinos.

Now getting back to George and how strong a case the airlines have against him. Ron thinks it's weak. They only have the front man's jilted girlfriend. The front man is in the wind, having heard from the angry girlfriend what she did, and she hopes he goes to jail for a hundred years. Even if they find him, they still have to extradite him, which will be difficult because they have to show criminal intent. He took a shot at a business and it didn't work out, and he didn't have any money left to pay off his debts.

However, they also know that George is the money guy and the mastermind behind this whole business. They know that he's done it before and that it is a continuing course of criminal conduct which they have to put a stop to. What they know or think they know is one thing; proving it is another matter.

Ron thinks that they are going to proceed because they can't continue to allow him to defraud the airlines. But Ron also thinks that he has a good chance of working out a plea where he will be sentenced to probation; but, only on condition that he no longer have anything to do with the airlines or work for any business that has anything to do with airlines.

He tells George their case is weak, and he is pretty sure he can win it, but there's always a chance that he could lose, and a loss to a felony count could mean several years in jail. He recommends if he can get it for George, to take a plea. George says he doesn't have to sleep on it, if Ronnie can get a plea to take it. He tells Ronnie he has more than enough money socked away, and he has some ideas for another business. At this point, Ronnie doesn't want to know what that other business is.

The next day, Ronnie goes to see Tommy, the head assistant DA and one of his closest friends, in the DA's office, and after some haggling, the plea deal Ronnie hoped he could get is agreed upon. The DA agreed for a couple of reasons. They had a weak case, and with Ronnie trying it, there was a good chance they could lose it, and they would have accomplished their mission in that they had stopped George from continuing in the travel business. Ronnie also pointed out that the injured parties were the airlines who were not out for blood. They just wanted it stopped, and this plea deal accomplished that.

As to the owner who sold the business, he had gotten 10 percent down and 5 percent over the months George had the business. He received about 40 percent of the purchase price in total and he had his business back. He wouldn't have the credit line he had when he left, but eventually, he would also get his credit line back as the airlines knew he had been defrauded too.

When Ronnie told George he was able to work out the plea deal he had hoped for, George almost collapsed. Underneath that cool exterior, he was frightened to death of going to jail. He hugged and thanked Ronnie as did his father, who was aware of what was going on. George said, "Let's celebrate. I'm going to make reservations at Windows on the World at the World Trade Center for next Saturday night. Besides me and Maria, I want to have my mom and dad, you and Lisa, Bonnie and Bobby, Pablo and his girlfriend, Dr. Joe and his wife, and a couple of my close friends and their wives, maybe eighteen in all."

Ron asks if he can get reservations that quickly. George says he'll give it a shot. He somehow manages to get the reservations. A couple of people are busy but told George they are changing their plans because they have never been to Windows on the World.

Bonnie and I had been there several times. I think it was on the 102nd floor. It truly was a glorious place. If you were to get a table next to a window, you felt like you were dining in an airplane. I remember they had one of the largest wine selections in the world. The food was excellent, although the portions were small. Bon and I once went with close friends, Fred and Ann, a doctor friend, and his wife. He was in private practice and a great doctor.

We got into a conversation with the maître d' whose name was Max and who took our order. He was from Queens County where both of our offices were and knew someone who had been treated by Fred for life-threatening obesity.

Whatever Fred did was successful. The maître d' mentioned he had an obese sister and asked if Fred could help her. Fred said, "Sure, here's my card, have her call my office, and when she makes the appointment, tell her to mention you."

I remembered from my previous times there that the veal scallopini was world-class. It was Fred and Ann's first time, so I recommended it; they ordered it along with me and Bon. Each plate came covered by a silver top, very fancy, but when the waiters removed the silver top, each plate had enough veal scallopini to feed a bird. To add insult to injury, each plate had peas, about six of them on each plate.

Fred looked up at Max and said, "May I speak to you for a minute?" He got up, put his arm around Max's shoulder, and walked away with Max.

A minute later, the waiters came back and removed our plates and came back with big empty plates. A couple of minutes after, Max shows up with some other waiters pushing a big cart upon which is a large covered silver tray. When the cover is removed, there is a mound of veal scallopini enough for twenty people, literally sliding off the platter. Next to it is a giant bowl of peas. Max looks at Fred. "Will that do, Doc?"

Fred looks at Max. "Thanks, Max."

I said, "Fred, what the hell just happened?"

"I was pissed off and told him to give the portions he had served us to his fat sister. He apologized and said he would replace the dishes just served with larger portions but asked if he could count on me to help his sister. I promised I would."

Well, it's the Saturday night we are celebrating George's plea deal when we arrive at Windows on the World. I picked up Ron and Lisa in my Silver Blue Rolls Royce, which I had bought after hitting for a big number on a case I thought the lawyer who was trying the case for me had no chance of winning. I never took the car seriously, keeping a jar of Grey Poupon Mustard in the car, and when I got dirty looks from people who thought the car was obnoxious and the driver insecure (which it was and I am), I would roll down the window and say, "Would you care for a jar of Gray Poupon?" There was a TV commercial for

Gray Poupon with a guy in a Rolls asking another car stopped for a red light if the driver by any chance had any Gray Poupon he could spare.

Of course, Bonnie, for the most part, refused to ride in it as she didn't want to be seen in it. One the few occasions when she agreed to ride in it, she would put her feet (sometimes she had sneakers on with red clay on the bottoms) on the dashboard in utter disdain for the car.

After buying the car, I noticed that the gas gauge didn't work. I called Rolls Royce and was told to bring in the car the following week. I took the car to the gas station to get it filled because I didn't know how much gas was in the car and didn't want to run out of gas while driving. As I pulled out of my driveway, being pissed off that I had to be inconvenienced, I banged the gas gauge, and guess what? The gas gauge needle popped into place, showing a full tank of gas. Well, I never got around to getting it fixed, and for all the time I had the car, whenever I wanted to know how much gas I had, I would bang the gas gauge, sometimes once, sometimes a couple of times. Of course, every time I did this, Bonnie would roll over laughing.

As we drove into the World Trade Center, we put out the joint we had been smoking and pulled into valet parking. The kid working for valet parking ran over to take my car and, as we started to walk away, got into the car to park it, smelled the pot, got out of the Rolls, and yelled after me, "Mister, you're my hero!"

We all got into the elevator, and taking it up to Windows on the World was a trip in itself. It was very fast, and you felt like you were ascending into heaven. As we get out of the elevator, there is a big area leading into the restaurant with a magnificent view of Manhattan. Every time I went there, I felt like I was walking around in a 747. As we entered, the maître d' (not Max) approached us, and we told him we were with the Guseman party.

He said, "Yes, sir, follow me." He knew where the Guseman party was.

With all those people in the restaurant, George must have tipped him well.

When we get to the table, George comes running over to us and gives Ronnie a big hug, then George's father does the same. Ronnie is certainly the hero of the night. George had already started ordering. There were several appetizers already on the table, two platters of caviar with blinis, and others that

I knew to be outrageously expensive. One platter of caviar alone was several hundred dollars.

Also on the table were multiple bottles of Dom Perignon champagne which cost about $150 a bottle if you bought them in a liquor store, but here at Windows on the World, it must have been marked up to be over $500 a bottle. Also on the table were several bottles of Grand Cru red wines which had been opened so that they could breathe. Grand Cru wines are from France. They are first growth wines and probably start at $400–$500 a bottle. I thought, *My God, there must be around seven or eight thousand dollars' worth of food, wine, and champagne on the table, and we haven't even ordered dinner yet.*

To make a long story short, we had the best time. The wine and champagne were out of this world. The appetizers and food were great, and we all ate and drank probably too much. It was late when we started to say good night to everyone. We all thanked George and Maria for an unforgettable night, George says he's going to stay a little longer to finish his coffee and settle the bill.

As we are leaving, the head waiter comes over to George and hands him the bill for the evening, which looks like a small phone book in a very ritzy leather binder. He says, "If you have any questions, Mr. Aguila, please let me know."

Ron and I look at each other. *Mr. Aguila? Did the Maître d' just say Mr. Aguila?* Without thinking, Ron and I had the same reaction. We quickly grabbed Bonnie and Lisa by the arm and hustled them toward the elevator. Bon turns to me, saying "What's the rush?"

As we approach the elevator's doors, one of them opens as if on cue. There's no one in the elevator since it's the end of the evening, and people are mostly leaving and not coming up.

We get right in, and down we go. I look at Ronnie. "Can you believe it?"

Ronnie says, "I had no idea! If I knew what he intended, I wouldn't have come! I was worried that if the card was no good, we would get stuck with the bill. I'm afraid to think about what the bill was." We fill Bon and Lisa with what just happened. They can't believe it.

Ron says, "I'll call him tomorrow morning, and if he's home, then he got away with it." Ron turns to Lisa and asks her to please not tell Maria about this. She says, "Of course not." Besides, she would never believe George would do anything like that.

The next day, on a Sunday morning, Ronnie calls George, who answers. Ronnie tells George he wants to meet him for breakfast at a diner they both know. George says, "What's up?"

Ronnie, not wanting to talk on the phone, tells him, "I'll tell you when I see you."

They meet. I see Ronnie later that day, and he tells me what happened. George tells him that since he can't be in the Travel Agency Business, he has decided to go into the credit card business. He says it's a victimless business and only the credit card companies get hurt; and they're mostly banks, and who feels sorry for banks?

Ronnie says, "When you screw credit card companies and banks, they pass on the losses to their customers who pay more in interest and for services."

George tells Ronnie, "See, I knew you were going to make me feel bad."

Ronnie gets serious. "George, you know what I went through to allow you to be sitting here, having breakfast today? I gave my word that you would be not be doing "con" bullshit in New York."

George tells Ronnie that he is also considering another business which will make the credit card business look like small potatoes. The problem is he will be out of the country a lot. Ronnie asks what it is. George, who trusts Ronnie with his life, tells him, "It's money laundering for some drug cartel. It entails moving large amounts of money from South America to Europe and the United States." He says, "One year, and I'll be a multimillionaire, and then I'll retire."

Ron looks at him incredulously, tells him he has lost his mind. "You're already a multimillionaire. You would be dealing with people who would kill you and your family if they caught you stealing a hundred dollars."

He says he knows, but he would never fuck around with them, and in less than a year, he'll stop.

Ronnie asks him, "What makes you think they will let you stop?"

He tells Ronnie, "The longer you do it, the more people get to know you, and the likelier you are to get caught, and they don't want you to get caught with a lot of their money, so pretty much after a year or so, they let you walk." George tells Ronnie, "Since I can't do the credit card business, what choice do I have?"

Ron tells him, "Don't put this on me. You have enough money never to have to work again. Why don't you go into the jewelry business with your father?"

George tells him that Pablo is working with his father, and the three of them together wouldn't work. He tells Ron he has to think about it. He'll keep in touch. Since the travel agency is now closed, at least temporarily until the old owner starts it up again, Ron does not see George on a daily basis. He speaks to him occasionally, but George is evasive about what he's doing.

Before Ron first agreed to represent George, he told him, "If I ever catch you lying to me, I will withdraw from representing you. That's like being sick and going to a doctor and lying about your symptoms. I want to know everything. I don't want to be blindsided. If I am, I may lose your case, and you know how much I hate losing; but you will be the one going to jail for a long time."

Ronnie believed George never lied to him, not even once. For that reason, he never asked what he was doing when he spoke to him. George knew how he felt about money laundering, and Ron hoped he listened to him. He didn't want to force George to lie to him for the first time. He just hoped George, who was exquisitely bright, would listen to him. He always did in the past.

About three months later, Ronnie comes into the office, just as I'm about to leave. He looks upset and distraught. I ask, "What's going on? What happened?"

He looks at me and says, "George is dead." I can't believe it. I ask, "What happened?"

He says, "Against my advice and warning, he decided to do money laundering. He had been doing it for over a month. His father called and told me as much as he knew. He died in Venezuela. They found him tied to a tree with a knife through his heart."

I'm in shock. I can't believe it. We both sat there quietly for a minute. Ron says, "I warned him."

I ask, "What do you think happened?"

He says, "He probably started skimming some money off the top. When you're dealing with millions of dollars, he probably figured they would never miss a hundred grand or so, at least that's my best guess."

There was no funeral, He was buried in Venezuela. I ask why they waited so long to tell him but he doesn't know. He said, "Let's go get a bite and a few drinks. I don't feel like being alone."

We went and had dinner and got pretty loaded. We laughed and cried, talking about George and what a brilliant, special person he was. He had the ability to be anything he wanted to be and be successful at it, yet he chose to be a criminal. He had so many unique qualities. Yes, he was smart, but to Ronnie and me, that was just a small part of it. He was kind, the softest touch I ever saw (well, maybe next to Ronnie).

When you practice law, you try not to get too close to your client, especially criminal law clients. Some are just plain dumb and others are just too plain lazy to go out and make an honest living. I don't think I ever met a criminal who didn't think he was smarter than everyone else. You have to make decisions based on the facts you have before you. Once you get emotionally involved, you lose your objectivity, and that can be disastrous for the client.

Then every once in a while, you get a client like George. You see all the potential, all the good qualities, and you just can't help yourself. You get closer than you should. In the end, even Maria's prayers and Statue of the Virgin Mary and the candles couldn't save him.

The People of the State of New York versus Frank R Aliazzo, Esq.

It all started about two weeks before the "incident." Bon and I had just gotten home after a night out. We, along with a close friend, Mike Cohen, and his wife had gone to New York City to see Al Pacino in a play. We had season tickets to Circle in the Square, which is a Broadway theater in midtown Manhattan. The name of the play, as I recall, was *Salome*. I'm not a big Broadway play kind of guy, more a *Three Stooges* fellow, but Mike talked me into it, telling me it will give me a little culture, a little class. Besides, Bonnie liked going to plays.

Now a little about Mike Cohen. We both lived in Lloyd Harbor and had daughters. Mine was Alison, and his was Deborah (Ali and Deb). They were in the same class in grade school and became close friends. So, through our kids, we got to know each other and eventually also became close. Mike was born and raised in Boston where he went to Boston Latin grade school (a very ritzy school, hard to get into with lots of famous graduates), followed by Harvard University and Harvard Law School. He was exceptionally bright and had a slight Boston accent.

When I first met him, I thought he was a stiff; and with that accent, he sounded like a snob and a hopeless intellectual. Ronnie felt the same way when he met him. Boy, were we wrong. He came from very modest beginnings; his father was a tailor who made clothes for people in the theater. He earned money while at Harvard as a comic in the Jewish Alps, otherwise known as the Borscht Belt located in New York's Catskill Mountains.

He was billed as Comedian Myron Cohen (Myron was his real first name, although no one other than his wife ever called him that) and would come on stage, saying, "Yes, I'm Myron Cohen, not *thee* Myron Cohen (a famous comedian), but nevertheless, here I am."

I asked Mike, 'Didn't they boo you when they found out you were not the famous Myron Cohen?"

He said, "Nah, most knew I wasn't the real Myron Cohen, and the ones that didn't laughed at being fooled."

He became a senior partner at Hunton & Williams, a big-time law firm with several hundred lawyers. He was one of their senior trial lawyers, and one of his clients was AT&T. One New Year's Eve, he was in an auto accident and was critically injured. Bonnie and I, along with Ali and his daughter, Debbie, were coming home a little after 1:00 a.m. after being at Ronnie's and had to pull off of the main road in Lloyd Harbor. We were told there had been a horrible accident and they were waiting for the ambulance to go through as someone may have been killed. The ambulance and the police, with sirens blasting passed us heading to the hospital.

The next morning, we get a call from Mike's wife, Carol, saying she and Mike had been in an accident the night before and that he was in serious condition. She had only suffered some broken ribs, and they had released her from the hospital. It appeared some young kid had been drinking and driving very fast and had gone on to the wrong side of the road and hit Mike head on.

To make a long story short, Mike recovered after several months. One of his many injuries was a broken jaw, which had to be wired shut for several weeks. Bon, mostly, and I would stop by to see him and bring him strawberry milkshakes which he would sip through a straw as his mouth was wired shut. The first time I came by with the shake and a straw, as he was sipping it, I said, "You know, Mike, I'm sorry for your trouble, but this is kind of nice for me. Two lawyers, and only one gets to do all the talking."

I didn't realize what I had just done. He began to laugh with a mouthful of strawberry milkshake in his mouth and started to gag. Somehow, he managed to swallow the milkshake without choking to death. My God, he scared the life out of me. After that, whenever I saw him, until the wires were removed, I always tried to be serious, which caused him to laugh at me being serious, but he didn't have anything in his mouth, thank God.

After he had recovered and been back to work for a couple of weeks, he called me and said he wanted to see me. I asked if everything was okay. He said yes, but he wanted to stop by my office on the way home. He said he wanted to go to Don Pepe's after speaking to me and asked Ron to come along if he was available.

He shows up a little after 5:00 p.m., and as we're in my office, having coffee and waiting for Ron, he tells me what he wants to speak to me about. He wants me to represent him in his auto accident case which was a big case with serious money involved. I look at him incredulously. I said, "Mike, you're a senior trial attorney at one of the biggest firms in New York with literally hundreds of Yale and Harvard lawyers to pick from."

He gives me a long hard look and says, "I'm aware of that. I want you to represent me, and if the shoe was on the other foot, I would do it for you in a minute."

I said, "Mike, I am beyond flattered, and of course I'll represent you." I immediately put the case in suit, but apparently, the insurance companies wanted no part of us, especially after Mike Cohen's testimony at his deposition. They settled the case for basically what we were asking for.

Now that you know a little about Mike Cohen, let's get back to the night out when we were all going to see Al Pacino in the play *Salome*. This was after his accident, and he had fully recovered. I picked him and Carol up at their house since we were all going in one car. As I ring the doorbell, I hear what appears to be loud indistinguishable screaming. I'm taken aback. What the hell is going on?

Mike opens the door, and I come in, and as I walk toward the kitchen, I see this very large birdcage like the size of a small aviary. In it are two large exotic birds. As I recall, I think they were Lear's Macaws. They were blue and beautiful, but my God, it was as if someone was screaming in the house.

I turn to Mike. "What's going on? Where did these birds come from?"

He says, "Carol has gone crazy again and bought them today." "Where did she get them from?"

He says, "From the pet store in town." "How much were they?"

"Eight hundred dollars each, plus the big cage, plus all this other stuff."

"Are you kidding, Mike? How are you going to live with them screaming all the time?"

He says, "they mostly scream when the doorbell rings or if they get excited." I say, "Just like dogs."

Carol, his wife, was a beautiful actress when he met her; she was eventually diagnosed as a manic depressive who, as long as she was on lithium, was okay. But when she stopped taking lithium, which she did every three or four years, she went crazy (as Mike, that most sophisticated Harvard man referred to these episodes), and go on buying sprees; this always was the first indication that she was off her lithium.

I said before we went to the play, "How bad?"

He says, "It just started. Hopefully, I'll get her back on lithium tomorrow morning before the real craziness kicks in."

"Why did she go off it at all?"

Bonnie's guess was because she liked the high that the manic part gave her where she became totally unfiltered and outrageous in her behavior. Every time she went off her lithium and "went crazy," he would call Bonnie and me, and we would try to talk her into going to the hospital, where she would be forced to take her lithium, and usually, in a few weeks, she would be back to normal. If she refused to go to the hospital, Mike would call the Lloyd Harbor police who knew her well, and they would manage to convince her to go.

The last time she "went crazy," she agreed to go with Mike and Bonnie to Stony Brook Hospital. I wasn't home at the time; it was in the early evening, and by the time they got her admitted, it was late evening. Bonnie called to tell me what was going on. I got home late that night, around eleven-thirty, and Bon was still not home. Cell phones were not popular at the time, and so after not hearing from her by twelve-thirty and figuring she was probably still waiting for Carol to get admitted, I went to bed. I was woken by Bonnie at around three thirty in the morning just as she was getting into bed. I asked, "What happened? Why did it take Carol so long to get admitted?"

She said, "Carol was admitted around twelve-thirty." When she and Mike left the hospital, they headed home, which is about a forty-five-minute drive. After they had been driving almost an hour, they didn't know where they were and didn't see any familiar signs. They finally saw a sign that said "Montauk Point, Thirty Miles." They had been driving in the wrong direction for over an hour. It turns out both Bonnie and Mike have what is called directional dyslexia. What is it? It's a condition. The definition is "extreme difficulty distinguishing right from left and following a sequence of directions or retracing a path."

Now I knew they both had it, although I didn't know what the medical term was. I just thought they both had a bad sense of direction. Once Bonnie was in criminal court and had a policeman testifying, and the cop said, "I first saw the defendant on the southwest corner, and then he crossed the street to the northeast corner." She was hopelessly lost. She told me that when she went into large courthouses or large buildings, she was always frightened that she would not be able to find her way out.

As for Mike, I think he was as bad as Bonnie. We both belonged to a country club that had a beautiful golf course. We had played it hundreds of times, and whenever he drove the golf cart, he would always ask, "Where's the next hole?"

Back to the day we leave Mike's house with the birds screaming and head to Manhattan to see *Salome* with Al Pacino. Part of the play is about Salome doing the Dance of the Seven Veils. When the seventh veil is removed, Salome is naked. Pacino, believe or not, is playing the part of King Herod with a very slight New York accent. He asks her to do the Dance of the Seven Veils. She says, "Only if you bring me the head of John the Baptist."

He says he cannot do that because he has committed no crime. "But I will give you two beautiful Arabian horses."

She says no, she wants the head of John the Baptist.

He offers her several other things—diamonds, rubies, etc. But she only wants the head of John the Baptist.

Finally, as a last resort, he tells her he has two beautiful peacocks and tells her even Caesar himself does not have such magnificent birds, and before she can reply, Mike leans over to me and says, "Tell him I'll throw in my two birds."

Writing about Mike brings back memories of the wonderful time we had when we lived in West Hempstead, before we moved to Lloyd Harbor in a beautiful brick colonial, a short time after we were married and had our daughter, Alison.

The previous owner was a doctor named Lou Able who had died a year earlier. His wife decided to sell the house because it was too big for her alone and her children had all left. One of Mrs. Able's sons had been a law student, had a fight with his roommate and subsequently tried to poison him. He was in all the papers, charged with attempted murder. This happened shortly after we moved in.

The newspapers who were on the story knocked on our door one day and wanted to know if I ever met the son and if I knew anything about him. I said, "You mean Killer Joe." And as he got excited and started to ask questions, I closed the door. I didn't know Joe, never met him, but I thought I would have some fun.

He knocks on the door again, and I answer.

He says, "Did you say Killer Joe?" And can I quote you on that?" I told him he must have heard me wrong. "I never said Killer Joe."

When I was ten and living in Ozone Park, there was a hurricane, and a large tree came down, blocking the street. The first thing the following morning, I went out to see the damage with a couple of friends. We went over to the fallen tree and were looking at it when a newspaper reporter came over to us. He was with a photographer who was taking pictures. He asked if we saw the tree come down. We said, "No, we just saw it this morning."

The next day, our picture next to the fallen tree, was on the front page of the newspaper with a story that said "Boys Were Nearly Killed by Falling Trees." That's when my distrust for newspapers began.

Anyway, one evening, after we came home from a dinner with friends, Joan, our housekeeper, was up having a cup of tea. She was from Barbados and was a very spiritual person. We asked, "Everything okay and are there any messages?"

She said, "Everything is quiet, except I saw a spirit on the stairway."

I said, "Joan, have you been smoking our pot?" I know I mention smoking pot here and there, but you have to understand, growing up in Ozone Park, smoking pot once in a while was like having a Pepsi, no big deal.

She laughed. "No, Bobby, he was a very friendly spirit." I asked what he looked like.

She was very specific, describing a man, not a tall man, about five-seven or five-eight, very handsome, with gray hair parted on the right side, with blue eyes and a mole on the right side of his chin. She said she paid him no mind as she felt he was very friendly. She said he walked past me and disappeared as he walked up the stairs and into our bedroom.

I get cold chills. I look at Bonnie, and she appears okay, not as spooked as I am.

I ask, "Aren't you spooked?"

She says, "No, Joan says he's a friendly spirit."

I whisper, "Joan said he went into our bedroom. Suppose he's a pervert and watches us when we fool around."

She looks at me as she usually does when she thinks I'm nuts and walks up the stairs, shaking her head.

I have an idea. I walk out of my house and look over to my neighbor's house. His name is Hal Warren, one of the closest friends

I will ever have. I loved the man. More about him in a minute. I know he stays up late some nights. I see the living room lights are on. I go over and ring his bell. He answers the door and looks at me. What he says to me I swear I'm not making up. He looks at me and says, "Are you okay? You look like you've seen a ghost." He says, "Come in."

We go into his living room and sit down. He goes to his liquor cabinet and pours me a drink. I don't know what it is, but I drink it. He says, "Hell, I think I'll have one myself."

He asks again if I'm okay. I say, "Yeah" I asked him if he knew Lou Able.

He looks at me with a look like, why am I asking him that? He says, "Of course, he was my neighbor for many years. He checked out on the golf course about three and a half years ago. He really wasn't my cup of tea, pretentious and stiff. We were kind of like on a hello, how you doing basis."

I asked him what he looked like.

He asks why I wanted to know. I tell him I'll tell him in a minute. He says, "He was not that tall, about five-eight or so, a handsome guy with blue eyes, gray hair parted on the side."

I asked him if he had any marks or moles on his face. Hal says, "This is starting to get weird, what's going on?" "Hal, did he?"

He says, "Yea, he had a noticeable mole on the right side of his chin." He looks at me and says, "Bobby what's going on? You look fucked up."

I tell him what just happened. His first words to me were, "No shit, really?" He says, "Don't worry, he won't bother you, he was always a bit of a pussy."

I say, "I don't believe in spirits, but how do you explain what Joan saw?"

I told him I once asked Dr. Joe to explain this spirit phenomena (Hal knew Dr. Joe through me and, like everyone else, liked him and couldn't help but admire his brilliance, especially because he was so modest about it).

Hal asks, "What was Joe's take on it?"

"From what I could understand, he said that all matter has energy. We as human beings have this energy, and when we die, this energy doesn't die with us but continues on in different forms. I remember asking him how long this energy lasts, does it eventually dissipate? He said no one can prove that this energy even exists, but he thinks it does. That's the only way to explain this spirit phenomena. There are these old mansions and sightings of people who died over a century ago, still inhabiting these mansions, so the energy may never dissipate." I say, "I have to call Joe tomorrow and ask him if there is any way to get rid of unwanted spirits."

I got back home, and everyone is sleeping. I go into Alison's room and check on her. She just turned three. I go into my bedroom, and Bonnie is sound asleep, which is unusual as she is a tortured soul and has a hard time falling asleep. I, on the other hand, could fall asleep at the drop of a hat. Sometimes I will get into bed and look at her as she is trying to fall asleep and can't and say, "Bon, count to ten, and I'll be asleep." And I am. She explains the reason I have the ability to fall asleep so quickly is because I have an "empty head."

I get into bed and turn out the lights and say my nightly prayer, which I do because of my religious upbringing, Catholic Grammar School, Catholic High School (the last two years), and Catholic College. I think the same thing. Why do I say a prayer every night when I'm really not a believer? I think the earth is a tiny star among trillions of stars in the universe, and yet we have the audacity to believe we and our God created the entire universe. I think it's highly unlikely. That's my legal training at odds with my religious training.

So why do I say that prayer? Simple, I like to hedge my bets. It's like going to the race track, betting five dollars to win, and two dollars for second in case I'm wrong about my horse winning. That's called hedging your bet.

When I think about the millions of people who have died over religious beliefs and are still dying, I sometimes see religion as a destructive force. So then why is religion still practiced by most of the world? I think mostly because of one thing: the fear of death. Almost all religions promise life after death. Don't get me wrong, religions have some worthwhile things. They have rules to live by. Christians and Jews have the Ten Commandments and they have a sense of community, of belonging.

The problem starts when one religion believes theirs is the only true one, and those who are not part of their religion are not worthy of living (in extreme cases). My point is that religion has surely caused a lot of misery, heartache, and pain, and for what? So that when we check out, we will go to this place called heaven where seventy-two virgins (in some cases) will be waiting for us. What about the women? There will be seventy-two guys waiting for them? One of my favorite songs is by John Lennon called "Imagine," and part of the lyrics are: "Imagine there's no country, it isn't hard to do, nothing to kill or die for, and no religion too."

I try to live by a simpler code called "the Golden Rule." It's straightforward, but just imagine if we only had that rule to live by. I have tried to teach my two children (Alison and Amy) my belief in the Golden Rule as a way to conduct your life, and my other belief which I once wrote down in my office so I would remember it every day and which I tried to impress upon my kids. It goes like this: "Net worth does not equal self-worth."

We live in Lloyd Harbor now a very affluent neighborhood; and I didn't help matters by buying fancy cars, including a Rolls Royce. It was a bad example to set, and of course, Bonnie did not want me to buy it even though I never took it seriously. My younger daughter, Amy, when she was very young, asked me what it meant, and

I told her simply when you get older, don't judge people by how much money they have.

Anyway, enough of my philosophy of life. The last thing I said that night in West Hempstead, out loud, before going to sleep was, "Lou, if you're listening, it's time to leave." Little did I know and only found out later that's one of the things you're supposed to do. Bon and I asked around, and one of my friends knew of a medium who got rid of spirits. We hired her. She came to the house and informed us that her fee for getting rid of spirits was five hundred dollars. I agreed.

I told her that I had several friends who were coming to witness the expulsion of a spirit from our home. She said fine, she will conduct a seance. As my friends arrived, I told them what was going to happen. And what a group they were. Ronnie and, of course, whichever beautiful lady he happened to be going with; a couple of my other lawyer friends; a doctor friend who I was very close to and another friend; a plumber and contractor; and last but not least, my friend Stephen, who got us the medium and whatever girl he was presently dating.

What a crew. I don't think anyone there drew a fully sane breath. Before she started, she went to each of our bedrooms and put a bowl of water and a red light under each bed. The medium then instructed us to sit around the dining room table and hold hands, keep our eyes closed, and put our heads down. She dimmed the dining room chandelier so we could barely see each other and started the seance. She asked if we knew who the spirit was. We told her his name was Lou, and he had lived in the house before he died. We told her about Joan and Hal and everything that had happened.

She closed her eyes and took the hands of the two people sitting to the right and left of her (I was peeking) and began. She said, "Lou, this is Madame Bishop, and I have been brought to your home to ask you to leave." And then went on and on. I don't remember everything she said, but nothing happened. I asked her how we would know if he left. She said we would hear unexplained things like the opening of windows or of kitchen cabinet doors and a whole bunch of other things which I don't remember. She asked us to be patient as sometimes it takes a while for her to connect to the spirit, and sometimes, she cannot connect at all if the spirit does not wish to connect. After trying for a while, continuing to call out, "Lou, Lou, do you hear us?" and nothing happened, some of the people at the table began to get a little restless.

My doctor friend, Stuart, started whispering to his wife, June, who was a pretty lady and in her former life a Playboy bunny, "June, don't fall asleep on me or get tired. I want to get laid when we get home."

Because we were all being silent, nearly everyone heard him, and there was some muffled laughter. June looks at me and says, "Did you hear your wonderfully refined friend, Bobby?"

I say, "Stu, cut it out."

He says, "How long before something happens?"

Madame Bishop asks for everyone's silence. She says, "While we are waiting for Lou to contact us, is there anyone else who would like to try to connect with a departed loved one?"

Several people try, and no one connects.

I can see that everyone is getting impatient and probably nothing is going to happen, so before I call it a night, since we had been at it for over an hour, I tell Madame Bishop, "I have someone I would like to connect with."

She says, "Very well, may I have the person's name?"

A couple of people moan, but I tell them if we can't connect with this person, we'll call it a night. I gave her the name, "Maurice Horowitz."

A couple of people ask, "Bobby, who's that?"

I tell them, "You will find out shortly if he connects. He passed away over ten years ago."

Everyone quiets down, and she slowly starts to say, "Maurice, Maurice, can you hear me?"

After several attempts, I interrupt, "Madame Bishop, I guess this is not a good night to connect with the spirits. Some of my friends are getting a little antsy, and I think we should call it a night. Thank you so much for all your efforts."

She says, "Very well," and we turn on the lights.

As we are getting up from the table to have some coffee and cake, my friend Stu asks me, "Who the hell is Maurice Horowitz?"

I tell him, "One of my favorite people of all time. You may have heard of him. He was an actor whose stage name was Moe Howard. He worked with a partner and brother. His partner's name was Lawrence Fine, and his brother's name was Jerome Horowitz, otherwise better known as the Three Stooges; Moe, Larry, and Curly."

Stu says, "We took this seriously and you are fucking around?"

Of course, everyone cracks up, except Madame Bishop. She is not amused.

I apologize. The house was quiet for a while after the seance, no strange things happening. We thought maybe the seance worked.

Then, one evening, I was in the living room by myself, reading a brief that I had to have ready for the next day, when suddenly, all the windows in the living room opened by themselves, making a large banging noise. I was startled. The windows were the old-fashioned casement windows that you had to turn with a handle to open. I saw the handles spinning fast as the windows opened. At first, I thought a strong wind had caused them to spin, but it was not windy outside.

I called Bonnie to tell her what just happened. She remembered what Madame Bishop said about doors or windows or kitchen cabinets opening unexpectedly. Maybe it was Lou. We called Madame Bishop. She confirmed what we were experiencing was a sign that Lou was leaving with a grand gesture. After that, we never again experienced another sign from Lou. Apparently, Lou had left.

The following Saturday, while I was having breakfast, Bon reminded me that we were going out to dinner with Jovette and Harry, friends of ours. Both were teachers. Harry had a PhD and was very bright and also very serious. I found his seriousness funny on lots of occasions. An example: the four of us were going into the city to see a play. Harry was complaining about a couple they went out with on occasion. He said the wife was okay, but the husband, who was a trial lawyer, didn't speak at all. Harry found it impossible to have a conversation with him.

Harry thought he would only speak if he was being paid to speak. He said, "If only he would say hello." The way he said it caused me to laugh.

I said, "Harry, listen to me carefully, you're not responsible for his actions.

Fuck him."

But Harry felt sad. He was just a good soul. How could that prick not have a conversation with Harry, who was so smart and knowledgeable, was beyond me.

Jovette, besides teaching, was a very good tennis player who entered tennis tournaments all over the place, traveling out of state sometimes.

After meeting for dinner, we head over to Greenwich Village to see Dennis, a gay friend of theirs, who plays piano and will be singing this night at a place called Don't Tell Mamma. It was a music venue, and that evening, the place was packed to the rafters. Dennis had reserved a table for us close to the stage. We got there a little after eleven as we knew Dennis would not go on until after twelve. It was one of those nights when there were lots of gay performers, and we were all having a great time. I had a couple of drinks, which is unusual for me as I'm not a big drinker and have no tolerance for alcohol, and two drinks is enough to get me feeling really good.

Dennis finally comes on, and he's great; singing and playing the piano, and after every song, there's lots of clapping and cheering for him. It gets to be around twelve-thirty, and I realized I have to pee really badly. I get up, excuse myself, and head to the men's room. There is one stall with someone in it and someone waiting to go next. There are two urinals with no partition between them and a line of four or five guys behind each urinal. There are several gay guys, all pretty lit, talking and laughing. Every time someone steps up to the urinals to urinate and exposes himself to pee, the guys are yelling and clapping. I'm a reasonably modest guy, and I think, *oh my god, I can't do this, it's too embarrassing.*

I leave and go outside, looking for another bar on the street since there were several. I go into two, but both bath rooms have lines waiting to get in. I'm desperate when I walk out of the second bar. As I'm walking to the third bar, which looks crowded, I see a dark alleyway between two buildings. I'm almost floating. I have to go so bad. I cross the street and start walking toward the alleyway. There is no one around. I walk down the alleyway, and at the end of the alleyway is an empty lot. It's pitch black. *Thank God.* I relieve myself and head back to the street. As I reach the sidewalk, there is a cop standing there.

He looks at me suspiciously and asks what I was doing in the back lot. I tell him the truth. Most of the cops I knew would laugh upon hearing the story. Not him. He was very young and looked at me sternly and said, "Follow me."

I think he's kidding. It turns out one of the two buildings was his police station. We go into the station, and he tells the desk sergeant he's going to ticket me for public urination. He goes to the side to write up the ticket, and I ask the sergeant if there's any chance, he can talk him out of it. "I'm an attorney, and my brother is an ADA in the homicide division of the Queens County DA's office."

He asks, "What happened?"

I quickly told him the whole story. He's laughing as he hears it. He tells me the cop just started a month or so ago and is breaking everyone's balls, but this is ridiculous. "Let me see what I can do, Counselor."

He comes back a minute later and tells me he has almost finished writing up the ticket and he will not cancel it. I thank the sergeant as the cop comes over and hands me the ticket. There is a pause, and I look at him. "Do you expect me to say thank you?"

The sergeant laughs as I thank him once again for trying and leave.

Now the problem with getting the ticket was that public urination is a misdemeanor, requiring an appearance in court; and if you plead not guilty, an additional appearance. I'm pissed off and embarrassed by the whole thing.

The cop's name is on the ticket. I know a lot of people in the police department, and Ronnie knows even more. I'm going to get this prick transferred to the worst posting in the police department. Then I calm down. I think revenge in the end comes back to bite you in the ass.

Many years ago, I read *The Diary of Anne Frank*, and there was a passage I try never to forget. Although I have failed many times and I continue to fail. It goes like this: "In the long run, the sharpest weapon of all is a kind and gentle spirit." I think I'll just let it go and I do.

I go back to the bar, and everyone is asking where the hell I've been. I tell them what happened. They, of course, think it's funny.

Bonnie is laughing and tells me, "It's no big deal, you'll get an ACD (adjournment in contemplation of dismissal). That means the case against you will be automatically dismissed if you don't get into trouble for six months."

I say, "Yes, but I still have to appear in court, maybe twice before I get the ACD." I say, "I think I will have to be represented because there's an old saying: 'The person who represents himself has a fool for a client.'"

I tell Bonnie she'll have to represent me. She says, "No thanks." I ask her, "Are you kidding me?"

She says, "I don't represent perverts."

Of course, everyone is laughing, unfortunately, at my expense.

This happened on a Saturday. The following Monday evening, I have plans to have dinner with Ronnie and a couple of friends. Ron shows up at about six, and while we're waiting for the other guys to show up, I tell him what happened Saturday. Of course, he thinks it's funny and says it's no big deal. He asked me when it's on, and I told him that it's at 100 Center Street in Manhattan. I tell him, "Bonnie will represent me I don't want to represent myself."

He says he thinks he has something on in the city that date and looks into his calendar book. He says, "You're in luck. I have to be the city on that Tuesday and Wednesday, so tell Bon I'll take care of it."

I remind him that he is an ADA and can't represent private clients.

He says, "I don't know anyone in the misdemeanor part, and even if someone recognizes me, they can see that you're my brother, that the charge is bullshit, and no one is going to say anything."

I say, "Okay, I'll tell Bonnie."

That Wednesday, we went to court; and the court was so packed that there was a line outside the courtroom at least fifty yards long and three people wide. I will be here all day. The court officer standing at the courtroom doors is telling anyone who approaches to go back to the end of the line. We approach the court officer. Ron takes out his ADA ID card, says something to him, and he nods and opens the door and lets us in. Ron walks over to the ADA who is in charge and whispers something to him. He nods and then comes over to me. We'll be the second case called in about two minutes.

One of my favorite movies of all time was a movie written by Mel Brooks, called *History of the World Part One*. There was a scene in the movie when Mel Brooks, playing King Louis XIV, walks around at an outdoor party and goes up to all the pretty girls he sees and squeezes their breasts, and then looks into the camera and says, "It's good to be the king."

Today, he probably would be stoned to death for that scene. That's how I felt that day, kind of like it's good to be an ADA on this day. I tell Ronnie what I'm thinking. He laughs. I asked him if he remembers the end of the movie. It's one of my favorite movie endings. As the movie ends, the credits are running, and as people are getting out of their seats, you hear Mel Brooks voice saying, "Wait, don't leave. See *History of the World Part Two*. See 'Hitler on Ice.'" And then there is an ice skater dressed as Hitler, figure skating. "See 'Jews in Space.'" And then there was a scene of Hasidic Jews in a spaceship, shooting down an enemy spaceship and dancing around arm in arm, celebrating. What a comical genius he is.

I took a thousand dollars cash with me just in case we got a crazy judge. He looks at me. "There is not going to be any bail set. You're an attorney, and the charges are bullshit."

I'm not taking any chances. I tell him, "You remember what happened last time?"

He looks at me and says, "You know, you're crazy."

What happened last time was that I didn't have enough money to pay a speeding ticket, and because I was a law student, and to teach me a lesson, the judge fined me more than twice the normal amount. Since I didn't have enough money, he sent me to jail.

This ticket incident reminded me of the earlier one. It was a day I will never forget. It happened several years earlier. I was on my way to college on the Whitestone Bridge. I was stopped for going fifteen miles an hour over the speed limit. When I got to school, I knew I would not be able to get back in time to appear for the speeding ticket so I called my older brother, Vin, who was a lawyer. He told me to send him the ticket, he would take care of it.

I sent him the ticket and forgot about it. Several years later, on November 22, 1963, a day I will never forget, at about seven in the morning, the front doorbell rang, and there was a pounding on our front door. It woke up everyone in the house. My mother got to the front door first, and there were two policemen. They told my mother there was a warrant for my arrest. My mother tells them they must be mistaken. "What did my son do?"

They tell her, "He failed to pay a speeding ticket years ago, and the city is going after all scofflaw defendants." As they come into the house, we are all up and going into the kitchen.

My brother Vin sees one of the cops and says, "Brian, what are you doing here?"

He says, "Vin, I didn't know you live here." Apparently, they knew each other from the courts; Vin had been a court officer for a year while he was waiting to take the bar exam and start his law practice.

Now everyone sits down as my mother starts to make coffee. They explain what's going on and that the city has gone nuts, having cops go to people's homes and take them into custody for not paying tickets. They have been arresting people for parking and even for jaywalking. They figure once it gets into the papers, it will scare everyone, and there will be a mad rush to pay outstanding tickets, which is exactly what happened. They have been ordered to only do this for a week. I asked him if I could see the ticket in question. They show me. I look at it. "That's the ticket I sent you when I was on my way to college."

Vin looks. "I must have misplaced it and never paid it," he explains to Brian.

Brian says, "No problem, we are not going to take you in, but I suggest you pay it within the next day or so."

Vin and I thanked him, and as they were about to leave, I asked him if they were heading into the city. They said, "Yes, we are going to 100 Center Street traffic court," which is where I have to pay the ticket.

I have a bright idea, which turned out to be a big mistake and cost me three months of not being able to be admitted to the bar after I graduated law school and passed the bar exam. Here's what happened. My bright idea: I asked Brian if I could catch a ride with them into the city to pay the fine. The courthouse is a short walk to my law school, which is also in the city. They say sure. I tell them I'll be ready in five minutes. They say, "Take your time" as they are now having more of my mother's coffee with warm Kaiser rolls and butter and catching up with Vin.

As we're heading into the city, with me sitting in the back of the police car, they get a call that they have to stop at the Maspeth Police Station and pick up some more scofflaw tickets to serve later on. They tell me it will only take a minute; they have to pick up the tickets and change cars. I say okay. When we get to the station, they tell me to come with them since they are changing cars. I go with them into the station. As we are walking through the station, I hear someone calling my name. It's someone who is behind bars. I look to see who's calling me. It's my friend, Lou Dennis. He's in the cell with a dozen men and looks frightened to death. Brian is doing some paperwork, so I go over to him. "Lou, what are you doing here?"

"They came to my house at six-thirty this morning and arrested me." "What for?"

"They had a ticket that I got almost three years ago for jaywalking in New York City. I don't even remember getting it." He says, "Bobby, don't leave me here, I'm scared to death."

Now who is Lou Dennis? First, he is an Italian who changed his name to get into show business, and he made it. He was the host of a TV show which was on Sunday mornings called *Continental Miniatures*. It was a show about opera. He interviewed opera stars and talked about what operas were worth seeing and where. He was a big celebrity in the world of opera, yet here he was in a jail cell, frightened to death. He lived with his mother in Forest Hills. He was in his fifties, always impeccably dressed, and very refined.

If you remember, I mentioned that I had a cousin Ron and I were very close with who was a pretty famous opera singer. Her stage name was Franca Duval. When in the United States, she lived in Forest Hills with her husband, Carlo Nell. He had a very popular TV show in Paris, which was where she met him when she was a guest on his show. Ron and I became very close to him. Most people thought he was our older brother because he was the same height and build as us and looked like us. He was smart, talented, funny, and a bit nuts, and Ron and I loved him. More about him later.

Franca had been a guest on Lou's show many times and, since he lived in Forest Hills, became a family friend. He and his mother had been at Franca's house often for dinner or just to hang out. My Aunt Sara, Franca's mother, would often cook for him, and she always called us all to come over. For some reason, Lou really liked Ron and me. I was never sure why. As I said he was so refined, and we were like two roughnecks next to him. He was a little effeminate, but not gay and fun to be around. Of course, we always made fun of fat opera singers, Franca being the exception. She was beautiful and thin and like an older sister to us.

Anyway, getting back to Lou, I tell him I can't stay with him. "I'm going to the city to pay a speeding ticket."

He says, "So am I. Only it's a jaywalking ticket."

I say, "Hold on a minute." I go over to Brian, who's doing some paperwork, tell him about Lou, and ask if we could take Lou with us. He says ""Lou is formally under arrest but if you want, you can go with him because Lou will be following us into the city and going to the same court". We will all be leaving in a couple of minutes." I'm looking at poor Lou who is staring back at me with pleading eyes. I think, *What the hell...*

I asked Brian to put me in with Lou. He says, "Okay, just a second," and gives me something to sign so I can go with Lou. I asked him what I'm signing, and he says, "This allows you to go with Lou." I later found out that the little piece of paper I signed put me officially under arrest if only for an hour and until I got to court and paid the fine.

We get to court, and I am put in a jail cell with Lou and all the other fine gentlemen. After a couple of minutes, we are taken from our cells and into the courtroom. Since I am the only one other than Lou that is dressed and carrying a briefcase, the judge asked me what I do. I tell him I am a third-year law student. Before I have a chance to explain why the ticket was not paid, he says, "You're going to be a lawyer; you should be an example to the community" and hits me with a $100 fine. The usual fine for 15 mph over the speed limit at the time was $25, but since I didn't pay it in a timely manner, Vin figured the judge could double the fine, so he gave me $50 just to be safe.

After paying his fine, Lou only had $28 left. Since he only needed a dollar for train fare to get home, he gave me $27. I only had $50, so I still couldn't pay the fine. I told Lou that when he got home to call my brother Vin and have him send someone here with enough money to pay the fine so I could get out of jail.

I got to the holding pen where people were trying to raise money. I managed to get to the phone and called my law school and asked for Jackson, the elevator operator who I knew well and really liked. I told him what was going on and asked if he could get Bonnie who, of course, he knew well. I told him what class she would be in. She comes to the phone in a minute, and I tell her what happened. She, together with a couple of my classmates, get the balance of the money I need and, in about fifteen minutes, shows up with the rest of the money to pay my fine. I call Vin and tell him what happened and not to send anyone since I have managed to raise the money. Five minutes later, we were in a cab, heading back to law school.

While in the cab, the driver said, "Did you hear President Kennedy was shot in Dallas today?" That's why I will always remember November 22, 1963, so well. When we got to school, we did not go back to class but went to a local bar/restaurant which had a TV. We were hoping he would recover. We walk in and see what appeared to be half the school packed in there. As we enter, we hear Walter Cronkite on TV announcing that President Kennedy had been killed. Everyone was shocked. It was a sad, sad day. We all loved him. At the time, most of us were liberal Democrats. I believe it was Winston Churchill who once said, "Anyone who is twenty and not a liberal has no heart, and anyone who is forty and not a conservative has no head."

Well, we were all in our twenties. As a result of helping Lou out and signing in and going with him in the police van, I was considered officially under arrest and had to put that on my papers to be admitted to the New York State bar. Having been arrested for any reason caused a delay in my swearing in as they checked up on you. I had to appear before the Board of Inquiry which caused me to miss one swearing in until the next one, which I believe was several months later. I finally got there, but, thanks, Lou.

So here I am, standing next to Ron in a courtroom again, and after a few minutes, my case is called. Ron and I go before the judge, plead not guilty, and are given a date to appear for a final disposition of my case. There is no mention of bail. Ron, of course, was right. The date is in a little over three weeks.

We get back to the office and we go into the lunchroom to have a coffee and relax. As we walk in, I see my secretaries have put up a big sign on the blackboard we had back there, saying results of the great PP case have not been determined yet. Of course, they're all in there, waiting to see my reaction. I look at them. It's very funny. Of course, they are all laughing.

A little over three weeks later, we're back in court. As I approached the courtroom, I told Ron, "This really sucks. It's so embarrassing."

He says, "Why are you making such a big deal out of this?" I say, "Wouldn't you be embarrassed if it was you?"

He says, "Absolutely not."

I tell him, "Since that's the case, I have an idea." He says, "What?"

I say, "How about you be me, the defendant, and I'll be your lawyer representing you?"

He says, "Are you crazy?"

I say, "Why not? No one will know, and since you don't get embarrassed, it won't matter to you." As I'm suggesting this, we approach the courtroom doors where my case is being called.

On the left-hand side is a glass-enclosed case with the name of the cases being heard that day. The first case being called is "The People of the State of New York" against Frank R Aliazzo, Esq.

I look horrified. Ronnie look at that. "The People of the State of New York" are after me. I can't believe it."

He says, "Would you stop?"

As we walked in, I told Ronnie, "Waive the reading of the complaint."

He says, "No, I want to hear what they have to say." Now I know he is breaking my balls and wants to have fun at my expense. "The complaint states what you already know, that is what you are charged with. If the complaint is read, then the whole courtroom knows what you are charged with. That is public urination."

I look at him as my case is called and we approach the bench. "All right, I'll waive the reading" he says.

"The ADA stands up in the matter of The People of the State of New York against Frank R Aliazzo, Esq. How do you plead?"

Ron says, "Not guilty."

The ADA asks, "Do you waive the reading of the complaint?" Ron says, "Yes."

Thank God.

Ron then asked the judge, who is a woman and is looking at us because we are not the normal attorney and defendant as she can tell we are brothers, for a sidebar. She nods yes. A sidebar is where you go over to the side of the judge's desk and speak about the case to the District Attorney and judge.

They talk for a minute, then Ron comes back next to me. The judge then addresses the court, In the Matter of the State of New York against Frank R Aliazzo, Esq., the defendant has been offered an ACD (adjournment in contemplation of dismissal)."

Ron turns to the judge. "May I have a moment to speak to my client?" She nods, yes. He whispers, "What do you think?"

I say, "What, are you fucking crazy? Do you think I'm going to go out in the street and pee in public in the next six months? And if I don't, the case will be automatically dismissed."

He says, "Okay, okay." He addresses the court, "The defendant agrees to accept the ACD."

Judge says, "Very well. Next case."

As we walked out of the courtroom, people were looking at me, wondering what I did. I said, "Screw them, they'll never know."

Patrick Lucie

It's a Friday morning, and I'm on the phone with Marty Asner, a criminal lawyer friend of mine. He called me because he is pissed off at Ronnie and wants me to talk to him. As he starts to tell me why he's angry at Ronnie, I get another call from Pat Lucie. I tell Marty to hold, and I pick up Pat. He is calling to remind me of the time we are meeting tomorrow night. He and his partner and Bon and I are going to dinner, then to see an off-Broadway musical called *Boy Meets Boy*. Yes, he's gay, and so is the show, but he told me he saw it a couple of weeks ago, and it was so good we would love it. I tell him Bon has all the info, and I'm looking forward to it. I hang up and get back to Marty.

Marty Asner is a very well-known criminal lawyer, has had some famous clients, and is well-liked by everyone, including Ron and me. He starts telling me what's going on. He has a client, a burglar who got caught inside a 7-Eleven at four in the morning. He was stealing cartons of cigarettes and other stuff. He got out on bail and hired Marty.

Marty's fees are very high, and the client gave him a retainer with a promise of paying him the balance of the fee before trial. Marty knew that he couldn't win the case but felt if he got lucky, he would get an ADA in Queens County who would have the balls to drop the C felony his client was being charged with, which carries three and half and up to fifteen years or so, to an E felony, which carries one and a half to four years. He hit the jackpot or so he thought when he got Ronnie.

He goes to see Ronnie about dropping the C felony to an E felony. Ronnie knows the client was overcharged, and an E felony is what it should be. Why? Marty's client has a relatively clean record, only one other arrest for burglarizing a candy store years ago, and no history of any violent crimes. Marty tells Ronnie his client will not plead to a C felony which means Marty would have to try the case, which he had no chance of winning, especially against Ronnie. In addition, his client could not pay the balance of his fee which meant Marty would be working for only the retainer. Ronnie asked, "How come he can't come up with the balance of the fee?"

He said the client planned to do another burglary to pay him, but he couldn't get the money needed to do the job; and so, Marty thought if Ronnie doesn't drop the C to an E felony, he's fucked, to say nothing of the client.

Ronnie says, "Okay, I'll drop it to an E felony on one condition." Marty says, "What's the condition?"

Ronnie says, "You've got to get rid of the pompadour."

Now you have to understand Ronnie and I have had a thing about bad hair styles. My older brother, Vincent, was the one who started this. He was twelve years older than us, and whenever he didn't like the way our hair looked, he would say, "Let me fix your hair, and he would then get a comb and restyle our hair. Ninety percent of the time, it looked worse, and we would wait a little while and then recomb it.

As we got older and refused to let him recomb our hair, he would bribe us with a quarter or so. Ron and I figured a quarter was a quarter, and we could always put it back to how it was when he left.

After a while, he was up to a dollar to fix our hair and ended when he came up to me one day and said, "You can't go out looking like that." He said, "Let me cut it for you, and I'll give you two bucks."

I said, "Absolutely not."

My mother hears this and says, "Vinnie, leave him alone. He looks fine."

He said, "I can't let you go out looking like that. I'll give you five bucks if you let me cut your hair."

Five dollars was five dollars. I figured; *how bad could it be?* I said, "Okay." We went into the bathroom where he normally would recomb my hair. When he finishes, before I even look at myself in the mirror, I go into the bedroom to put my shirt back on as I don't want hair all over my shirt. My mother looks at me and screams.

I looked like the bride of Frankenstein. Half of my hair was sticking up; the other part was going in seven different directions. My father comes in, looks at me, and starts laughing. He tells Vin right after dinner to take me to the barber to get him a crewcut. "That's the only thing you can do with his hair." That was the last time Vin cut my hair, but he made us extremely conscious of hairstyles.

Ronnie and I once thought Vin should have become a barber instead of an attorney, but after some careful thought, we both agreed he would have starved as a barber.

Getting back to Marty Asner and Ronnie's demand that he fixes his hair and gets rid of the pompadour. I understood and completely agreed with Ronnie. I tell Marty, "You know he's crazy, what's the big deal? You can comb it back right after you get the plea."

He says, "No, I can't, he wants me to go to his barber, and I don't know what his barber will do to my hair." I tell him the barber he is suggesting is my barber. He's only nineteen years old and is going to be a legend in the haircutting business. The fact is the barber would become pretty famous, but not for cutting hair; that story is for later on. "Well," Marty says, "I guess I have no choice." And he goes to Frankie (the barber) and gets the haircut. Frankie was told by Ronnie, he wanted him to get rid of the pompadour and make him look good.

Ronnie tells me what happened the next day. Marty goes to court with the new hairdo to officially get the C felony reduced to an E and get rid of this nightmare of a case. As he enters the courthouse, he goes to the counter where you have to show what's in your briefcase. There are two court officers there that check everything. Marty knows them both very well as he has been going to the courthouse for many years. One is a man, and the other is a very pretty woman who Marty has been flirting with for years.

She looks at him. "Is that you, Marty? I hardly recognize you. What have you done to yourself? I know, you changed your hair. My god, you look so handsome."

He's flabbergasted. He doesn't know what to say. Finally, he says, "Thank you." Embarrassed, he walks away. He doesn't know what to make of it. He takes the elevator to the third floor where Ronnie's offices are. As he enters the outer office, the receptionist who knows him well looks at him and says, "Mr. Asher, is that you? My god, you look terrific, you look so different."

He says, "Yeah, I got a new haircut from Mr. Aliazzo's barber." She says, "Well, whoever cut your hair did a great job. Let me tell Mr. Aliazzo you're here." As he walks into Ronnie's office, Peggy is taking dictation.

She stops and starts to get up, and as she turns around, she sees Marty. She stops and does a double take. "Marty, what the hell? I hardly recognize you. You look so different. I know, it's your hair. My god, the new hairstyle is very becoming."

He says thank you, and as she walks out, Ronnie stands up. "I fucking told you."

Marty says, "What can I say? You were right. Even I think I look better."

As a result of his new look, his confidence grows, and now he really becomes a man about town. A short time after this, Marty is in court and bumps into Bonnie who he knows well as they have both been criminal lawyers in the same court for several years. Bonnie told me that most of the time, when she would bump into him in court, he would give her a quick hello. But not today. She had just left the matrimonial part, having represented a friend who had just been granted a divorce. Her name was Skyler, and she was with another friend, Page, both of whom were attractive with great figures. Marty, with his newfound confidence, asked Bonnie what she was doing in the matrimonial part.

"I'm representing my friend Skyler here who was just granted a divorce." He starts to chat with Skyler, and she responds, smiling.

He says, "Well, I was just going for lunch, can I invite you ladies to join me?"

Bonnie and Page are unable to do so, but Skyler accepts his invitation.

That evening, Skyler calls Bonnie to tell her that she has a date with Marty. Bonnie is surprised because she knows that Marty had just gotten married for the second time just a few months ago. She tells Skyler. Skyler says she doesn't care. After such a miserable marriage, she was just interested in having a good time, and a good time they had until it got too weird. Marty would call from his house while his wife was in the shower or while he was out walking his dog. Bonnie told me that after a while, it just fizzled out.

So, getting back to Patrick Lucie who had tickets for me and Bonnie to see the Broadway musical, Boy Meets Boy. Let me tell you a little about him. He was the youngest brother of my childhood friend, Ralphie, whom I wrote about previously. He grew up in that crazy family, and it was difficult. He was studious, smart, always reading, handsome, slim, soft spoken, an A student, and gay. We all knew I think before he even knew.

Being gay in those years in Ozone Park was not easy. However, no one in the neighborhood really bothered him because he was Ralphie's kid brother. Only once did I speak to Ralphie about him. Ralphie said he can't control what he is or how he feels anymore that he can control the color of his eyes. He's my kid brother; you could not ask for a better brother, and I love him. For a guy who grew up in the streets with no education, boy, was that an enlightened view. I was proud of him. All our crowd accepted him and cared for him. Pat was especially close to Ronnie and me because he thought we were smart, got good grades in school, and recommended books that we knew he would like.

What he didn't know was that we had not escaped the Ozone Park mentality of quitting school at sixteen, getting working papers, and saving up so that at eighteen, we could buy a car because with a car came lots of girls. We did not tell my father what we planned. We figured we would tell him when we graduated high school because we knew he would not allow us to quit high school. Somehow, while having dinner one evening while still in John Adams High School and before being sent off to Mount Assumption Institute, we let slip out what our plans were. My father listened as we told him.

When we were finished, he calmly said, "You boys can do that if you want, but then you have to be very careful crossing streets from now on."

We said, "Why?"

He said, "Because I will run you over with my car before I let you do that. Your older brother is a lawyer already in private practice, doing well. Didn't I always drum into you that you had to go to college? What the hell happened? Where did I go wrong?"

Vin said, "It's their friends, that's what they do. They want to be part of the group."

That evening, when my father wasn't around, Vin said he wanted to talk to us. I'll never forget what he said. He told us that we didn't really understand how fortunate we were to have parents who would sacrifice anything for us to get an education. He said whatever it takes moneywise, they were willing to do. They cashed in their life insurance policies later on to take us out of John Adams High School and sent us to Plattsburgh New York and Mount Assumption Institute. My father died at forty-nine while we were in our second year at Mount Assumption, and guess who paid for us to finish Mount Assumption and go to college? My big brother, Vin.

Now back to Patrick. As Pat got older and graduated from high school, he knew he wanted to go to college, but did not have the money. He thought maybe he could get some sort of scholarship, but a scholarship for what? He didn't play sports, and although he was an A student, that alone wouldn't get him into college. I suggested Queens College, remembering that some schools offer unusual scholarships. Maybe he could work at the school to pay for some of his tuition and get student loans if no type of scholarships were available. He said he was going to give it a shot.

He called me a week or so later and told me he applied for a scholarship and thought he might get it. I tell him, "I want to hear all about it. Let's have an early celebration. Let's go for dinner, my treat. Can you meet me around six at Don Pepe?"

He says, "I'll be there, and thanks, Bobby."

At this point, both Ron and I were like older brothers to him. I call Ron, and he says, "I'll be there." I call Bonnie and tell her what's going on.

She says, "Good for Pat," but she just got home, had showered, was in her pajamas, and didn't feel like coming out; so, I said I would give her the full report after dinner.

At this time, Pat was around eighteen, and Ron and I twenty-seven, and I was already practicing law, and Ron was in the District Attorney's Office.

We met Pat at Don Pepe's. He's excited. He says Queens College is offering a scholarship if the recipient was willing to major in Chinese. I said, "What happens if you can't handle it and quit?"

He said they discussed that. What happens is the scholarship turned into a student loan if he understood them correctly.

Ron says, "What do you know about Chinese?"

He says, "Nothing, but if it means going to college for free, I'm willing to learn."

I say, "What are you going to do with a degree in Chinese?" He says, "I don't know."

Ron says, "Maybe you could work at the United Nations as an interpreter."

Pat says, "Gee, I never thought of that. Maybe." He says, "I still have to take some tests, but I'm excited."

To make a long story short, Pat is awarded the scholarship and gets immersed in Chinese. We keep in touch. He tells us that he's doing great and can already get by pretty well in this new language. He thinks part of the reason is some of his classmates are Chinese, and in school, he is only allowed to speak Chinese. Several months after that conversation Ron, Ralphie, me, and some of the guys make plans to go to Chinatown to rib it up (you remember, all the spare ribs you could eat for $18.50). I have an idea. I call Pat and invite him to come with us. He hesitates, then says okay.

That Friday night, the six of us went to Chinatown. The waiter brings us the menu, which is in Chinese, with tiny little printing in English at the bottom of each item. Ron says, "Okay, Pat, we want you to order for us in Chinese."

He says, "Oh no."

Ron says, "How do we know when you say a Chinese word for us (we are always asking him how do you say this or that in Chinese) you're not talking gibberish and can't really speak that language?"

He looks at us and knows he can't get out of it. He says to Ronnie, "Okay, what do you want?"

Ron says, "I'll tell you when the waiter comes."

The waiter comes over with a pen ready to take our order. Pat starts to speak to him in Chinese. The waiter looks up from his order pad in shock, looks at Pat, and starts to jabber away, and before you know it, there is a conversation in Chinese. Now we are all in shock and all have the same reaction. We get up and start to hug him. We are so proud of him. The waiter looks at us like we were crazy. Pat was happy, proud, and embarrassed.

After graduation, Ron and I took him out for dinner and asked him what he planned to do now. He says he was thinking of working for a real estate agency in Chinatown. I said, "I have a better idea. Go to law school. When you get out, you can come work with us."

He said he never thought about it but would. The next thing I know and without telling Ronnie or me, he took the law boards, did well, applied to law school, and was accepted. Since he didn't have any debt from college, he could get student loans. Ron and I were in shock and were so happy for him. He asked if he could use our office in the evenings as it was impossible to study at home. I said, "Of course. I'll have keys made up for you."

Three years later, he graduates, passes the bar exam, and we have a big party with his family and friends. Pat and I are chatting outside, and I tell him I haven't forgotten my offer to him and he can start anytime he wants. He thanks me for the offer but tells me he would like to try something else. I tell him, "Pat, that's fine, and if it doesn't work out, you always have a place with us."

He hugs me and thanks me for the offer and for being so understanding. He says knowing he has a place to come back to gives him the courage to try.

"May I ask what you plan to do? If you feel comfortable talking to me about it."

He says he would not feel comfortable moving forward without telling Ron and me. I say, "Give me a second, let me get Ronnie." I get Ronnie. We sit down with some espresso and cigars; that is, me and Ron. Pat has regular coffee, no cigars. We started to chat.

Pat says he has some really good news. He has met someone who he really cares for. His name is Val. He lives in Manhattan, and he is going to be moving in with him in a couple of weeks. We are surprised. Pat has always been very private about his personal life. In all the years we've known him, he has never brought a boyfriend around, so this is a big deal.

He says Val owns a beautiful apartment on 57th Street, comes from Wisconsin, is two years older than him, and works in the entertainment business. He is a set designer for Broadway plays and has designed the sets for major Broadway shows and is in great demand. Ron and I look at each other, thinking the same thing (after all, we are twins). We can get tickets to Broadway shows. We tell Pat. He laughs. "Not only can you get tickets for almost any of the shows you want but also the best seats available, and most of the time, you will not have to pay for them."

We say, "Patrick, we love you." He laughs.

He says he is going to be living for free as Val makes a lot of money and doesn't need his help. He has managed to save up some money all the years he worked for his parents in the restaurant and thinks he has enough to make the payments on his student loan and still keep him going for a year or more. He then tells us what his plans are.

He is going to open a law office/real estate practice in Chinatown. He says he doesn't want to let his knowledge of Chinese go to waste. He has found a place in Chinatown, which is a short subway ride from his new apartment. He's going to sign a year lease. He says it's a suite of offices with a common waiting room/conference room. The other seven lawyers share in the rent and the receptionists. The office is a nice size with a window. It's furnished already and ready to go.

We ask if he's met any of the other lawyers. He says he's met two, both of whom are Chinese. He thinks he's the only lawyer who is not Chinese. We tell him it sounds great to us, and whatever we can do to help him, let us know. We tell him, "If you find that you are getting in over your head, let us know, and we will always be there for you."

And now for the most important part: "When do we get to meet Val?"

He says he has told Val all about us, and he wants us to meet him before he meets the rest of his family as he wants to start off with a good impression. We tell him we will be on our best behavior. He says, "No, please, just be your crazy selves."

We made a date to meet. It's at the apartment, and they will be cooking dinner for us.

The night arrives a week or so later. It's Bonnie and I and Ronnie and his current flame, Elsa, who we tell Ronnie to please marry as she runs a gourmet catering business and we have never eaten so well, although it seems to me Ronnie has put on a pound or two. Ronnie, who is somewhat vain to say the least, has noticed and has indicated she may cook herself right out of his heart. We meet Val who is tall and handsome. He asks, "Are all the stories Pat told me about you true?"

Before we could answer, Bonnie pipes in, "He probably tones them down a little." It turns out that he is smart, very warm, welcoming and a terrific cook. We had a great time and, over the years, became very close to him.

One day, a couple of months after meeting Val, and Pat starting his practice, Pat calls and says, "Bobby, I have some exciting news" and tells me the story. He said it all began when he was reading the *New York Times*, and there was an article about the Chinese looking for a building for the UN embassy. He found out where they were temporarily staying and went over to introduce himself.

I said, "Pat, you went over just like that without knowing anyone?"

He said, "I had nothing to lose, so I gave it a shot." I said, "I'm sorry to interrupt."

They were occupying two floors of a hotel. Somehow, he found out who was in charge of purchasing the new property and in what suite of rooms he and his staff were occupying. He knocked on the door, and when the man answered, he introduced himself, speaking in Chinese, telling the person he was an attorney and also a licensed real estate broker, had his own firm, and that he was confident he could find a place for their new embassy.

The guy listens politely, says, "No thank you" and shows him the door.

Pat, not to be deterred, shows up the next day, and this time, he gets to leave his card. The weekend comes, and on Monday, he's back again. In the several times he's been there, they never once told him that they had someone showing them the buildings.

Many years ago, I smoked. My cigarette brand of choice was Rothmans, an English cigarette, which I first bought while I was on vacation in England. How did I come across Rothmans cigarettes? I was staying at a hotel called Sherlock Holmes. In the lobby, there was a smoke shop, and I wanted to try a different cigarette. I went into the shop and, in my best British accent, said, "I say, can you recommend a good cigarette?"

Without missing a beat, he said, "Hey, Yank, you're from New York, right?"

I guess my accent wasn't that good. He recommended an English cigarette called Rothmans. I smoked them, liked them, and until the day I quit smoking, I never smoked another brand of cigarette. Pat, who also smoked at the time, tried Rothmans, loved them, and I told him the place where he could get them.

Little did we know that terrible habit would be the key to him getting to meet the Chinese ambassador. While making his pitch for the third time, the person whom he was speaking to was smoking. Pat noticed that the smoke was really strong and harsh. Pat said, "Why don't you try one of mine? I think you will like them."

The guy loved the cigarette. Pat showed him the pack and tells him to take it. The guy said, "No, no," but Pat said, "There are just a few cigarettes," so the guy accepts them and thanks Pat. He still is not given a chance to speak to anyone.

A couple of days later, he gets a call from the guy he gave the cigarettes to, saying the ambassador would like to meet him. Pat is in shock.

The next day, when Pat shows up, he is greeted very warmly, and the guy says the ambassador is waiting for him. He takes Pat to a suite of rooms, and he's introduced to the ambassador who is sitting at a long conference table, drinking a cup of tea. He stands and welcomes Pat, speaking Chinese, and as they get into a conversation, the ambassador asks Pat how he learned Chinese. Pat tells them the truth that his family could not afford to send him to college and about the scholarship. The ambassador tells him he comes from humble beginnings also. The ambassador is very warm towards him, and Pat thinks it's because of his humble beginnings.

As they are chatting, a woman in a white chef's jacket wheels in a tray of food. It smells delicious. The ambassador tells him the chef has prepared some of his favorite snacks as he usually has a late dinner. "Please have some tea and try some."

Pat says, "Thank you, I would love to."

The tea comes in, the server tells Pat it usually is sweetened with a little milk the way the ambassador likes it. Pat says, "May I try the ambassador's tea?"

The ambassador is delighted that Pat wants to try it. The tea is beyond great. Pat has never tasted tea like this.

The ambassador tells him the tea is his favorite from China and says "Wait until you try my delicious snacks." Some of the snacks were hot and some were cold and one more mouthwatering than the next. Pat wanted to try to be refined, but the food was so good he was digging right into it without thinking. With his mouth almost filled, he looked at the ambassador and felt embarrassed that he was eating so much.

The ambassador looks at Pat and smiles and says he loves people with a good appetite, but save some for him, and they both laugh at this. That was the beginning of a very warm friendship for years to come.

Pat tells the ambassador that perhaps he could come to his mother's house in Ozone Park since his mother and Aunt Anna are two of the best Italian cooks in the world. The ambassador says that sounds lovely, and he will be looking forward to it, but first he wants to know a little about Pat. He said, "Let me tell you what I know, and maybe you can fill me in on what I'm missing."

With some notes in front of him, he basically tells Pat the story of his life. Pat is shocked, and when the ambassador is finished, Pat asks him how he found out all this. He said, "You left your card with my secretary, and we did a little research because there is a chance we will do business with you, and we want to make sure of who you are."

The ambassador never mentions Pat being gay, so Pat makes the assumption that he doesn't know. His heart jumped up in his chest. There is a chance that he will get the listing from the Chinese ambassador.

The ambassador says, "My secretary tells me you are a very persistent young man and will not take no for an answer. I like that. We have had many calls from real estate people. My secretary did not like most of them. They were from big real estate firms. He liked you. None of them spoke Chinese." The ambassador asks, "Pat, do you have the same access to real estate that these big brokerage firms have?"

Pat explains how multiple listings work and how everyone has access to the same properties. The ambassador asked him to explain how the whole system works. Pat is starting to catch on. This ambassador is extremely smart. Under that polite demeanor lies a very shrewd, very sharp mind. Pat takes twenty minutes to spell out how multiple listings work and also tells the ambassador that some real estate firms get exclusive listings, listings that no one else has.

"These listings are time sensitive, and if not sold within that time, they will probably go on multiple listings, and then everyone will have access to them. However, those properties that are exclusively listed can be bought."

The ambassador says, "How?"

Pat says that even those exclusive listings are known by all brokers as it is almost impossible to keep it quiet for a very long time. "If I see one of these exclusive listings, and I think you might like the property, I can approach the real estate broker and tell him I represent the great country of China, and my client may be interested in your property. Of course, they would show it to you for a couple of reasons, even though they would have to split the commission with me. If they had no other buyers, they would rather get half of a commission than none at all, and to have in their resume that they were the real estate firm who sold the government of China the property that is now their embassy is very prestigious and great advertising for future sales."

The ambassador then asks Pat simple questions, which shows Pat he understood everything Pat just explained, and he asked some questions that only an experienced real estate guy would ask. Pat thought, *Boy, this guy is sharp.*

Finally, after more than an hour, the ambassador tells Pat why they might actually give him a chance and that he has the full authority to make that decision. He tells Pat he does not like to deal with big American corporations and would rather engage with a small real estate firm. The fact that he is a lawyer was also a consideration as Pat would be able to address any possible legal problems that may arise.

As they are having dessert and drinking tea, the ambassador lights up one of Pat's Rothmans cigarettes, and it's obvious by the way he is smoking that he is enjoying it. Pat lights up one of his own, and together they are smoking and sipping tea and are quiet for a moment. Finally, the ambassador says, "Thank you for the Rothmans, they are the best cigarettes I have ever had. It is an indulgence I allow myself."

Pat tells the ambassador, "If you're thinking of giving me the listing, I can prepare a standard real estate listing agreement. You could tell me how long I can have the listing. Whatever you say will be fine with me."

The ambassador asked him, "What is the normal time to give a real estate brokerage firm a listing?"

Pat replies, "Anywhere from one month to six months."

The ambassador says, "Let's settle on three months, and we will go from there."

Pat says, "I can have the listing agreement prepared in the next couple of days, and if I can make an appointment now, I will be back with the agreement. The agreement will be the standard listing agreement. When I give it to you, please take as much time as you need to have your attorneys look at it, and if they have any questions or changes, I would be happy to discuss it with them."

The ambassador agrees, and they make a date to meet the following Monday.

The following Monday, Pat is back and meets with the ambassador. The listing is only three pages long. The ambassador is surprised. The ambassador tells Pat to come back in a couple of hours as he would like to have his lawyers review the document.

Two hours later, Pat returns, meets with the ambassador, and the listing is signed. Pat is in heaven; he now has an exclusive listing to sell the Chinese their new embassy.

After the listing is signed, the ambassador takes Pat aside and asks him if the invitation to his mother's home for the Italian home-cooked meal was real.

Pat is shocked. He says, "Mr. Ambassador, I would be honored to have you in our home anytime you're available."

The ambassador says, "I'm available any time."

And so, they make a date for that Sunday evening at five o'clock. Pat asks how many people will be coming. The ambassador says, "Just me and my assistant, if that's okay. I will have my driver drop us off and pick us up later."

Pat gets home that evening and calls his mother and tells her that he got the listing. He also tells her about the dinner he set up for Sunday at five o'clock. They discuss the menu, typical Italian—lasagna, salad, meatballs, veal cutlet parmesan. His mother is about to go on, but Pat stops her. "Ma, that's enough."

That Sunday evening, about an hour before the ambassador is due to show up, two men appear at Pat's mother's house and tell her that it is normal for them to come and check out a place where the ambassador will be visiting if he's never been there before. Around five o'clock, the ambassador shows up with his aide. The house is a small typical Ozone Park house. Pat welcomes the ambassador and tells him, "Welcome to my mother's humble home."

The ambassador tells him, "In China, this home would be a rich man's home." Pat later told me that the ambassador and his aide loved his mother's cooking. Pat had the feeling that the real reason the ambassador wanted to come to Pat's home was to make sure Pat was who he said he was, even after all the checking on him that had been done before.

To make a long story short, Pat found the building that became the Chinese embassy. To this day, I'm not sure how he found it and if there were other people involved, but I do know he received a large commission because with part of the commission, he bought a home in the Hamptons which we visited many times.

Now the story really gets interesting. A short time after the sale, the ambassador, with whom Pat had become very friendly, invited him to a dinner with some of his friends and colleagues. It was a formal dinner, with a couple of the ambassador's colleagues standing up, all praising Pat for the wonderful job he had done finding the building for them. Then came the big surprise. He was officially invited to be a guest of the Chinese government.

What did that mean? He would be, as a guest of the government, flown to China. Once in China, as an honored guest, he would be treated as a dignitary and given a tour of different parts of the country. Included in the tour would be visits to hospitals, factories, and other places of interest. At that time, China was still closed, and he would be one of the first Westerners to be touring China. It would be quite an adventure, and we were really excited for him. We had a small going away party for him the night before he left, and the next day, off he went. When I thought of the family he came from and the obstacles he had overcome, I just marveled at how special a country we had and how a kid from his background was able to take advantage of the opportunity to go to school and achieve such wonderful things.

So off he went to China, going for over a month. When he came back, he toured the country for several months, speaking at various colleges. He had taken several hundred pictures and, in his lectures, included a slideshow of his time in China. He got an agent to help him book his tour. When we finally all got together—that is, me, Bonnie, Ronnie, Pat, and Val—at dinner, we asked him to "start from the time you got on the plane to China and stop when you got back home."

He looked at us like we were nuts but said he would do his best. Ronnie and I attended one of his lectures. I believe it was at Queens College in New York City. I probably could write another book about his trip (he should have but never did write a book about this trip to China), so I will give you a couple of the stories that I remember Pat telling us. I don't know why I chose these three because there were hundreds of others.

The first story I remember is about him having dinner with some Chinese hosts on his first night there. After dinner, as he and his hosts were walking along a river on a beautiful warm evening, he noticed a crowd of people following them.

He realized it was because they had never seen a Westerner before. After a while, he turned to them and said, "Why are you following us?" in Chinese.

They started to laugh.

He asked, "Why are you laughing?"

They said, "Because you speak with a funny accent."

I don't know why I remember that story, but I do. The other two stories I remember were that as he was visiting a hospital with his Chinese hosts. They asked if he would like to see a surgery using a Chinese method to anesthetize the patient. Although he wasn't particularly keen on witnessing a surgery, he didn't want to seem squeamish and therefore said yes. He was in the room above an operating theater that was enclosed in glass. He was looking down. A man, the patient, walked to the operating table. He had a large goiter on his neck. The man got on the operating table. Some of the doctors started to insert needles around the goiter and different parts of his body. They then proceeded to remove the goiter.

Pat did not see an anesthesiologist and couldn't believe that the man survived the surgery with no obvious pain and, with the help of some of the surgeons, walked away after the surgery. I didn't believe it at the time, but now I realize it must have been acupuncture, which I had never heard of back then.

Pat had pictures of him arriving in small towns with people waving flags as he stood in a convertible car, like a visiting dignitary. He said it was quite surreal. He said he tasted foods that were unbelievably delicious and some that he declined to try, always being aware that he did not want to insult his hosts and always declining gracefully.

He was expected to give speeches, which he did. They were always short and basically were speeches welcoming the Chinese to the United Nations and thanking them for their hospitality toward him. Before he left the United States, he was told by someone that the Chinese did not have bubblegum. He wasn't sure whether this was true or not but decided to bring Bazooka bubblegum. A couple of hundred Bazookas wrapped in the iconic Bazooka wrapping. He gave them to children who had never seen bubblegum before and showed them how to use it. He said it was a tremendous hit with the kids, especially when showing them how to use it.

This trip was one of the highlights of his life. He loved the Chinese people and their culture and remained friends with the ambassador for years.

Upon his return and after his tour, he returned to work, selling real estate in Chinatown. About a month after returning, as he was walking back to his office after lunch, he was approached by two men in suits. They asked if they might speak to him. He asked what about, and they identified themselves as CIA agents. He was shocked. They addressed him by his name as they obviously knew who he was. They asked if he would come with them as they wished to speak to him. He asked again what this was all about, and they said they would explain everything to him. He told them that he had to get back to his office, but if they would give him an address, he would meet them this evening. They agreed.

That evening, at about six o'clock, he walked up to what looked like a brownstone house at a location he agreed never to disclose. He rang the doorbell; he noticed a small camera almost hidden at the top of the door which he figured was a camera to see who was entering. A man in what looked like a policeman's uniform answered the door. They walked through the vestibule and into a large room with desks and people working. The man who answered the door had a gun attached to his belt. As he walked up to a desk, the woman behind the desk said they were expecting him. Another man came up to him and asked him to follow him up to the second floor.

Upon entering a large room on the second floor, he was greeted by the two men who had spoken to him on the street as well as another gentleman sitting behind a desk. The man behind the desk introduced himself, gave his name, and asked Pat to sit down. The two other men who had initially approached him left. The man behind the desk told Pat that he would like to show him something and, with that, turned on the television and inserted a tape. He then started to play it.

The disk included pictures of Pat from the first day he entered the hotel where the Chinese were staying. They had pictures of him getting off the elevator on the floor where the Chinese were staying. They had pictures of him knocking on the door of the Chinese suite. They had pictures of him walking away and pictures of going back. It seems everything Pat had ever done with the Chinese had been photographed. He couldn't believe they had photos of him walking down the hallway the first time. He couldn't imagine where or how they took those pictures. They had images of him throughout his trip to China, and they were not pictures he had taken but ones that they had taken. They also had his phone tapped and played recordings of almost all his conversations with the Chinese. Pat was in total shock.

Then the man behind the desk began to tell him what they wanted. They wanted Pat to become a CIA agent and to work with them. Since he had such a special relationship with the Chinese ambassador, he would be of tremendous value to them. Again, he was in shock. He thought about it and said he would like to sleep on it and he would get back to them in a couple of days. He had no intention of spying on the Chinese but didn't want to seem like he made the decision without thinking about it.

About a week later, he made an appointment to see the man behind the desk whose name he never told me and made it clear to them that he did not want to spy on the Chinese. He considered the Chinese ambassador a friend and did not want to betray his trust. The agent behind the desk became quite upset and told Pat his loyalties should be to the United States, not to the Chinese ambassador. Pat told him he had made up his mind and he did not wish to work with the CIA.

The next day, he called me and met with me and Ronnie to tell us about this whole CIA incident and to discuss what the CIA could do to him to compel him to work for them. We thought about it and didn't see any way they could force him to do it. We told him to hang tough and, if they contacted him again, to refer them to us.

He called me seven days after that meeting to tell me that he could swear that his phone was being bugged as he heard strange noises on it. I told him, "Pat, it would not make any sense changing your phone number (as he wanted to do) because they would get it again if, in fact, your phone was being bugged." After a while, he would pick up the phone without intending to call anyone and would say in Chinese to whoever he thought was listening, "The sun always rises in the east."

"Why that saying?" I asked.

He said he liked the rhythm of it when he said it in Chinese.

Bob Viccara

Bonnie and Bobby

I DON'T KNOW HOW TO begin to describe Bob Viccara. I guess I can start by saying he was probably the most brilliant attorney I have ever known. He was at one time one of the heads of the Legal Aid Society in Manhattan and was a legend among all the lawyers and judges in the court. They all respected him and feared him. Why? Simply because he knew far more than any other attorney or judge. He was the quickest thinking lawyer I ever saw. He could quote sections of the law ad infinitum. He had an encyclopedic knowledge of the law and, for fun, was writing a book about legal terminology and legal words. He was also quite nuts and had been under psychiatric care for years.

Occasionally, he would do all the arraignments at 100 Center Street in Manhattan; 100 Center Street is one of the busiest criminal courtrooms in the world.

Now what is its arraignment? If someone is arrested for a crime, he or she is taken to court to be arraigned. This means, at that time the district attorney will apprise the court of what the person is being charged with and the amount of bail they deem necessary to ensure his or her return.

Now why would one of the heads of the Legal Aid Society be doing arraignments? Since an arraignment is considered the very beginning of learning how to be a criminal law attorney, the reason Bob did arraignments was to teach his young new legal aid lawyers how to do them. Whenever he was scheduled to teach new attorneys how to handle an arraignment, the courtroom, which fits a couple of hundred people, was booked to the rafters. When Bob Viccara taught young attorneys how to do arraignments, it was more than a legal proceeding, it was a show not to be believed.

On these occasions, half of the spectators in the courtroom were lawyers, both new and experienced. He was such a legend that everyone wanted to see how he did it. No one could control him simply because he knew more than anyone else. The judges, when they knew that Bob was handling the arraignments, were extremely happy and sometimes quite upset. Why? Because they knew it was going to be an incredibly entertaining fun night, and they also knew that the arraignments would take much longer than usual. I will give you an example of one of Bob's legendary arraignments that I remember before telling you how and when I first met Bob Viccara.

I happened to be there that evening for the arraignment of one of my clients. I was sitting in the third row of a fully packed court. Of course, I had heard about the infamous Bob Viccara but I was later to learn it was because the famous Bob Viccara of the Legal aid Society was handling the arraignments that the court was so packed.

The doors of the courtroom opened, and in walked Bob Viccara with several legal aid attorneys in tow, following him like ducks behind their mother. He was about six feet tall, a little stocky, good-looking, with a small mustache. Looking at him as he walked by, I felt he was special. I don't know why, but that's how I felt. There was an aura about him I can't explain. Little did I know then that he would become one of my closest friends and Bonnie's boss. He put down the papers he was carrying on his desk and directed the young lawyers to the empty benches behind him that were reserved for them. He then slowly looked around the room, turned, and sat down.

After about a minute or so, the court clerk stood up and said, "All rise!" as the judge entered.

The judge was carrying papers as he walked up the steps to the bench. He put his papers down and observed the room, saw Bob Viccara and slowly started to shake his head.

He looked at the court clerk and asked him to begin. The first case called was a legal aid case and therefore assigned to Bob. As the defendant was brought in, Bob stood up, ramrod straight, and said, "Good evening, Your Honor."

The judge said, "Good evening, Mr. Viccara. You know we have a very heavy schedule this evening, and therefore, I would like to proceed as expeditiously as possible."

Bob said, "Of course, your honor, we will proceed as expeditiously as possible, but we must proceed carefully as the rights of all defendants should be carefully guarded to preserve the integrity and fairness of our judicial system, for as our forefathers would have wanted—" And then Bob started to go off into a long speech.

The judge shook his head, stopped Bob, and said, "Please, Mr. Viccara, we have a busy schedule. Can we proceed?"

Bob stood ramrod straight, clicked his heels like a Nazi, and said, "Of course, Your Honor."

The people in the courtroom already began to snicker and laugh. The judge shook his head. The first defendant was brought in. Bob knew him as he had represented him several times. "Rodney, what are you doing here?"

"Hi, Mr. Viccara. I was doing my normal rounds when some rookie cop, I had never seen before saw me taking a number and decided to arrest me." Rodney had been a numbers runner for over twenty years; lately, he had not been bothered since most of the police considered it a harmless, almost necessary service to the community. When he first started, he was arrested many times, but then slowly, the arrests became more and more infrequent. However, this new rookie decided that he was breaking the law and arrested him.

The ADA stood up and started to recite the section of the law that had been broken. Bob did not know him as he was new. After reciting the section of the law that Rodney had broken, he asked for $1,000 bail. Bob looked at him incredulously and told the judge $1,000 bail was ridiculous. The DA then proceeded to go over to the judge and show him Rodney's yellow sheet. A yellow sheet is a history of arrests. Rodney's yellow sheet was over seven pages long with arrests going back twenty years.

The judge looked at his yellow sheet and said, "My god, Mr. Viccara, have you seen this yellow sheet? It goes back twenty years?"

The court clerk went up to the judge, took the yellow sheet, and brought it back for Bob to see.

Everyone in the courtroom was on edge to see what possible response Bob could have. After reviewing it very carefully, he looked up at the judge with a confident smile and said, "Well, Judge, it just goes to show you the man can hold onto a job."

An explosion of laughter in the courtroom erupted with the judge banging his gavel. "Mr. Viccara, is it going to be one of those nights?"

Bob says, "I'm sorry, Your Honor."

The judge says, "And by the way, this yellow sheet has seven pages of arrests?"

Bob looks very carefully again and then looks up at the judge with a smile and look of confidence and says, "Yes, Judge, but if you'll notice, the arrests are double-spaced."

Laughter in the courtroom as the judge shakes his head. Bob says, "Will you give me a moment, Your Honor, to confer with my client?"

The judge says, "Go ahead, but make it fast."

Bob speaks to Rodney for several seconds, then looks up at the Judge and says, "After a lengthy conversation with my client, I am convinced beyond all doubt that he is not guilty."

This time the laughter is so loud that even the judge starts to laugh and turns his swivel chair around so as not to be seen laughing. Finally, the judge turns around and says, "Come on, Mr. Viccara, what do you want to do?"

Bob says, "My client was arrested for taking numbers, which is probably a service to the community as he always pays his customers, and they are happy with him. I suggest my client plead guilty and pay a fine of $111.25."

Judge asks, "Why that amount?"

Bob says, "Because that's all he has on him."

More laughter in the courtroom as the judge says, "Fine, defendant having pleaded guilty is fined $111.25. Next case."

There are so many of these Bob Viccara stories I could go on and on. I'll tell you about one or two more I remember a little later on.

So, this was my introduction to Bob Viccara, one I'll never forget. Now how did he become Bonnie's boss? Here's how:

Bonnie, when she graduated from law school, got a job with a law firm in Manhattan on 42nd Street, right across the street from the New York Public Library. She worked there for a short time and hated it. While working at the law firm, she met one of our classmates who was working for Legal Aid. His name was Sal, and she was telling him how much she disliked working in a private civil law practice.

He told her, "Why don't you get a job with the Legal Aid Criminal Division?"

She asked, "Are there any openings?"

He said, "They're looking for lawyers" and he did not think she would have a problem getting a job with Legal Aid. At the time, they were so desperate for attorneys that there were two requirements: one, that you had a license to practice law in New York; and two was the mirror test; if you breathe into a mirror and it fogged up, you were hired. Today you have to be a genius to get a job with Legal Aid.

She applied for the job and, of course, was hired and started the following Monday morning. That's when she first met Bob Viccara. Most of the new young lawyers were afraid of him, and he could tell. Bonnie, however, was not.

Her first impression of him was that he was exquisitely bright but, underneath that stern exterior, was a tortured soul. He was a troubleshooter for the New York City Legal Aid Society. He was too restless to sit behind a desk and so delegated paperwork to other lawyers who would rather do that than have the pressure of representing people in open court. Bob once told me, "One generally tends to be good at things they like."

So why put a lawyer who likes to be in court in a room, doing paperwork, and why put a lawyer who likes to do research in the courtroom when he doesn't want to be there? Not all lawyers are meant to be in court. Some are meant to do research and write legal briefs and rarely talk to clients. So, I ask these new young lawyers coming in and try to match them with what they want to do most. It generally works out pretty well.

Since Bob was incredibly good in court and loved being in court and did not like sitting behind a desk, that's what he did. But taking on a major case was a problem for Bob. Why? Because major cases could tie him up for weeks or months at a time, and he was needed in too many places; there were always problems popping up all over the courthouse that had to be resolved. So, Bob became the ultimate troubleshooter for the Legal Aid Society. Over 60 percent of the problems that arose in court were questions of law, and since Bob was a walking law encyclopedia and everyone knew it, he naturally fell into it.

The admiration and adoration from other lawyers and judges rolled off his back. He was so used to it and hardly noticed it. When he did, he found it annoying.

Now getting back to Bonnie and her first meeting with Bob. When Bonnie was hired by Legal Aid, there were hardly any female attorneys. Most of the women who worked for Legal Aid had secretarial jobs. She was the only female attorney that was hired in a recent group of new attorneys, so she was kind of an anomaly. It was her second day at Legal Aid, and she was in one of the courtrooms, observing a legal proceeding, when there was a tap on her shoulder, and standing behind her was Bob.

He leaned over to her and said, "Are you one of our new attorneys?" She turned and saw him and said, "Yes, Mr. Viccara."

He said, "So you know who I am?" She said, "Yes, you're my boss."

He said, "What are you doing here? Why are you here? Why do you want to be a criminal lawyer?"

The questions kept on coming on and on. She told me she immediately liked him because she could sense he was nuts.

She would see him often in court, and on occasion, he would come into the courtroom she was working in and interrupt the proceedings to ask her a question or speak to her. All the judges knew him. He would come in and say, "I'm sorry to interrupt you judge, but I have to speak to my attorney."

Naturally, the judge would say okay and wait for him to speak to his attorney. Sometimes, the judge would call for a five-minute recess.

On this occasion, the judge waited for Bob to speak to his attorney, Bonnie. He guides Bonnie to the side wall and then in a whisper, with a German accent, asks her if she had seen the Johnny Carson show the night before. Bonnie, who had been in the middle of cross-examining a policeman when Bob first came in, was now totally confused. There was a courtroom full of people, and here Bob was asking her if she had seen the Johnny Carson show the night before and doing it in a German accent.

Bonnie now was completely perplexed. She had been questioning the policeman and did not know what Bob was talking about; and, she was nervous because she was new at cross-examination. Bob says in the German accent, "Did you see the Johnny Carson show last night?" once again.

She says no.

He says, "There was a German comedian last night, and he was talking about the different airlines. First, he spoke about the Jewish airlines, El Al. He says the pilot comes into the passenger compartment and says welcome to Israeli airlines, El Al. This is flight number 495, reduced from 500."

And then Bob starts to laugh. The judge is looking at them as are all the people in the courtroom, but the judge says nothing. Then Bob tells Bonnie the best one of all was the German pilot who comes to the front of the cabin and tells the people, "Welcome, this is Lufthansa Airlines, you will all go to your seats, you will sit down, and you will be quiet. Today, we have for you the World War II movie *The Longest Day*…with a surprise ending." And, again, Bob starts laughing.

Bonnie is mortified. Bob looks at the judge and says, "Sorry to have disrupted the proceedings. My attorney can now continue." He turns to Bonnie and says, "I expect you to win this case." Then he turns around and walks out, leaving Bonnie standing there with all the people and the judge looking at her.

Bonnie walks up to the front, a little bit dazed and confused, and asks the judge if she could have a ten-minute recess. The judge says since it's almost one o'clock, we will break for lunch. "See you back here at two-thirty."

Bonnie is relieved; now she will have time to gather her thoughts and figure out where she left off with the policeman. Even with Bob driving her crazy and with the responsibility of representing people who could go to jail for a long time if she screwed up, she liked the job. She enjoyed the mental challenge, the Legal Aid attorneys, and even started to become very fond of Bob Viccara.

One evening after a couple of months working for the Legal Aid Society, Bon, Ronnie, and I were having dinner. Bon was talking about a case she was working on, a very interesting criminal case, and Ron was fascinated by the case. Out of the clear blue-sky, Ron asked Bonnie if they had any openings at Legal Aid. She said she thought so, and if he wanted, she would ask Bob.

I was in shock. Ron had just started working with me and Vin a couple of months before. He didn't seem that enthused about practicing general law, although he was very good with the clients. I would, however, catch him on occasion practicing writing his signature over and over.

I spoke to him about it, and he admitted that he found it somewhat boring and started to complain to me about one of the clients that was assigned to him. His name was Mr. Ferrara. I asked him what seemed to be the problem.

Ron tells me, "Mr. Ferrara comes in every day, asking him the same question, and when I explain over and over what I'm doing, Mr. Ferrara wants a receipt that he spoke to me." At first, Ron signed a piece of paper saying "Alan

J. Ferrara, our client, was here to see Mr. Aliazzo" and signed his name. It obviously had no legal significance. The guy was crazy, and I told Ronnie that. After a while, Ronnie signed his name to any piece of paper he had lying around to keep Mr. Ferrara happy.

One day, I hear Ronnie raising his voice. I go into the office, and he is yelling at Mr. Ferrara not to come in any longer for these ridiculous receipts. My brother Vin hears this and goes running into the office to apologize to Mr. Ferrara for Ronnie's unprofessional behavior. He asks Ronnie, "What happened here?"

Ronnie explains what's been going on. Vin looks at Mr. Ferrara and says to him in a very loud voice, "Get the fuck out!"

I try to calm everything down. The secretaries and some of the lawyers have heard all this and are laughing. Mr. Ferrara starts to run out of the office, then stops to come back in to ask for a receipt for which Vin goes really nuts and tells him again to get the fuck out.

I tell Ronnie, of course, "We always get some nutjob clients, that's just part of practicing law." But I could tell he wasn't happy and wanted to be in a courtroom all the time, practicing criminal law. I figured he eventually would get over this and settle down, but apparently asking Bonnie if they had any openings in the Legal Aid Society meant that he really wanted to do something else.

After the shock wore off, I told him if he really wanted to do this, then go for it. And that if it did not work out or if he ever wanted to come back, the door was always open to him. I told him

I would tell Vin. He thanked me, gave me a hug, and the next day went and met Bob and got the job at Legal Aid.

He took to Legal Aid and the criminal division like a duck to water, and of course because he was, in a way, as nuts as Bob Viccara they became very good friends very quickly. Bob recognized Ron's ability, how good he was with people, and how well-liked he was. He immediately got him out of arraignments and into hearings with cross-examinations, which is the next step up the ladder to becoming a criminal trial lawyer. Bon was several months ahead of him, and they occasionally appeared in the same courtroom together when there was more than one defendant.

Bon told me, "Can you imagine what it would be like working with both Ronnie and Bob, two nutjobs? They find everything funny."

It turned out that Bob Viccara lived in Rockville Center, which was a short distance from where Bon and I lived, in West Hempstead. Bonnie, Ron, and Bob would often go out for lunch together. They finally made plans to get together for dinner with their respective spouses. Bob wanted to meet me as he had heard so much about me from Bonnie and Ronnie. Plans were made for the following Saturday. We were to meet at Bob's house in Rockville Center and go out to dinner, the six of us. Ronnie brought one of his girlfriends, although I don't remember which one.

The following Saturday night, Ronnie comes to my house with his girlfriend, and the four of us go over to Bob's house. It was the first time we met his wife, Nancy. Let me tell you a little bit about Nancy. She was a blonde, blue eyed wasp who grew up in Vermont. Her mother and father were wealthy and traveled the world often for long periods of time. She was raised by her nanny who happened to be a spectacularly, wonderful woman. I once asked Bob, since she was basically left alone most of the time, without parents, how she turned out to be such a stable, normal person. He said she suffered the benefits of benign neglect. I'll never forget those words: benign neglect. It seemed nothing bothered her. I used to wonder about her because she seemed so solid, so normal. How the hell did she get involved with a nutjob like Bob?

As I got to know them, I started to figure it out. First of all, everything rolled off her back. Bob's most outrageous behavior simply elicited an, "Oh, Bob." She was so used to him. When we became really close friends, we would go into the city to see a play or go to dinner, and Nancy, always a good driver, liked to drive sometimes. When she drove, Bonnie would sit next to her in the front, and Bob and I would sit in the back. Bob would then tell everyone how much he loved me and would grab and hold my hand. I would say, "Nancy, Bob is holding my hand again."

And she would say, "Oh, Bob, let Bobby's hand go." The way she said it just made me laugh. She was obviously used to his outrageous behavior.

They had two children, both teenagers, a girl named Brooke and a son named Matt. Both were very bright with Brooke bordering on genius. She wanted to be an architect, and in the end, that's what she became. She was beautiful and had lots of different boyfriends; all the ones I met were really smart. That was the thing with Brooke; she did not suffer fools. If she went out with someone and he wasn't intelligent, then no matter how good-looking or athletic, she would cut them loose.

Her relationship with Bob was difficult to describe. She was a senior in high school when I first met her. She, on the one hand, adored him and, on the other hand, did not understand him and his nutty ways. His rules for her were no rules; she could do whatever she wanted to, come and go as she pleased. He would never argue with her. I once asked Bob how come he never argued with his daughter. He said he never reprimanded her because just about every time he did, she was right. As I said, she was exquisitely bright.

Nancy, on the other hand, was the one who set the rules. But since she grew up with hardly any rules, the rules for Brooke and Matt were almost nonexistent. Yet both kids were normal, bright, interesting, and very sensible, unlike Bob. I loved those two kids and had a great relationship with them. Matt was a year younger than Brooke and a star on the varsity basketball team. He practiced basketball every chance he got. He was sweet, and naïve and just special.

Bob called me one day on a Sunday and said, "You can't believe what just happened." He says he went with Matt to the Rockville Center Park because Matt wanted to practice shooting some hoops. Matt practiced, and Bob read the newspapers. On this particular day, there was a tall Black guy who was also shooting hoops. They started to chat and laugh, and before you know it, they were playing a game of 21. Bob watched as the Black guy seemed pretty good, but Mark seemed to keep up with him, and the scores, he thought, were close.

After a couple of games, they chatted some more and shook hands, and Mark came back to where Bob was sitting. Bob said, "That guy looks pretty good, but you gave him a good game, I thought."

Matt looks at Bob and says, "Are you kidding me? That was Dr. J, Julius Irving, and he was just playing with me."

Well, now getting back to my first meeting with Bob. We drive up to the house, and the four of us ring the bell. Bob answers the door. Of course, Bonnie and Ronnie knew Bob and introduced me to him. For some reason, the first words I said to him he never forgot. What were the words? I said, "Hi Bob, I'm Bobby, and I want to thank you for the largesse you have shown to Bonnie and to Ronnie." Well, I should've never used the word *largesse* because he never forgot it. He marveled that I would know the word and gave me a history of the word. How did I know the word?

Bonnie's brother, Howard, while in law school several years before, had ordered a prune Danish in a diner. I never knew something like that existed. As we left the diner, I picked up the check, and Howie said, "I want to thank you for your largesse."

I said, "Howie, largesse? I think I read that in a Dickens novel."

He said, "That's correct. It means I want to thank you for your generosity and kindness." I never forgot the word and always used it when I could, more for fun than anything else." When I used it with Bob, who was a word nut and was in the process of writing a legal dictionary, he immediately took a shine to me. That was it.

And so, we became friends. He loved to play tennis, but was just an average player. Bonnie taught me; I was a bit above average. He knew all about Bonnie and her tennis career and asked if I played tennis. I said I did, and he said, "Would you like to play with me here in Rockville Center? They have great indoor tennis courts." After all the largesse he had shown Bonnie and Ronnie, how could I say no? And so, a weekly tennis game started every Wednesday evening at six o'clock, followed by dinner with Bonnie and Nancy.

Now getting back to that first meeting with Bob, after chatting a moment, he said, "By the way, Bonnie told me about your first legal win." I was surprised, even though I didn't remember my first legal win. There were so many wins and losses coming when I first started. He said, "No, no, this was before you became a lawyer."

I said, "Bob, you got me, I don't know what you're talking about."

He said, "Let me refresh your memory. This is what Bonnie told me. Your first legal win was when you were in law school."

I still didn't know what he was talking about. Then he refreshed my memory, and of course, I remembered it vividly. Here's what happened. Our whole law school class was taking Evidence, one of the mandatory courses. It was a course which explained how to present evidence and basically everything about law and evidence. It was taught by a Professor Schwartz who, if I recall correctly, wrote several books on the topic for law schools. He was a wonderful guy and a terrific teacher who everyone liked. It appeared, however, he would not be able to complete the course to his satisfaction in the required time; therefore, for the next four weeks, every Wednesday, we would have to stay for one to three hours so that he could satisfactorily complete the course. Another teacher would teach those Wednesday afternoon classes.

The problem was that a lot of the students had afternoon jobs. Our classes were only from nine to one. Some of the students were married and had families, and not being able to work their afternoon jobs was a major problem.

The solution they found was to ask Bonnie to sign in for them so that they could go to their jobs. Bonnie agreed to help them out. There were over fifty students in the class, and more and more people asked Bonnie to sign them in, until a day came where there were fifty signatures on the sign-in sheet and only twenty-five or thirty students. At that point, the professor teaching the course realized that someone was signing in the absent students. He asked the students who were there. No one raised their hands. Bonnie did not.

He reported what was going on to Professor Schwartz, and everyone showed up for class after that.

Professor Schwartz was upset and asked that the person who signed in for all the missing students come forward. Bonnie did not. Apparently, handwriting samples were taken, and it was determined that Bonnie was the one who was signing in everyone who was not present. Nothing further was said until finals were complete at the end of semester; we were then called in one by one into Professor Schwartz's office to get our grades.

I being Aliazzo with an A was one of the first called in. I received my grade which was a passing one. I thanked Professor Schwartz, and as I left, he asked me to have Miss Bonnie Mencher come in next. This was unusual as he was taking her out of turn, her last name starting with an M.

I left the room and told Bonnie that she was the next one in. She was surprised as we all were but went in. Several minutes later, she came out in tears. We were all surprised and asked her what was wrong. She said although she passed the written test, she failed the oral test – obviously, because she had signed in all the students who did not attend. None of the students whom she had signed in for came forward.

I was pissed off at the injustice of it all. I told the next student who was to go in if he would mind if I went in before him. He inquired why as I had already received my passing grade. I told him I wanted to speak to Professor Schwartz about a personal matter and, without waiting for his reply, walked into the room.

Professor Schwartz, upon seeing me, looked surprised as he had already given me my passing grade. I walked up to Professor Schwartz and asked if I could speak to him.

He sat back curiously and said, "Yes, what can I do for you?"

I said I was there on behalf of Bonnie Mencher. I don't remember everything I said. I was only there for a few moments. I do remember reminding him of some of what he taught us; that is, we as lawyers, when we saw an injustice, had to have the courage to try to do something about it. We had to defend those people who could not defend themselves. Bonnie, although studying to be a lawyer, was so caught off guard she was momentarily unable to defend herself. "I know you asked her who she signed in, and knowing Bonnie, I know she would not say anything. She is going to fail the course rather than be a rat, as we say in the old neighborhood, and squeal on the people who didn't attend. In my book, that's called courage, integrity, and real character."

"The thing about it is she attended all the classes as required, yet you're failing her and passing all those that did not attend. They are all out there. They saw Bonnie come out in tears, yet not one of them thought to come in to defend her. I attended all the classes because I was forced to by Bonnie because we both live in Forest Hills and carpool, and she insisted we attend all the classes. I don't think this is justice as you taught it to us, and since you told us to speak up whenever we see an injustice, here I am, speaking up."

He said, "Is that all?"

And I said, "Yes, Professor, except I want to thank you for giving me the opportunity to speak on Bonnie's behalf."

This is most of what I remember, although I'm sure I said more. As I walked to the door, Professor Schwartz called after me, "Mr. Aliazzo."

I, turned and said, "Yes, Prof?"

And he said, "You're going to make one hell of a lawyer." I was stunned. I said, "Thank you, Professor."

And as I was turning the doorknob, he said, "Mr. Aliazzo, is Miss Mencher still here?"

I nodded yes.

He said, "Please send her back in."

I went out, and everyone wanted to know what happened. I said, "Bon, he wants to see you again."

She looked at me, surprised, but went in and came out a couple of minutes later, smiling, and said, "Professor Schwartz has changed his mind and is passing me." I guess that was my first legal win, and the compliment I received from Professor Schwartz was one I cherish and will never forget.

One day, I'm in my office, and my secretary buzzes me and says, "There's a Bob Cabello that wishes to speak to you."

I tell her, "I don't know any Bob Cabello. I do know a friend called Yogi, but not Bob Cabello."

She says, "Very well, I'll tell him." She buzzes me back and says, "He says it's Yogi and to stop breaking his balls."

Now Yogi was my college roommate who I was very close with and loved to drive crazy. He gets on the phone and says, "You have nothing better to do than to break my balls."

I ask Yogi, "What's cooking?" He says, "My father is in jail."

I say, "Yogi, that's impossible, it's more likely the pope would be put in jail than your father. Why?" Did I say that I have known his father ever since I knew Yogi, and I met Yogi my freshman year in college? His father was a CPA and one of the most low-key, conservative, wonderful men I've ever met. He was a Jersey guy with a Jersey accent and a slight stutter that made him even more endearing to Ronnie and me.

He loved to have Ronnie and me around as he thought we were bright and funny and a good influence on Yogi. In shock, I asked Yogi, "How is that possible? And what the hell is your father in jail for?"

He says he doesn't know. He got a call from his father saying that he was locked up in Manhattan and they were going to set bail on him that night. He didn't explain why he was in jail. He did, however, give Yogi the section of the law that he was charged with violating, but didn't understand it.

I said, "Yogi, give me the section, let me look it up and I'll get back to you."

He gives me the section, and I immediately call Bob Viccara and am lucky enough to get them on my first try. I tell him what's going on and recite the section of the law that his father is charged with. Bob, being a walking encyclopedia of law, of course knew the section and told me his father had been booked for patronizing a prostitute.

Bob says, "Give me his name, and I'll see what I can find out."

He calls me back ten minutes later and tells me that he was arrested by an undercover cop, a woman, who was posing as a prostitute. Her name is Barbara

Folone, says he knows her but not really well but that Ronnie knows her well because she worked with him on some cases when he first went into the District Attorney's Office. I asked if he was doing arraignments tonight.

He says, "As a matter of fact, I'm on, so if you need me to take care of the arraignment, I will."

I say, "Thanks, Bob, I'll get back to you as soon as I have more information."

I call Ronnie, and again I'm lucky enough to get him on the first try. I tell him what's going on. He says, "I know Barbara well. I can't believe she would bust Yogi's father, especially since he's pretty elderly now. You know what? I'm going to come down and handle the arraignment so that I can speak to Barbara."

I say, "Ronnie, you can't you work in the DA's office."

He says, "It's okay, I'll say I'm you. Nobody will know the difference." He asked me to have Bob meet him in the hallway outside of the arraignment part at about 9:00 p.m. when the arraignment starts. I say, "I will do it and will try to make it myself, and maybe afterward, we could go to Little Vincent's clam bar for some baked clams."

He says, "It's a great idea. See you later."

I then call Bob and tell him the arrangements we are making and not to eat anything as we will go to Little Vincent's clam bar afterward for some baked clams and pasta. Bob says, "Now you're talking, see you a little before nine."

I call Yogi back and tell him what's going on and to meet me and Ronnie at 100 Center Street, the arraignment part at eight-thirty.

I call Bonnie, tell her what's going on, and that I will stay at the office rather than coming home and then schlepping all the way back into the city. She can't believe Yogi's father got busted and said, "Let me know what happens."

I say, "Okay, speak to you later." I then call Ronnie and tell him I decided to come in and suggest we go in together. We make plans to meet at the DA's office at seven, figuring we will get there by eight-thirty, before the arraignment part starts. I find a parking spot right in front of the Queens Supreme Court and run up to get Ronnie. As I get there, he's having an argument with Pete Andino, the second-in-command in the District Attorney's Office, and his boss. It seems Pete (who is married) wants to borrow Ronnie's apartment for a couple of hours since Ronnie will be in the city late. Pete has a girlfriend he would like to entertain there.

Ronnie asked him, "Why don't you take her to a hotel?" He says, "She's not that kind of girl."

Ronnie says, "She's not that type of girl? Are you kidding me? Knowing you, I would check her for venereal diseases." Ronnie says, "Okay, but be out of there by twelve. I should be home by then, and use the spare bedroom, not my bedroom."

Pete says, "You're just so damn picky." Pete asks Ronnie if he has anything to eat as she may want a snack after their little romp in the bedroom.

Ronnie says, "I think I have some tuna and some Cheerios around." Pete says, "Jesus Christ, what am I supposed to do if she's hungry?" Ronnie says, "You figure it out and keep my place clean."

Now you may be surprised at how an employee and his boss speak to each other, but understand Ronnie and Pete are really very close friends. As a matter of fact, it was Pete who took Ronnie out of the arraignment part after only a few weeks and brought him up to the felony part which was unheard of. Why? Here's how it happened.

While Ronnie was in the arraignment part, a case was brought to him with a defendant who was charged with a B felony. That's a serious charge, and if one is convicted, he/she can be sentenced to many years. Ronnie reads the charges. Here's what happened. The defendant had an argument with his girlfriend when both were drunk. As he dropped her off in front of her parent's home the argument continued. She went inside and slammed the door in his face. He got angry and began to pound on the door. She refused to open it.

He then went to his car and opened his glove compartment and found a cigarette lighter and a can of lighter fluid. He went back to the door and pounded some more, and when she refused to open the door, he poured cigarette lighter fluid on the door and lit it and yelled, "I'm burning down your door!"

She didn't open the door at first, so he went to his car and fell asleep. His girlfriend, after a minute, opened the door, saw the door on fire, and called the fire department. When both fire department and police arrived, she told them what happened and pointed to the car where he was sleeping.

They arrested him, and the charges against him included arson and attempted murder. Now in the District Attorney's Office, as an attorney, you can only drop the charges one count lower, and that's with permission of your superior. Ronnie dropped the charges for the B felony two and A misdemeanor. That was unheard of and was immediately reported to his superior who happened to be Pete Andino.

Ronnie was called up to Pete's office, figuring he was probably going to be fired. Pete, who had only met Ronnie once before, asked him to explain himself. Ronnie told Pete that the charges were ridiculous, and he did what he thought was correct, and if Pete and the District Attorney's Office intended to charge the defendant with arson and attempted murder, this wasn't the kind of place he wanted to work and would hand in his resignation.

Pete looked at Ronnie and said, "Before I make my decision, would you please tell me what went down with this case?"

Ronnie told him. Pete looked at Ronnie, said nothing at first. Then, after a moment, he told Ronnie to go back to the arraignment part, and he would think over what to do and wanted Ronnie back in his office at five o'clock. At five o'clock that afternoon, when Ronnie reappeared at Pete's office, he told his secretary that he had an appointment with Mr. Andino at five o'clock. She asked for Ronnie's name, and when he told her, she looked at him for a moment and said, "So you're the attorney everyone is talking about."

Ronnie had no idea what she was talking about. She buzzed Pete who told her to show Ronnie into his office. Upon entering, Pete was sitting at a round table he had in the corner of his office with two cups of coffee, one for him, and as Ronnie came in, he told him to come sit down and have a cup of coffee with him. That was the beginning of a very close personal friendship.

Pete told Ronnie that he agreed with what Ronnie had done and that most of the young new lawyers didn't have the balls or the smarts to act the way Ronnie did, and that's why they always put restrictions on their ability to make decisions on cases. He told Ronnie that most of the new lawyers he hired were bright with impressive resumes from ivy league schools, but sadly, no street smarts and, in some cases, no common sense.

He told Ronnie, "This is the first time in a long time that someone had the balls to break the rules and do what you did, which was to change those ridiculous charges to what they should have been and what you changed them to." He said that after speaking to the DA himself, he had decided to move Ronnie up to a felony part which would be opening in about six weeks, and until then, he would move up to a misdemeanor part to try a couple of small cases before assuming his duties in a felony part.

Ronnie, who was in shock, thanked Pete and told him he did not know what to say. Pete told him, "You don't have to say anything, and I know you'll do great once you get up to the felony part."

Now the subject changed as Pete mentioned to Ronnie that he had seen him several times around the courthouse, getting picked up by some beautiful girls. Ronnie wondered what this had to do with anything, but it seemed Pete was as impressed with his success with girls as he was with his legal abilities. Thus began a very close personal friendship.

Now getting back to Yogi's father, charged with patronizing a prostitute. (Ronnie hands over the keys to his apartment to Pete, reminding him that he and his girlfriend leave it no later than 12:00). Ronnie and I arrive at the courthouse sometime after eight and go to the arraignment part. As we get there, we see Bob Viccara speaking to what appears to be a couple of Legal Aid attorneys. He sees us smile, comes over to us, and gives us both big hugs; seeing this, I thought the Legal Aid attorneys would faint. He was a legend and a strict disciplinarian with them. I remembered when I was in grammar school, being taught by the nuns and seeing one of the nuns hug someone. As a kid, I thought the nuns descended from heaven to teach us and then went back up because they weren't really humans – especially, because they rarely hugged anyone and – more especially, because they dressed in those scary black-and-white habits.

Ronnie asked Bob if he'd seen Barbara Folone, who was the arresting officer. Bob says yes, she was here just a minute ago with her team which consisted of three cops dressed in street clothes who would assist her in making arrests. Just as Ronnie was asking for her, she and her partners came from around the corner, walking toward Bob, Ronnie, and me. Ronnie walks up to her. When she sees him, she goes running over to him, hugs him, and says, "Ronnie, you handsome fuck, how have you been? I hear you're kicking ass in the DA's office over in Queens."

Barbara is about five-eight with long blonde hair and blue eyes and is an absolute knockout; that's why she was put into what they called the Pussy Posse, which was a police unit designed to arrest possible Johns looking for prostitutes, so as to discourage it. Everyone knew it was an impossible task, but hopefully, it would keep the number of men looking for prostitutes down. The way it worked with the Pussy Posse was that prostitutes would gather at a special location together. In the evening, there were cars pulling up for the prostitutes. Eventually, what would happen was that the store owners would complain to the police precinct. The precinct would arrest some of the girls and chase the others away. Then someone like Barbara would be sent to the location to make some arrests.

The Johns soon found out the new location and stopped going to the old one, and so Barbara was not needed until the store owners of the new place where the prostitutes were congregating started to complain. Then Barbara was sent into action.

This evening, Barbara was in court to address some of the cases where she had made arrests. Barbara was dressed in her working clothes which consisted of a short minidress and a blouse that exposed her breasts, except that now she was wearing a sweater over her blouse. After greeting Ronnie so warmly, she looked at him and noticed that he did not return the warm greeting and asked what was the matter.

Ronnie says, "Can we talk, Barb? Let's go around the corner so we can speak in private."

Barbara says, "Sure," and they walk away and around the corner. Barbara says, "So what's up?"

Ronnie says, "How could you do it, Barbara? How could you arrest that old man?"

She says, "Ronnie, who are you talking about?" He says, "Robert Cabello."

She says, "Robert Cabello? Who the hell is Robert Cabello?" and then suddenly, she says, "You mean the old guy?"

He says, "Yeah."

She says, "Ronnie, let me tell you what went down." She says, "So I am at my post with my team, looking to make some collars. This old guy comes up to me and propositions me. I look at him. He's a little long in the tooth, and I tell him to move on. He insists and starts waving money at me. I tell him I'm not interested, move on, and then suddenly, as I start to walk away, he grabs my arm. The deal with my team is anytime someone touches me, they move in, so they move in and arrest him. I didn't want to arrest the old guy. I had no choice."

Ronnie looks at Barbara and says, "I knew you wouldn't bust an old man like that."

Barbara asks, "Is he your client?"

Ron says, "He's my brother Bobby's college roommate's father." Barbara says, "What can I do to help?"

Ronnie says, "I need a favor, Barbara." She says, "Sure, anything."

"I'm going to ask you not to show up tonight and not for the next few times this case is called so that it will eventually be dismissed."

She says she is happy to do it.

Ronnie says, "Barbara, I owe you one."

While they were chatting, Yogi showed up, and I gave him a warm hug and then introduced him to Bob Viccara. He looks worried, scared, and out of his element. He is still not sure what's going on. I introduced him to Bob, explaining that he is the head of the Legal Aid Society and familiar with the case.

Yogi asked me, "Is Bob going to represent my father?"

I tell him, "No, Ronnie knows the detective who arrested your father. He is charged with patronizing a prostitute."

Yogi is mortified and doesn't believe it. As we are talking, Ronnie comes walking up to us, sees Yogi, and gives him a big hug. He sees Yogi is upset. Yogi says, "I can't believe the charges against my father."

Ronnie and I know that his mother has been sick for over a year and was starting to recuperate. We tell Yogi, "Your old man probably hasn't had sex in over a year and, while he was in the city, saw Barbara, figured she was a prostitute, and approached her."

He says, "Who's Barbara?"

Ronnie points out Barbara who is down the hallway speaking with her crew. Yogi looks at her and says, "Are you kidding me? Is Barbara a prostitute?"

Ronnie tells Yogi, "No, she's a cop posing as a prostitute, and because of the way she was dressed, your father mistook her for one and approached her. Fortunately, Barbara is a friend of mine, and a deal has been made with her."

Yogi says, "Thank God, I got you guys. So, what happens now?"

Ronnie explains the cop will not show up, and the case will eventually be dismissed. Ronnie asks Bob if he can handle it going forward, and Bob says, "Sure, no problem, but Yogi, your father will have to come back at least two more times, and then it will be dismissed."

I say, "The big problem we have here is how to make your father save face.

He is going to be mortified that he was caught propositioning a prostitute."

I tell them I have an idea. "What we do is tell him we spoke to the cop, and she thinks she made a mistake arresting him and can get into trouble for false arrest. She is willing not to show up so that the case will be dismissed if the old man doesn't sue her and the police department for false arrest."

Bob thinks my idea is brilliant and comes over and gives me a big kiss on the cheek. We all agree that's how it will go down, and Ronnie will explain it all to him.

As Ronnie is leaving our group to go to the pen where prisoners are held until arraignment so that he can talk to Yogi's father and give him the story we just made up, a pimp comes walking down the hallway. The pimp, who is Black, is dressed in a light tan suit with a dark coat over his shoulders, wearing a white fedora with a feather in it with the crease in the hat down the center. He stops, walks up to Ronnie, and says, "Hey man, you an E-attorney?"

Ron says, "No, I'm the man."

The pimp says, "You ain't the man, the man don't dress the way you do. I got two bitches been locked up. Ain't doing me no good with them locked up. I need you to get them out, $100 for each girl. It will take no more than five minutes of your time."

Ronnie says, "I'm not interested" as he continues to walk away. The pimp follows him and says, "Okay, man, $200 for each girl." Ronnie says, "I told you I'm not interested."

The pimp says, "I knew you was class. Okay, let's get right down to it, how much do you want? I can't have these sleazebag attorneys representing my women. I need someone with class like you."

As they are talking and walking, Bob comes up to them, looks at the Black pimp, and says, "Cecil, I love you, how are you?" and gives the Black pimp a kiss on the cheek.

The pimp says, "Mr. Viccara, I'm trying to talk this E-attorney into representing my women."

Bob says, "He can't represent your women, he's the man." Cecil says, "He ain't the man, I can tell."

Bob says, "He's not the police, he's an Assistant District Attorney in the homicide bureau."

Ronnie, in the meantime, is listening to this conversation. Cecil says, "I'll be damned, I would've never guessed."

Bob says, "Don't worry, Cecil, for tonight, I'll take care of your ladies." Now, normally, Cecil did not want a Legal Aid attorney to represent his women as it would look like he was too cheap to pay for a lawyer, but with the head of the Legal Aid Society representing them, who was indeed a legend, he was honored and thanked Bob.

Ron gets to the pen and asks to speak to his client, Robert Cabello. They bring him out to the attorney's conference room, and he looks ragged and frightened. He sees Ronnie go up to him and hugs him and says, "Ronnie, I don't know what happened."

Ronnie gives him the whole story that it was one big mistake; that the cop who arrested him misunderstood what he was asking, and would not appear in court any further if Mr. Cabello would not sue her or the police department.

Yogi's father could not believe what he was hearing, but said, "Yes, I will not sue anyone if I can just go home."

Ronnie explains what will happen and that he will have to come back a couple of times before the case is dismissed. He tells Mr. Cabello that he will be brought into the courtroom in a little while and that Ronnie will be there to get him released. He doesn't want to go back with the other arrested people, but Ronnie tells him he must but it's only for a short time.

Ronnie comes back out and tells us that he spoke to Yogi's father, that he understands and that he's very happy to be going home. As we are speaking, the doors to the courtroom open, and everyone starts walking in. I told Yogi to come with me. We take a seat in the back while Ronnie and Bob go up front as Bob has to handle the arraignments, and Ronnie's representing Yogi's father. I tell Yogi to sit back and relax. "You're going to see a show for as long as we're here."

He says, "What are you talking about?"

"Bob Viccara, who you just met, is a legend in the courtroom, and he will be handling the cases for Legal Aid; and, we may see a case or two before your father's case is called, although Bob has already arranged for your father's case to be called second."

The courtroom fills up within a couple of minutes, and then the judge walks out, steps up the stairs, and onto the bench. He sees Bob Viccara sitting there for Legal Aid and smiles as he is one of the judges who doesn't care how long the arraignments take. He just enjoys dealing with Bob Viccara.

The clerk calls the first case, and it is a Legal Aid case, and Bob stands up and says, "Your Honor, these defendants are being represented by Legal Aid for the arraignment."

The judge says, "Very well, let's proceed."

Bob says, "Before we proceed, may I just tell the court how pleased I am to be here before Your Honor?"

The judge says, "Thank you, Mr. Viccara, now may we proceed?"

Bob decides not to give one of these long speeches as I guess he's just not in the mood. The defendants that Bob is representing are Chinese and have been charged with a violation of Section 1003 of the penal code, gambling illegally. It seems they run a big card game every Wednesday evening with people coming and going. Complaints were made by the neighbors since there was so much traffic coming and going, and so the cops have charged the seven defendants with illegal gambling. Bob walks up to them and starts to chat.

Some of them speak English and some of them are speaking Chinese. He's trying to make sense of what's going on and explains to them that he suggests that the three plead guilty and pay a small fine.

After some more chatting with the judge banging his gavel to speed things up, Bob steps up to the judge and says, "Your Honor, I have made a deal with the district attorney that three of them will plead guilty, and the charges will be dropped against the other four."

The judge, anxious to move things along, says, "Okay, which ones are going to plead guilty?"

Bob turns to his clients who are in the group, and he says, "Let's spread out three on this side of me and four on the other side so that we can all face the bench."

They do that. He then huddles them up again and says, "Which three are going to plead guilty?"

After chatting with them another moment, he turns to the judge and says, "Your Honor, since they are all going to chip in to pay the fine, they don't care which ones plead guilty."

The judge says, "You have to tell me which three are pleading guilty."

The defendants are standing next to him, three on one side and four on the other. Bob suddenly has a brilliant idea. He tells the judge, "I have an idea, Your Honor, as to who is going to plead guilty."

The judge says, "Okay, what is it?"

And Bob says, "Your Honor, I suggest you pick two from group A and one from group B."

Laughter bursts out in the courtroom. Even the judge can't control himself and is laughing.

Yogi turns to me. "Bobby, your friend is really crazy."

I say, "I know, and too bad we are not going to be here for some of his other cases, but your father's case is being called next."

Just as we are speaking, the court clerk calls out the next case, The People of the State of New York against Robert Cabello. Yogi's father is brought in. Ronnie, who is sitting up front, walks up and addresses the court. "Your Honor, my name is Frank R Aliazzo, Esq., and I will be representing the defendant in this matter. I have already spoken to the district attorney, and together we have ascertained that the defendant has no prior criminal record. The district attorney has agreed to release the defendant without bail."

The judge looks at the district attorney, and the district attorney stands up and says, "Yes, Your Honor, we've agreed to release the defendant to his own recognizance."

The judge says, "Okay," bangs on his gravel, and says, "Next case." Yogi and I start to walk out. Yogi says, "That's it?"

I say, "Yes, except that he will have to come back one or two more times, but Bob Viccara will be here to represent him until the case is finally dismissed."

"Bobby, how come Ronnie used your name and you didn't represent my father?"

I said, "Since Ronnie knew the cop who made the arrest and she is in the courtroom on the other side, and since Ronnie said he would be representing him, we thought it best that he does so. And since he's in the DA's office, he isn't allowed to represent private clients. That's also why he used my name."

As we are talking, Ronnie and Yogi's dad passed us, and we followed them out of the courtroom. Yogi walks up to his dad. "Dad, are you okay?"

His father says, "Yes, yes, I'm fine. I just can't believe this whole thing."

I chime in, "This happens all the time, Mr. Cabello, cops make mistakes. They are human, like everybody else. Fortunately, this case will be dismissed after an appearance or two. I know it's inconvenient, but at least we got this taken care of."

Yogi's dad looks at me. "I can't believe you two came. Wow, they have all the big guns out tonight."

Yogi said, "You had a problem, so of course they came."

As we are chatting, Bob comes out of the courthouse and walks up to us. I say, "Mr. Cabello, this is Bob Viccara, the head of Legal Aid, and he will be the one representing you when you come back. Hopefully, you will only have to come back two times for this case to be dismissed."

Yogi's father shakes his head and says, "Wow, the head of Legal Aid. You guys have become some big shots." He looks at Ron and me.

I say to him, "We are not so big, we try to stay slim." And we all laugh.

Bob says, "I just have to take care of Cecil's girls. They are being called next, and then we can go downtown for some baked clams and pasta."

I look at Yogi. "Would you and your father like to join us?" Bob should be finished with the next arraignment in a couple of minutes.

Yogi's dad says, "I would like to, guys, but I really would like to get home and shower and see my wife."

Yogi says, "I'm going to take him home, guys; thanks for the invitation anyway." Then he comes up to Ronnie and me and hugs us, almost breaking into tears, and says, "Thank you."

We hugged him back and said, "No problem. Yogi, give me a call tomorrow."

He nodded yes, and just as he was about to leave with his father, Cecil came walking up to us. Yogi and his father look at him and the way he's dressed and are in shock. Bob looks at him and says, "Cecil, your girls are next." Bob then decides that he would like to introduce us to Cecil, so he says, "Gentlemen, I would like to introduce you to a man about town, the one and only Cecil Butler."

We all shake hands. Yogi's dad and Cecil are confused and a little embarrassed but smile faintly.

We say goodbye to Yogi and his dad and follow Bob into the courtroom. He assures us that this will be quick. As he's walking up to his place in the front of the courtroom, one of his Legal Aid attorneys is just finishing up an arraignment. Bob walks up to him and whispers something which we think is, "Sit down, I'll take over."

Bob then bends down to look at his papers as the two prostitutes, Cecil's girls, are brought in. Both of them are pretty Black girls, dressed in short miniskirts and tank tops that are very revealing. They see Bob who waves them over.

"Mr. Viccara, are you representing us?" He says, "For this evening, yes, I am."

Both are impressed as the head of Legal Aid Society generally does not represent prostitutes.

The judge looks down at Bob. "Mr. Viccara, are you representing the defendants?"

And he says, "Yes, it is my great honor to be representing Ms. Holly Star and Ms. Ruby Dee Silva." He knows them well as they've been in and out of the courthouse many times.

The girls chuckle, as do the audience. The judge shakes his head. "Mr. Viccara, can we proceed?"

He says, "Of course, it seems that the defendants are charged with Section 107 of the penal code, loitering for the purposes of prostitution. May I have a moment to confer with my clients, Your Honor?" He speaks to the girls.

After speaking to the girls for a moment, he says, "Your Honor, after conferring with my clients, they have informed me that this has been a terrible misunderstanding and they are innocent of all charges."

The girls chuckle, as do the audience. "I therefore request that no bail be set as the defendants assured me, they will return as required. They have assured me that they have firmly planted roots in the community."

The judge looks at Bob and says, "Please, can you have them plant their roots in another community?"

Everyone in the courtroom laughs, and the judge looks up, surprised as he did not intend his remarks to be funny. Bob requests $100 bail for each defendant. The judge looks over to the DA who is an experienced DA, and the DA nods yes. The Judge says, "Okay, $100 bail for each defendant. Next case."

Bob turns around and speaks to one of the Legal Aid attorneys for a moment and then leaves the courthouse. As he's walking out, we also leave and meet in the hallway with Bob rubbing his hands, saying, "Boy, am I starving!"

And so off we go to Little Vincent's clam bar in Manhattan. Back then, it was a very low-key place, but the food was beyond great. I got home about two in the morning and had to get up early as I had a very busy day.

I get into the office the next day at around eight-thirty as I have appoint-ments starting at eleven, and I needed some time to prepare for the them and also to discuss some of the upcoming cases with the lawyers who are handling them. Generally, from when I get in, in the morning until about eleven, I do not take calls because if I did, I would never get anything done. My secre-taries know this. However, one of them comes in and tells me that there is a girl on the phone named Jackie who I used to work with at a place called the Mayflower coffee shop. She has to talk to me. I can't believe it. I say, "Okay, put her through."

Now who is Jackie and what is the Mayflower coffee shop? After I got out of college, I applied to law school and was accepted, but at the last moment, I decided I needed a year off. I went to the law school and spoke to who I believe was the Dean and told him that I would like to start the following September. I wasn't ready for school and needed some time off. I told him, however, if that was not possible, I would start this September.

He said, "No, I think it's a good idea. If you're not ready to start, we will hold your spot for the next September class."

I was relieved. I didn't want to start school. I needed a year off. Funny how things work out because I didn't start that September, but the following September, I met Bonnie who was in that September class. Fate has funny ways of doing things. Had I started the previous September, I probably would not have met Bonnie or at least would not have gotten to know her well because we would have been in separate classes. So, after the Dean gave me permission to start the following September, I felt relaxed and renewed. No school pressure for a year.

When I first started college four years ago, Ron and I arrived at St. Michael's College in Winooski Park, Vermont, in the early morning. We went to the main administration building and were told where our dorm was and what our room numbers were. We were told to go to our rooms, unpack, and then go for breakfast at the Commissary building. The Commissary building was commonly referred to as the chow hall. We packed and then asked directions to the chow hall. The building was a small rectangular building with three steps and a porch as you entered.

At the top of the steps were guys who were handing out beanies to freshmen. You had to wear a beanie if you were a freshman to enter the chow hall. I looked at Ronnie and he at me. "Are they kidding we are not wearing any beanies? On the other hand, do we want to get into trouble the first couple of hours here on the campus? What to do? What to do?"

The guys handing out the beanies were sophomores wearing tweed sport jackets with brown-and-white shoes. Both were wearing shirts and ties and looked very preppy. One was smoking a pipe.

Ron and I were dressed in jeans and sweat shirts. We waited for a minute before approaching the steps and noticed they were stopping everyone entering and asking if they were freshmen. It seems, however, that they knew who the freshman were since it was a very small school. Just as we were about to approach the steps, a guy in front of us started up the steps. He was about six feet tall. They approached him with the beanies, asking him if he was a freshman. He said, "Yes" as he tried to walk by. They stopped him and told him he had to wear a beanie.

He said, "Are you kidding me? I'm a Korean vet, and I just came back from Korea."

They said, "Sorry, but all freshmen have to wear a beanie."

He said, "That's ridiculous, I'm not going to wear one" as he tried to walk past them and into the chow hall. They got in front of him to stop him. All this was happening as we were walking up the steps. He quickly grabbed one by the front collar and back of his pants and threw him down the three steps. As the guy landed on his behind, the other guy started to go toward the vet. As he did so, Ronnie and I reached the top step, grabbed the guy, and threw him off the steps. Now both of them were on the ground, and as they got up and approached the steps, the guy who threw the first one off the steps said, "Come up these steps and I'll rip your hearts out."

The way he said it made them realize that this guy was nobody to fuck with, and they stopped dead in their tracks. All three of us walked into the chow hall, and as we did so, we introduced ourselves. His name was Harry Andrews. He said, "Thanks for the help, guys." We shook hands and became friends for the next four years. I will not go on any further with my college days as that would be a book in itself.

The reason I'm telling you about my first day at St. Michael's College is because when we walked around campus, everyone looked smart. They were very preppy, carrying their books around campus, smoking pipes and wearing glasses. Ron and I, on the other hand, were dressed in Ozone Park attire, and the only thing we had to smoke were a couple of joints which we were saving for later on.

The point I'm trying to make here is that at St. Michael's, they all looked smart and studious and bright, yet at the end of four years, our class had shrunk to a smaller size. The students who we thought were brilliant either were not or couldn't take the pressure of college or flunked out or just decided to quit.

On the other hand, the students in law school looked bright and intelligent and were actually smart. Although we lost some guys, too, I think mostly because they could not take the pressure. When I started law school, our class consisted of all men with Bonnie and another girl the only women in the class. The other girl dropped out after a week.

Getting back to Jackie, the woman who just called me. Let me tell you how I met her. After getting the okay from the Dean of the law school to start the following September, I decided to look for a job, something that was brainless and had no pressure; anything that would make me a couple of bucks a week so I could enjoy myself and hang out. I found the perfect job; it was at the Mayflower Coffee Shop, a restaurant on 59th Street and Park Avenue in New York City. I saw an ad in the paper for a cashier, went for an interview, and was hired.

The job turned into something totally unexpected for me. The place was a very ritzy restaurant with an eclectic menu. They served both hamburgers and steaks, had terrific desserts and, because of its location on 59th Street and Park Avenue, had a clientele that was reasonably wealthy and high class. I was instructed by the manager, Sal, that when a famous person came in to take him or her around to the back seating area, where they would not be bothered. Some famous people I remember are Jack Parr, who, at the time, was the host of the *Tonight Show* on TV channel four. Also, his sidekick Hugh Downs used to come in a lot, along with Steve Allen and Ed Sullivan who all had TV shows. Sullivan used to live right across the street, I think, at Delmonico Hotel. After a while, I got used to seeing the celebs.

The restaurant had a couple of counters and two large seating areas. Most of the people who worked there were aspiring actresses or actors or models who wanted to get into the theater or modeling and came from all over the country. While trying to do so, they had to make a living and got jobs as waiters and waitresses. Most of them sought out locations like the Mayflower coffee shop because although it was a coffee shop, the name belied the real restaurant. The unique thing about the Mayflower was that you could go in for coffee and a donut at the counter or you could sit down and have a really good meal, and so people stopped in for coffee and dessert and others for hamburgers and other sandwiches that the Mayflower offered. The prices were at least one-third more expensive than other restaurants that offered similar fare, but because it was in a safe, ritzy area, on Park Avenue, the tips were extra good; and since the staff knew a lot of famous people came in, the hope was that maybe they would get spotted and be offered auditions or whatever.

I loved the job; it was easy and mindless, but I noticed that so many things could be done better. So, after a month or so, I told Sal, the manager, about some of my ideas. One them was to put the name of the waiters and waitresses on their uniforms so that instead of people yelling out "Waitress!" or "Waiter!" they could call the staff by their names. It turned out it was a good idea because the waitresses and waiters started to tell me they that they got better tips, and they think part of the reason was because instead of the impersonal waiter or waitress, they now had a name. I think if you're speaking to someone and you say, "Jane, can I have a hamburger?" instead of "Waitress," you somehow feel like you know them, and I think that was the reason for the better tips.

I recommended lots of other changes that Sal implemented, which helped the restaurant do even better. I won't go into all the changes as they're pretty boring, but it was fun doing something positive and helping to improve the restaurant. Sal, the manager, and I became good friends. He was really a very warm and nice person. I had been working there for about two months when Sal came into the restaurant one day, took me into the back room, and told me that his wife was ill and that she needed to be in a warm dry climate, and they were moving to Arizona in a couple of weeks. I told him how sorry I was and that I hoped his wife would get better. I asked him if he had notified the corporation yet and if he knew who would be the new manager.

Sal told me he spoke to Mr. Anderson, one of the vice presidents, and Mr. Anderson was somewhat concerned that Sal was giving him such little notice. Out of the blue, Sal told Mr. Anderson that I, in his judgment, would be capable of running the place, that I had already implemented small things that he thought made the restaurant better. Mr. Anderson, having no choice since no one else was available, agreed to let me become the manager for the next three months to see how I did, and if it worked out, I would become the permanent manager. I was in shock.

Boy, did my life change after that! I suddenly became a man about town. I was making almost four times the salary that I was making as a cashier and was having a good time running the restaurant, which in the end was really quite easy. Suddenly, a lot of the actresses/waitresses took an interest in me. They found out that not only was I the new manager, but it also came out that I was college educated, which I did not put down on the application I filled out as part of getting the job; my thinking was they would not hire a college-educated guy to be a cashier. I also did not tell them that I would only be there for a year and that I was starting law school the following September. I think one of the deciding factors in my getting hired was that Sal disclosed I had a college education and the reason why I didn't put it down. I believe that tipped the scales for Mr. Anderson in hiring me. I had never told Sal that I was going to law school, and so Mr. Anderson didn't know or I think he would not have hired me.

I never asked any of the waitresses out, although it was tempting because some of them were so pretty. One of the ones that was working there that I never asked out but I knew liked me was Jackie, the girl who was presently calling me. I didn't ask any of the waitresses/actresses out because I was concerned if the date didn't go well, I would still have to work with them. Plus, I'm sure they would gossip about me and our date, and I thought it would undermine the authority that I now had as manager.

My life, however, did change in so many ways. Firstly, the Copacabana was right around the corner from the Mayflower, and so I started going to the Copa after work. My hours were from four to twelve, and so after twelve, I was hardly tired and didn't want to go home and go to sleep. I now also started to meet lots of girls, attractive ones that came into the shop who I became friendly with and girls that I met on the street in New York City.

One day, I was at work, and I suddenly saw this most attractive lady walking by on 59th Street. I thought, *What an attractive girl. How will I ever get to meet someone like that?*

I saw the same gal pass by a couple of days later at the same time, around five-fifteen, quitting time. At work, as the manager, I usually wore slacks, a shirt and tie and a sport jacket. I said to myself, "I have to get to meet this girl." And so, I told the cashier to watch the place for me. I would be right back. I then went outside, and as the girl was walking from 59th to 58th Street, I walked up beside her and said, "Excuse me, but I am new here in New York. I have just gotten out of school in Vermont. Am I heading in the right direction? I want to go to 56th Street."

She said, "Yes, this is the right direction." And so, we started to walk together in silence, kind of awkwardly.

Then I would start to chat as we were walking in the same direction, saying something like, "Boy, is the city confusing. I just got a job at the Mayflower coffee shop as the manager, but I can't find my way around."

And before you knew it, we were in a conversation. I would then say, "By the way, I would like to repay you for helping me find my way about New York City. Perhaps I can invite you to be my guest at the Mayflower for coffee one day after you get out of work?"

Most of the girls knew I was flirting with them, and the usual response was, "Oh, thank you so much, maybe I'll pop in." The trick was to be impeccably dressed and be very polite. This wasn't today where everyone is afraid of everyone. In those days, people were courteous and polite to each other.

Before you know it, I had several different young girls stopping by the coffee shop, asking for me. When I invited them for coffee, I would give them my Mayflower card with my name as manager on it. It became a great way to meet girls, and all the waiters and waitresses knew what I was doing and used to get a big kick out of it. I was twenty-one at the time.

On a few occasions, I had two girls stop by at the same time. The new cashier who I hired handled it very well. When the first girl came in, he told me, and I took her in the back, and we were having coffee and chatting when the second girl came in. My quick-thinking cashier told the second girl that I had gone out and wouldn't be back for a while, and since I was in the back, she couldn't see me, and so, it worked out okay.

After several weeks of doing this, I got a much bigger response than I had anticipated and so stopped running after girls on the street. One day, after I had stopped pursuing girls on the street, I happened to see this incredibly attractive girl walking by. I couldn't get a look at her face, but she had an incredible figure, and I just couldn't resist. So, I put on my jacket and told my cashier to watch over the place for a couple of minutes and went outside. As I got to the corner, the girl that I wanted to introduce myself to had stopped walking and was waiting for the light to change again.

On Park Avenue, there is a middle divider with cars going in opposite directions. I was on the corner, and I could not cross, and the girl was on the center island, and she could not cross. The lights changed, and we both proceeded forward. She stopped on the opposite corner and was looking in the window of the Delmonico Hotel at something. I walked up to her and went into my spiel about, "Am I heading in the right direction to go to Lexington Avenue?"

She stopped, turned around, looked at me, and it was Elizabeth Taylor.

I couldn't believe it. I was embarrassed. I was shocked. I didn't know what to do. I figured she would say Third Avenue is the direction in which you're walking, and I would say thank you and just walk or run away from her as fast as I could.

It didn't happen that way. Before I describe what happened next, let me tell you about a little experience I had several years later when I was on vacation in Jamaica with Bonnie and some friends. I was swimming by myself with a snorkel, fins, and a mask, looking at the beautiful fish, and lost track of time and distance; when I finally looked up, I had swum out so far that I could hardly see the shoreline. I panicked. The first thing I wanted to do was yell for help, and the second thing I wanted to do was swim as fast as I could toward shore. But I knew no one would hear me. I was too far out. I said, "Calm yourself down," then I took a deep breath, put my goggles back on, put my head in the water with the snorkel, and slowly started to swim toward shore. After about a minute, I looked up to make sure I was heading in the right direction, which I was, and in another ten minutes, I was safely back onshore.

The reason I tell you about this was because my first inclination was to swim as fast as I could toward shore, but I knew I had to stay calm and swim slowly back to shore. Well, meeting Elizabeth Taylor years before was kind of the same thing. I met her by accident, not knowing who she was, and all I wanted to do was run away as fast as I could from her. I was so embarrassed. I knew that would not be the right thing, and so instead I said, "Thank you" as quickly as I could and turned to start to walk away.

Before I could even turn to walk away, she looked at me and, in a flash, I think she saw the whole scene of me walking up to her to try to pick her up, realizing it was her, and trying to leave as quickly as I could.

She said, "Were you just trying to pick me up?"

I looked at her, turning beyond red to purple, and didn't know what to say, so I said, "I beg your pardon?"

She gave me a long look, and I was too nervous to try to lie, so I said, as best I can recall, something like, "Well, yes, but I didn't know it was you."

She laughed. She then said, "Well, good-looking (I swear she said good-looking and to this day, on occasion, when I answer the phone and it's a friend, I'll answer, 'The good-looking guy here,' figuring if Elizabeth Taylor thought I was good-looking, I must be okay), I'm walking toward Lexington Avenue anyway, so come on." And with that, she put her arm in mine, and we started walking toward Lexington Avenue. She asked me to tell her exactly how I do it. What do I say and do?

I told her the truth once again about how it worked. She was laughing and seemed to be enjoying our little chat as we walked down the block, chatting away. As we were walking, two ladies walking in the opposite direction spotted her and say, "It's Elizabeth Taylor." And within a matter of seconds, there must have been several people around her, asking for autographs. I stepped away, not knowing what to do. She reached out to me and said, "Can you please help me get a cab?" as she is signing autographs.

I say yes. I go to the street. Almost like in the movies, I flag a cab which has to stop anyway due to traffic. He looked at me and said, "What's going on?"

I tell him who it was and asked him if he could give her a ride.

He said, "I have a fare in the back. If it's okay with her, it's okay with me."

The woman, having heard everything, nodded yes. I said, "Thank you, one moment."

I went over to Elizabeth Taylor and told her I had a cab waiting. I walked to the cab, helped her in, and said, "It was fun meeting you, Elizabeth (which is what she asked me to call her)."

She whispered, "Thank you." I closed the door, and off she went.

The funny thing about the whole experience was that it felt so natural. After twenty seconds speaking to her, she put me at ease. She was such an easygoing, pleasant person to speak to. I was twenty-one at the time. I guess she must've been twenty-three or twenty-four. Anyway, I went back to the Mayflower and told everyone what had just happened. They had a hundred questions, and it was a lot of fun telling them about it.

So now I'm getting back to the telephone call from Jackie in my office. She was one of the prettiest, sweetest, unpretentious waitresses of them all. I knew at the time I worked at the Mayflower she liked me and I liked her, but as I said before, I would not date anyone that I worked with. So here she is on the phone, and the first thing she says is how is Elizabeth. I can't believe after all these years she still remembers that story. I tell her, "Jackie, I can't believe you still remember that."

She asked me what's doing and how I was. I tell her I graduated law school, I'm in private practice, and married.

She says, "Who's the lucky girl?"

And I tell her about Bonnie. She says, "She sounds lovely. I'm so happy for you, Bobby."

I asked her how she is doing. She says, "Career-wise, I'm doing well.

However, I'm getting a divorce, and that's one of the reasons for my call." I tell her, "I'm sorry, how can I help?"

She asked me if I can handle her divorce. I ask if the divorce is going to be contested. She says, "No, we mutually agreed to the divorce. No one is asking the other for any money, we have no children, and I hope we can do this quickly."

I asked her where she was living. She tells me Manhattan. I tell her, "I generally do not go into the city but would if this was a seriously contested divorce, but since it is not, I think I can recommend a lawyer who can handle it for her expeditiously and for a reasonable fee." I asked her to leave her number. "I'll check it out and see who I want to recommend to you." We talked for a while longer about old times at the restaurant, laughing a lot over all the insanity that went on there, and finally, I said, "Goodbye. I'll be in touch."

I call Bobby Viccara. I asked him if he knew a matrimonial attorney that he could recommend. He said he knew several. "Is it going to be a contested or uncontested divorce?"

I told him, "Probably uncontested." And he gave me the name and phone number of the lawyer he would recommend. I said, "What else is cooking?"

He tells me he has some important news for me and he wants to meet me, Bonnie, and Ronnie for dinner. I say, "Is everything okay?"

He says, "Yes, sure, fine."

We make arrangements to meet the following evening for dinner. I called Jackie back, gave her the name and phone number of the attorney, and wished her good luck. I told her I'm here for her if she has any other questions.

I call Bonnie and Ronnie and tell them that I have made plans for the following evening to meet with Bob and Nancy because he has some news for us. They both say fine. "What's the news?"

I tell them, "I don't know. We'll find out tomorrow."

The next morning, I'm at my desk, checking on my schedule so that I can be sure to be out in time to pick up Bonnie and meet Ronnie; Bob is very punctual and hates when you come late, another one of his crazy pet peeves. I always tell him, "Bob, if you're waiting on a street corner and I'm late, that's one thing. But if I meet you at your house and I'm ten minutes late, what does it matter?"

He says it matters, and knowing he's nuts, I always try to be on time. As Bob says, "Being on time is the courtesy of kings." And who am I to argue with him?

As I'm at my desk, I get a call from Lenny. Now who is Lenny? He is a building contractor and my partner on five houses we are building in Howard Beach, New York. How long have I known

Lenny? I have known him so long that I don't even remember when I first met him. That's how young we were. He has always been a lifelong friend. I gave him the nickname Sluggo because he was always getting into fistfights.

He never started them, tried to avoid them, but once he was in the fight, he was a killer. Growing up in Ozone Park, a lot of the guys could handle themselves as it was a necessity for growing up there. However, Lenny was always exceptional, probably one of the best in a fight in all of Ozone Park. He was so good that when he went into the Navy, he went on the boxing team and had a winning record there also. He was unassuming. One would never expect that he was as tough as he was. I had an incredible warm spot for Lenny and still do. How did I get into being Lenny's partner in building five houses in Howard Beach? He came to me one day and said, "Bobby, I have these properties. I can build five houses on them. Want to be my partner?"

I said, "I sure do." And that's how it happened. "Len, what's up?"

He says, "You know that guy across the street from where we are building who got us a $500 ticket for air pollution when our tractors kicked up too much dust? That son of a bitch."

I said, "I remember, Len, calm down, it's over."

He said, "Well, I just found out that at nighttime, he is stealing some of our lumber and taking it to his house where he's building a new shed."

I asked him how he knew, and he said he noticed some of our lumber was missing (two-by-fours), and when he asked around, one of the neighborhood kids said that he saw a guy that lives around the corner taking the lumber at night. I asked the kid to show me the house, and sure as shit, it was that guy's house. I went in the backyard, and there was our lumber, and the reason I know it's our lumber is because it had blue tags on it. The schmuck wasn't even smart enough to remove the tags. What do you want to do?"

I say, "Let me think about it."

He says, "Fuck that. I know what you're going to do. You're going to try to work it out with him. Fuck that, I'm going to the police and report that he stole the lumber from us."

I say, "You didn't see him, how can you prove it?"

He says, "I'm going to tell them I saw him take it because he took it, and I know it's our lumber."

I said, "Lenny, you can't do that, that's perjury."

He says, "Either that or I go beat the shit out of him."

I say, "Lenny, calm down, calm down.' I'm thinking when he says, "I'm going to beat the shit out of him," he really will go beat the shit out of him which will be an assault, for which he will be arrested and then I will wind up having to defend him. "So, I think the better way to do this is to report the robbery to the police. After all, the guy did steal our lumber, and let's see what happens. Report it to the police."

He says, "Okay, Bobby. I'll tell them I saw him take the lumber late at night when I know he's not working and is at home."

I'm thinking, *yes, Lenny, I'm being reasonable agreeing to let you perjure yourself, but what else could I do?* Well, he was arrested, and his name was Jerome Harriman. The case went to trial with Lenny as the star and only witness. He called me after he testified. I asked, "How did it go?" It turns out that if the guy was found guilty, he would lose his job and his pension. Therefore, he got a pretty well-known criminal lawyer to represent him.

He tells me the first question the lawyer asked was what the weather was like that evening. Len says, "The weather was warm and nice."

The lawyer then takes out a weather report showing that on the evening in question, it was raining, and he had the weather report in front of him that had been taken at LaGuardia Airport.

So, I said, "It might have been raining at LaGuardia Airport, but in Howard Beach, it was not. There have been times when it was raining two blocks away from me but was not at my house."

The lawyer after giving him a long look says, asks him, "How long did it take him to steal the lumber you claim he was stealing?"

Lenny says it probably took him about thirty-five or forty minutes. The lawyer then asked him, "What was the lumber you claim he took?"

He said, "It was all two-by-fours." He then asked him how he got the lumber from the building site to his backyard.

Lenny said, "He carried it over his shoulder three or four at a time."

He then asked, "How much lumber do you claim he took?" Lenny told him, "I wasn't sure but probably over $1,000 worth."

He then said, "You mean to tell this jury that my client took over a thousand dollars' worth of two-by-fours from your building site to his backyard?"

Lenny said, "That's right."

"And you're claiming that he did this all in thirty or forty minutes?" Lenny said, "That's right."

He then said, "Wouldn't you say that's impossible to take that much lumber from the building site to his backyard in thirty-five or forty minutes?"

Lenny said, "Generally, it would take a lot longer; but when you're stealing you hurry." Lenny said the jury laughed a little bit as did the judge, but it only pissed off the attorney.

He then asked, "How much do two-by-fours weigh?" Lenny told him, "I don't know."

He said, "You're a builder and you don't know how much two-by-fours ways."

Lenny said, "No, I don't." As he's asking these questions, he keeps on waving a pencil in Lenny's face. Lenny got pissed off and asked him, "You're a lawyer, how much does that pencil weigh?"

Again, the jury laughed a little bit, which again pissed the lawyer off. He asked a lot of bullshit questions which Lenny answered as best he could, and then he was dismissed.

I told Lenny to keep me in the loop and let me know when he found out what happened if the guy got convicted or took a plea or what.

He called me the next day and told me he found out the guy was acquitted. I said, "Even though he was a hump and a thief, I hate to see the guy lose his job over some lumber."

Len felt the same way. He said it probably cost more for him to hire a lawyer to defend himself than the lumber was worth.

I said, "After what he went through, I don't think he'll be trying to steal anymore lumber from us."

Len said, "Yeah, I think you're right."

That evening, Bonnie and I met Ronnie and his present friend, Ginny, who was a model from the Ukraine. She is beautiful, sweet, kind, and very unpretentious. Bon and I liked her a lot. We, however, learned not to get too close to his girlfriends. One day, they would be around, and the next, he would have a new one. I remember asking him later on about Ginny and why it didn't work out. He said he knew it wasn't going to work out when he took her to New Hampshire to the Cathedral in the Pines. This was a place in the woods in New Hampshire that was like a church; it had an altar, and services were occasionally held there.

They spent the weekend there, and the first sign that there was trouble was when they were having breakfast Sunday morning. As they were having breakfast, Ginny picked up two sugar packets. The sugar packets had the pictures of presidents on the back with a little synopsis of their presidency. As Ginny was looking at the packages, there was a package with the picture of Chester

A. Arthur, the twenty-first president of the United States. The packet said he was elevated to become the twenty-first president of the United States upon the assassination of James Garfield, the twentieth president of the United States.

Ginny asked him what they meant by elevated. He said, "You know, elevated. Went up and became the next president." But he was concerned that she didn't understand the word *elevated* or the context and with which it was used. That was the first signal that things were amiss. I reminded him that her first language was Ukrainian and perhaps didn't understand the word, and he said, "Gee, I never thought of that."

The second signal was when they were shopping at a vegetable stand in New Hampshire, and Ronnie was looking at some sweet potatoes and, for some reason, asked Ginny, "What's the difference between yams and sweet potatoes?" He didn't know.

She thought about it for a minute and said, "I know. The difference between yams and sweet potatoes is that yams come in cans."

Well, that was the end of it. He was not sure that he could continue the relationship with her. I told him, "Are you crazy? She's a terrific girl."

And he said to me, "Do you think Bonnie knows the difference between yams and sweet potatoes?"

I said, "Probably not." So, we asked Bon, and she said she didn't know. I said, "See, Ron, you're being too judgmental."

And he said, "Yeah, but Bonnie said she didn't know. She didn't say that yams come in cans."

I think the real reason it didn't work out was because she had emotional problems. She came to America as a refugee, and her parents were old-school with old-school values. They were traumatized because they escaped a Communist country and had all the baggage which comes with that. They traumatized her too. She was fearful of everything. After a while, it was difficult for Ronnie to deal with. He tried to get her to go to a shrink, but she refused. He did try but, in the end, it was too exhausting and slowly ended.

We finally get to the restaurant where we're meeting Bob and Nancy, a nice little Italian place called Nello. They are already there, waiting for us. We sit down and start looking at the menus as we are chatting. Bob looks awfully quiet, and I can tell that there is something on his mind. I asked him, "Bobby, what's up?"

He tells Ronnie and our group that he has decided to retire from the Legal Aid Society and is moving up to Vermont with Nancy and the kids. "Nancy originally came from Vermont, as you know, and thinks that life would be quieter and easier and less expensive in Vermont."

We are all in shock. We love these two people and their kids and feel like we are losing part of our family. I ask him, "Bobby, you're too young to retire (he was only in his early fifties)."

He says he's going to probably work for Legal Aid or the District Attorney's Office in Vermont. He already has an appointment in Mount Montpelier, the state capital. We all know he will have no trouble working wherever he wants, and whoever gets him will be extremely lucky. We're happy for them and at the same time heartbroken.

Within a couple of months, they sold their house and were gone. Of course, we tried to keep in contact, but it wasn't the same. God, how we all miss them, especially Bobby. He was a genius and a very, very special man.

Frankie Cantone

How do I begin to tell this story? I guess it started when I was in my last year of law school. I had just dropped Bonnie off at her house and was heading to my brother Vin's law office (which eventually would be my office also). I was stopping by before heading for my Friday afternoon and all-day Saturday job at the Brooklyn Academy of Music High School. I had been working there for over a year as a driver education instructor.

I had a classroom with over sixty students. I would give an hour lecture a week about cars and how they worked; the engine transmission etc. and how to drive the car properly. After the lecture, I would take four students at a time out to teach them how to drive. I sat in the passenger front seat and one student drove with three students sitting in the back. The cars were equipped with two pairs of brakes, one for the student, and on the passenger's side, one for me. If I hadn't had those breaks, I think I would've been killed a couple of dozen times. Thank God for those breaks. It was a great paying job, and I'll tell you how I got it.

While in law school, there were identical twins in some of my classes. They were the Stavos twins. They always wore very expensive suits. I asked them how they could afford such high-end suits. They told me that they were both driver education teachers on the side. The pay was like fifteen bucks an hour, which in those days was really a lot of money. I asked them how I could get a job like that. They told me I had to take a class at NYU and then gave me all the information I needed. So that summer, I took the course at NYU and became a certified driving instructor who could teach classes in high school. The catch was that in order to get this job and teach at the high school level, you had to have a college degree, which I did.

The Stavos twins were both fighters. They had fought in the Golden Gloves in the 118 and the 126-pound divisions, I think. They had also fought in the Pan Am games and had met the then unknown Cassius Clay when he was a light heavyweight. They told great stories about him. For instance, he had no money and so would give the fighters a five-minute head massage for twenty-five cents. They said they knew he was special and that he had this incredible talent and thought that if he followed through, he would be the light heavyweight champ someday.

While they were in law school, the twins fought in the Golden Gloves, and I remember Ron and I going to see them. They both won. They were well-liked by everyone. I think one of them left law school and became a teacher, and the other one became a lawyer.

After completing my course at NYU, I looked for a teaching driver education job in a high school and got a tip that Brooklyn Academy of Music High School was looking for a driver education teacher so I applied and was interviewed by Mr. Bolin. The interview went something like this. "Mr. Aliazzo, you seem qualified. However, you will be teaching lots of minority students who are tough to handle, and if you can't handle them and send them to my office constantly for help, you will not last long at this job. You have the additional disadvantage of looking very young"—at the time, I had just turned twenty-three. "You look younger than some of the students in your class, and therefore, it may be more difficult than usual to control them. Do you understand?"

I said, "Of course, Mr. Bolin, and I think I can handle the students." I was given the job on a trial basis.

My first day of class was a total disaster, and I thought at one point, not only would I lose my job but I would be arrested. I saw my whole life go out the window, including law school. Here's what happened:

My first day of teaching class was on a Saturday. Saturday meant informal attire, and therefore, I dressed in jeans a t-shirt and sneakers. I had the textbook to teach the class with me and a notepad, and at nine o'clock sharp, I showed up at the school. I knew the classroom number, and so at 9:00 a.m., I walked in. The classroom was a long rectangular room with windows all on one side and on the other side a front and rear door. There were about sixty students. I walked in the front door to the desk, and put my book and notepad on it. The class ignored me and continued to speak to one another. I turned to the class and said, "Quiet, please." Everyone ignored me. I think they assumed I was one of the students horsing around. I said, "Everyone, quiet please" again. Some of them looked up at me for a moment, then continued to talk.

I picked up a book that was on my desk and slammed it very hard onto the table so that it made a very loud noise. Everyone stopped talking and looked at me. I walked over to the blackboard and wrote my name, Mr. Aliazzo. I then turned to look at the class again and said, "My name is Frank Aliazzo and I am going to be your teacher and driving instructor. If you listen to me and pay attention, you will pass this course, and I guarantee you will all learn how to drive, become great drivers, and get your licenses, I will make sure of it."

Total silence in the class, everyone staring at me. "I know I look young, and that's because I am young. I'm twenty-three years old. I graduated from college over a year ago and am presently a law student at New York Law School. I took a special course at New York University to become a certified high school driving instructor. I heard there was a teaching job available here, I applied, and was hired by Mr. Bolin. So, you guys and girls are stuck with me."

At this point, the room was quiet. I had their attention because I told them what they most wanted to hear, which was that they were going to get their driver's license and that I was going to teach them how to drive.

The program allowed them to get their licenses at seventeen instead of eighteen and, additionally, would get them a 10 percent discount on their car insurance because they had graduated from the driver education program. A 10 percent discount could mean more than $100 in savings which was the amount they were paying to take the course. That was the good thing. Nobody wanted to flunk out or not pass the course because it would mean the loss of $100 or so, plus they would not get their license, and if the parents were paying, they had to face them and explain why they didn't pass the course. So, the advantage to teaching this course was that everybody cared and wanted to pass, which would potentially make my life a lot easier.

Things were really going well; the classroom was quiet, and I had their full attention. As I started to tell them what the course would entail, there was a big bang at the back of the room. There was a tall Black kid sitting in the last row with his chair tilted, and he was rocking it back and forth and hitting the blackboard in the rear, making a loud noise. Everyone turned around to see what was going on and everyone chuckled.

I looked at the kid and didn't say anything, figuring it was an accident. Apparently because he got a laugh or a chuckle, he decided to do it again and banged against the blackboard as I was speaking. This time, I knew he did it on purpose. I looked up at him and told him to cut it out.

I started speaking, and after a moment or so, he banged his chair against the blackboard again, this time getting a big laugh. I thought, *Here I go, I'm losing control of this class, and things are going so well. What do I do?* I look up at the kid and tell him, "If you do that one more time, I'm throwing you out of this class."

Everybody quiets down. I start to speak again, and within a moment, he bangs on the blackboard again, and now the kids aren't laughing so much but are getting nervous because I think they sense a confrontation between me and the student, and I think they're starting to like me and are starting to feel comfortable with me.

I look up at him and say, "Okay you just blew a hundred bucks, get out of my class."

He doesn't move. He just stares at me with his chair leaning against the blackboard. I say once again, "It's time for you to leave and get out of my classroom."

He stares at me but does not move. You could hear a pin drop in the class. I start to walk to the rear of the room where the kid is sitting. He starts to say something, but I am pissed and speak over him and say, "Get out!"

He looks at me but doesn't move. I'm thinking, *I can't go get Mr. Bolin because it's Saturday morning and he's not here, so I will have to handle this myself.*

I make my way down the aisle where the kid is sitting, and as I get next to him, intending to grab him by the arm and escort him out of the classroom, he suddenly jumps up. I instinctively and without thinking punch him on the way up. One thing I learned growing up in Ozone Park, if you're going to get into a fight and you can't get out of it, throw the first punch because eight times out often, you will win. I, for that moment when he jumped up, legitimately thought he was going to grab me or punch me, and my instincts took over.

Now the student is on the floor, groggy, bleeding from the mouth, and all the students around him jumped up and pushed their chairs away. Luckily, it was a Saturday, and none of the other classes had students in them. I didn't know what to do. All the kids were staring, and there was total silence. I'm thinking, *this is it for me. I will go to jail for assault, law school is a thing of the past, and all my dreams about joining my brothers in a law practice are over.*

The student started to shake his head and get up. I grabbed him under his left arm and helped him get up. He didn't say anything to me. I started to walk him out of the classroom through the rear door.

As I got to the rear door, I turned to the students and said, "Everyone, put your chairs back in order." I pointed to one of the students, a girl, and told her to go to the front of the room and start to read chapter 1. "I will be right back."

Everyone did exactly as I told them and started to put the chairs back in order with the girl I spoke to going to the front of the room with her book.

As I got the student outside, I was about to plead for my life and tell him, "I am so sorry, I thought you were going to attack me."

And before I could say anything, he turned to me and said, "Mr. A, please don't throw me out of class. I have a job lined up delivering flowers as soon as I get my license, and my father will kill me if he finds out what happened."

I take a deep breath and say, "Okay, I will not throw you out of the class, but if you do anything like you did before, I will have no choice but to do so."

He said, "I swear I won't do it again, and the last time I banged my chair, I didn't mean to. The chair slipped."

I said, "What's your name?" He said, "Anton."

I said, "Anton, I'm sorry I hit you, but I thought you were going to attack me."

He said, "No, I wouldn't do that, I just got scared when you got close to me and wanted to get up quick." I said, "Are you hurt?"

He said, "Nah, I'm okay."

I said, "Go to the bathroom and clean yourself up and then come back to class."

He thanked me for giving him another chance. Was I lucky or what?

I walked back into the classroom as the girl was reading the first chapter. I tell her, "I'll take over," and she goes back to her seat. I sit on the desk in front and tell the students that what happened was an unfortunate incident and basically an accident. "I thought that the student, whose name is Anton, was going to attack or grab me, and that's why I acted the way I did. Anton has asked me to give him another chance, and I said I would. He will be back shortly to join our class once again. I would appreciate it if what happened in this class remains in this class."

All nodded yes, but of course, what happened in the class spread like wildfire. I don't think Mr. Bolin ever found out or if he did, he never asked me about it. I think he was just happy that I ran the class smoothly and had no complaints. The students seemed to like me, and my class was the first one students signed up for.

Over the course of the time I spent teaching at that school, I never had another problem with students behaving badly. I found out that one of the reasons was because that incident I had teaching my first day became something of a legend around the school, the word being "Don't fuck around in his class or he'll beat the shit out of you." I found this out because one of my favorite students of all time, whose name was Julius, told me.

Julius is one of the students who, when I asked if any of them had ever driven a car before while they were in a car with me, raised his hand and said, "Yeah, teach, plenty of times."

I asked him, "How come?"

He said, "I've been stealing cars since I was fourteen, but I stopped when I was sixteen because my father found out and told me if I ever did it again, I would have to deal with him, and if you knew my father, you know that the last thing you want to do is deal with him."

So, I said, "You know how to drive?" He said, "Sure."

I said, "Okay, you're the first one to drive." He got behind the wheel of that car and drove better than me. Plus, he was incredibly bright. I later found out he had a genius IQ, a genius with a Brooklyn accent and tough guy talk that I just loved.

Now getting to Frankie Cantone, the guy this chapter is all about. Let me tell you how I first met him. I was in my second year of law school and had stopped by my brother Vin's office before heading on to my teaching job. In front of the office was a young teenage kid sweeping the sidewalk. I stopped to ask him what he was doing and who he was. He said to me in a typical wise guy Ozone Park speech, "What's it to you?"

Right away, I liked him. I said, "I'm Vin's brother."

And he said, "Oh, you are one of Vinnie's twin brothers going to law school, right?"

I said, "Yes, my name is Bobby Aliazzo." And with that, I shook his hand, and we became friends. He had dirty blond hair and was good-looking. I noticed his hair, and as you know by now, I have a thing with hair, and I said to him, "That is the best haircut I've ever seen. Where did you get it?"

He said, "A friend of mine, Frankie Cantone, just opened his own barbershop. It's a one-man shop, just Frankie."

I asked him where the shop was, and he said, "Right here on 101st Avenue, a couple of blocks down, on the right, 3 or 4 doors down from Romanelli's Funeral Home. He just opened it a few months ago." I asked him his name, and he said, "Everyone calls me Johnny Boy."

I said, "Johnny Boy, I want to make an appointment for a haircut. Do you have his phone number"? He said he doesn't have a phone yet.

Before I tell you about Frankie, let me tell you a little bit about Johnny Boy. I got to know him pretty well. When I met him, he just turned seventeen, although he looked like he was fourteen. He was the sweetest, nicest, kindest, toughest kid you would ever want to meet. He was bright and always so friendly with a big smile once you got to know him. About a year and half after I first met him, he was drafted into the army. We had a small going away party for him in the back of the office. He was looking forward to going.

Well, he wound up going to Vietnam, and it turns out he had a special talent as a soldier, and the story goes he saw lots of action and killed a lot of Vietcong. The neighborhood gossip was that he was a hero, but he really had a taste for it; that is, the fighting and killing. I hadn't seen him since he came back, but the story was he was a changed man.

Then I started hearing stories that he came back with a screw loose and had become a hit man for money. Kind of like a mercenary who whacked people for pay. It came from some reliable sources, but I refused to believe it. About a month or so after I heard this, I happened to be coming out of my office, heading to Café Geo to get some espresso and a good cannoli. I had already started practicing law. Café Gio was a mob-owned place that had three televisions going at all times with soccer matches from Italy. They had the best coffee and espresso anywhere in Queens; the cannoli and Italian pastries were legendary. The problem was, although it didn't say private club, if they didn't know you, they wouldn't serve you and tell you to leave. It was an honor that even though I was a lawyer and not one of the mob guys, they served me, and even though my brother was an assistant district attorney, they served him as well.

I think part of the reason we were welcomed was because we were neighborhood guys and I had represented some of them who were members of the club. Ronnie went with me there often, and nobody ever questioned him about it, even though he was an assistant district attorney. Neither the guys at Café Geo nor people from the District Attorney's Office who knew he went there occasionally ever questioned him about it.

As I walked out the front door across the street, I saw Johnny Boy walking toward Woodhaven Boulevard. I yelled out, "Johnny Boy!"

He turned and saw me. He started walking toward me and me toward him, and when I caught up to him, we gave each other a big hug. He looked the same, still young and good-looking. It appeared nothing about him had changed. He still had that big wonderful smile. I hugged him again and said, "It's so good to see you."

And he said, "You too, Bobby."

We started to chat. I asked him where he was headed. He said, "To Café Geo to meet up with some friends and get some espresso and cannoli's."

I told him that's where I was headed. "Great, we can catch up."

When we get to Café Geo, we get a table in the rear and start ordering up some cannoli and coffee. I tell him, "I heard about Vietnam and that you're a fucking hero with all sorts of medals."

He says, "Yeah, it was tough, and I can't believe I made it out of there."

I could see he didn't want to talk about it much, and so we started reminiscing about old times and all the laughs and guys we knew and where they were now and so on. He seemed the same to me, easygoing and nice and very respectful and deferential to me. He asked about Vinnie and said he had heard all about Ronnie and the District Attorney's Office. He couldn't believe that Ronnie was a ADA but was very happy for him.

As we were chatting, I got a cold chill up and down my spine. It wasn't anything he said to me, it was the way the guys in the club treated him. They were very respectful to him and deferential to him, and right then and there, I knew that what I had heard about him was true. We chatted for a while, and then the people he was supposed to meet came in. I got up, gave him a hug, and said how good it was to see him again and said, "If you're around, stop by the office and have some coffee with me."

He said say hello to Ronnie and Vin, and with that, I left. I went to the counter to pay for the coffee and pastries, and he yelled out to Carlo who had been serving us, "Carlo, it's on me."

I thanked him and said goodbye.

About two months later, while sitting in my office, one of my secretaries came in, looking very upset. I asked, "What's the matter?"

She said she just heard that Johnny Boy was arrested and is in jail. She said it was on the local news and would probably be in the newspapers tomorrow. I asked her what happened. She said according to what she heard, he was in a bar late at night on 101st Avenue, literally seven or eight blocks from my office, when he got into an argument with a guy at the bar. It was pretty heated, and then a fight broke out, and the people there separated them. He left, went to his car, got a gun, came back into the bar, and shot the guy dead in front of a whole bunch of witnesses. He then went back to his car, lit up a joint, and stayed there until the police came.

The people in the bar told the police what happened, and the police asked if anyone knew who the shooter was. Everyone looked at one another. Anybody who knew him and his reputation wasn't about to say a word. One of the witnesses who didn't know who he was said, "He's right out front, sitting in his car." The police approached him with guns drawn and arrested him.

I was shocked. How did this happen? This beautiful young kid turned into a monster killer after going to Vietnam. The first thing I did was call Ronnie. He was at work. When I got him on the phone, before I could say anything, he said, "I heard."

I said, "Call me back."

He knew what I meant; I didn't want to speak on the phone he was on. He said, "I'll call you back in ten minutes."

We spoke for a while. I said, "Is there anything we can do to help him?" He said, "I'll stop by the office after work to chat, but I don't think so."

That evening, he came by; we were both a little depressed because we both knew this kid from when he was sixteen and knew what a good and kind heart he had and what a sweet young boy he once was. We just couldn't believe what had happened to him. As we spoke, Ronnie said, "Let's go drown our sorrows in a nice plate of linguine and clam sauce." So off we went to Don Pepe.

After finishing dinner and a couple of glasses of Don Pepe's secret red wine (we called it secret because it came in an unmarked bottle, and nobody knew what kind of wine it was, but it was delicious), we got down to the business of figuring out what, if anything, we could do for Johnny Boy. The shooting happened in Queens County, and therefore, he was arrested in Queens County and would be indicted in Queens County, which meant there was a good chance Ronnie, who was in the homicide bureau, would get the case. We both knew he had to recuse himself and could not get involved or try the case for obvious reasons. We both knew and loved the kid. The next thing we discussed was if there was any way we could speak to the ADA who was going to try the case if Johnny Boy's lawyer decided not to take a plea.

Ronnie said he probably knew which ADA was going to catch the case. They were all his friends and colleagues. He said it's kind of a slippery slope because he could be accused of influencing the ADA who caught the case. We spoke about it for a while, and then Ronnie said, "Fuck it, I'm just going to tell the ADA who catches the case about our relationship with Johnny Boy and how Vietnam screwed him up." One of the problems was if he pleaded insanity, due to the circumstances of his being in Vietnam and coming back messed up, he would be sent to a mental facility which could be worse than being in prison.

The good point about going to a medical facility was that if someday the doctors felt that you were cured, you could be released. The big problem was that the ADA who caught the case would find out his reputation as a contract killer, and all bets would be off the table, meaning they would probably not make any deals with his attorney and he would have to plead to the indictment. The case against him was strong. If they had only one witness, that witness could be intimidated by his reputation, but they had several witnesses and, in addition, he was caught in the car with the gun that he killed the other guy with.

Johnny Boy never called me to ask for help or advice. I think he was too embarrassed. Since he was a freelance hit man and got paid by the job, there was no obligation from the mob to help him. He got a Legal Aid attorney and pleaded guilty. He just didn't care anymore because if he did, he would not have sat in the car and smoked a joint until the cops came. He was sentenced to life in prison, which at the time meant that he would be eligible for parole after twenty-five years. I believe that's what it was at the time. I tried contacting him subsequently. I wrote to him and asked him if he would like to see me. I never got a response. I think he was just too embarrassed to face me. I think he was too embarrassed for what he had become. I felt sad for the person he killed and his family, and I felt sad for Johnny Boy.

I guess this has been a long introduction to how I met Frankie Cantone, the subject of this chapter of my book. So, after Johnny

Boy, while sweeping our law office sidewalk back then, told me where he got the terrific haircut, I made it a point to go to Frankie the next time I needed a haircut. I had been getting my haircuts in a little barbershop on Liberty Avenue in Ozone Park. The barber Carmine was an old-timer, and sometimes he gave me a great haircut, and other times, I was not pleased with the haircut; in other words, he was never consistent, and you never knew if you're going to get a great haircut or bad one. Johnny Boy's haircut was so terrific that I knew I had to try Frankie, and so a couple of weeks later, I walked over to his barbershop.

Since he had no phone and didn't take appointments anyway, this was the only way I was going to get a haircut from Frankie. I walked into his shop. It was tiny, probably twelve-by-ten feet. It had a mirror in front of the barber's chair and three chairs for people who were waiting. At the time, Frankie must have been around five-foot-four. The barber's chair was a new one that went up and down, but sometimes, if there was a tall customer in the chair, the chair didn't go down far enough, and so Frankie had to stand on a box. It was quite unusual and funny, but he was a master haircutter. He could just look at you and tell how he could cut your hair so that you would look your best. He really was gifted. Within one year of me going to him, he grew to almost six feet tall.

Frankie was Hollywood handsome, spoke fluent Italian, and had a personality that just made you love him. When I walked into his barbershop for the first time, there was no one there. I introduced myself and told him that Johnny Boy had sent me. He said, "Oh thanks for giving me a shot at cutting your hair."

I told him, "If you cut my hair as well as you cut Johnny Boy's, you are going to have a customer forever." I sat down, and that was it.

He had to stand on his box the first couple of times he cut my hair. The first haircut was spectacular, even I didn't know I could look so good. Ronnie, upon seeing me, went nuts and said, "Where did you get that haircut?"

I told him about Frankie, and needing a haircut, he went to see him that day. Of course, he hit it off with Frankie immediately. Frankie didn't know that I had a twin brother and thought it was me at first and couldn't understand how my hair grew back so quickly. It was really funny.

Over the next couple of years, his reputation grew. Both Ronnie and I started sending all our friends to him. Lots of our friends were lawyers and doctors. Since Ronnie was in court all the time as an ADA, he became very friendly with a lot of the judges, and since by now you know how crazy we are with hair, he would recommend some of the judges who had terrible haircuts to Frankie.

Before you know it, Frankie with his father, Joseph, and his two brothers, Gino and Sal, opened up a gigantic barbershop on Woodhaven Boulevard in Ozone Park. His father had been a barber for many years and worked in the city, and his two younger brothers, upon seeing the success of Frankie, went to school, and so all four were barbers. His father stopped cutting hair and ran the business, and his two brothers were almost as good as he was at cutting hair. Of course, Frankie was the master, and the way the barbershop was set up, Frankie had a private room for his customers in the back of the barbershop, which was on the first floor. He only built this special room after he had been working for about three years. The room had a private door that you had to knock on to enter.

Generally, when you came for a haircut with Frankie, you had to, of course, book it in advance. Once you got there, the receptionist would bring you to Frankie's room. It was like one of those sunrooms, all glass, except for the roof, with one chair and mirror for Frankie and two comfortable, very large leather chairs for his customers. The room itself was surrounded by a small backyard with grass and flowers, and along the borders, during the summers, tomato plants and basil plants and peppers and other vegetables which Joe, Frankie's father, tended to. There was also a large fence, so you couldn't see into Frankie's room.

When you walked in, on the left was a long marble table. The table contained an espresso and regular coffee machine and little bowls of biscotti and other Italian pastries. There was also a small cabinet next to the table that was closed. That cabinet, when opened, had a middle shelf that slid out. That shelf contained a bowl of rolled joints, and on occasion, a marble slab with lines of coke and straws. Only special customers knew what was in that cabinet, and if you were one of those special customers as I was, and felt like having a joint or a line of coke, if it was available, you simply asked Frankie. Lots of times, he ran out of both. Most of the time, joints were available, and coke occasionally, but then only for special customers.

There was always music playing mostly popular tunes of the day. He also had tapes with different artists like Frank Sinatra and Dean Martin. When my brother Vin went, the first thing he would do is tell the receptionist to turn down that music and put on Dean Martin or Frank Sinatra which, of course, they did because Vinnie was older, and Frankie loved Vinnie. And if he knew he was coming, in advance, he would tell them to put on Dean or Frank. He did that for very few people.

So, what had started as a small one-man barbershop became one of the busiest and biggest shops in Ozone Park. Frankie, by this time, was a rock star and would not take on any new clients unless they were recommended by someone Frankie knew and respected. He was booked for weeks in advance, and his customers were an incredible mix. Every wise guy in Ozone Park or maybe Queens County got their haircuts from Frankie. The tips were outrageous with the wise guys outdoing each other; tips of $100 or more were not uncommon. I felt like a piker giving him a tip of $20.

But Frankie would've given me haircuts for free because he knew that Ronnie and I were the first ones to get his business booming. It got a little tricky booking customers, and the receptionist had to be very careful. For instance, you didn't want John Gotti getting a haircut when one of the Supreme Court Queens County judges or detectives or policemen, who were also Frankie's customers, were waiting around in the same room. I helped solve the problem because one day, as I was getting a haircut, he told me about this problem and that the receptionist had screwed up a couple of times. He said he couldn't blame her because she didn't know the names of all the judges and, for that matter, all the high-profile wise guys. I said to Frankie, "I think I have a solution for you."

I told him to give the receptionist the names of all those guys, including their nicknames. Although it would be a problem at first, since she would have to go down the list every time an appointment was being made, she would get to know them eventually. This would cut down on any embarrassing encounters between his customers. He thought that was a great idea, and eventually, it worked well. He also, on occasion, would go to the Hunt and Bergen Fish Club that was on 101st Avenue (John Gotti's club) and give private haircuts to the wise guys in the evening.

After a time, Frankie hired a couple of female barbers. Two of them were from Russia but spoke English and a couple others were American girls. They were all incredibly pretty and sexy and wore revealing clothes. The place was wild but a lot of fun, and although the girls were pretty and sexy, they also knew how to give great haircuts because Frankie taught them. As wild as it was, they were always treated respectfully because Frankie would have it no other way.

One day, as I was getting a haircut a couple of years after Frankie started, he told me that he and his family had been doing so well that they bought a beautiful place in Sicily on over an acre of land (which I did not know at the time I would eventually visit).

Things were going well for Frankie and his family, and I became the family lawyer for Joe, Frankie's father, who basically ran the whole business; Frankie and now his brothers were the stars. His brothers were also very talented and extremely good-looking, and both of them developed big followings of their own. Joe, Frankie's father, who was my client, was also like his sons, thin with gray wavy hair, always dressed impeccably with good manners and perfect taste. His sons adored him and, more importantly, respected him and treated him very deferentially. I noticed on occasion, when Joe would encounter some of the wise guys who were his customers, that they also treated him very deferentially and with great respect, more so than I thought was customary. I didn't think much about it, but later on, I discovered exactly why.

Frankie, I found out, was hanging out more and more with the wise guys. I asked him about it and told Frankie to be careful. "Don't become too involved. You give them haircuts and you're friendly with them, but be careful."

He kind of blew me off saying to me, "Bobby, you're a lawyer and very friendly with a lot of them, and you represent them also."

I said, "You're right, Frankie, but remember, I grew up with some of them, and so they are my childhood friends. Some of them are easy to like because they're exciting and crazy and fun, but I don't hang out with them."

I think that was the last time I ever spoke to Frankie. He had been cutting my hair for about seven years at the time. What happened? I'll tell you.

Shortly after that last conversation with Frankie, I came into the office. I think it was on a Wednesday morning, and one of my secretaries came running up to me, almost in tears, because she knew Frankie very well and liked him. She said, "Did you hear what happened?"

I said, "Anne-Marie, what the hell are you talking about?" She said, "It happened last night."

"What happened last night?" I said as I was walking toward my office. I enter my office, turn on the lights, and begin looking at messages left for me the night before, as she tells me what happened.

Apparently, Frankie was in a bar on 101st Avenue, several blocks from my office, (not the same bar that Johnny Boy was in when he shot and killed a man in the bar.) He was having drinks and hanging out with some of the wise guys when he got into an argument with the bartender. The bartender insulted Frankie and either threw Frankie out of the bar or insulted him so that Frankie left. He insulted him in front of all his friends and some of the wise guys. Frankie went home, got a gun, came back, and shot and killed the bartender. I couldn't make this up if I tried. Almost déjà vu of what Johnny Boy had done a few years before.

It was unbelievable. I never thought Frankie could or would do such a thing. I think it was because he was hanging out too frequently with the wise guys. He just couldn't let himself be insulted that way and had to save face, but what a way to do it. Jump over the bar, get into a fistfight, that's one thing. But killing someone? I couldn't believe it. I didn't think he was capable of it. He was such a nonviolent person. I was in shock. I didn't know what to do.

I go back to the lunchroom to have a coffee and try to digest what happened when I get a call from Joe, Frankie's father. He asked to see me right away. I told him to come immediately to my office. He says he'll be there in five minutes. I call Ronnie. He doesn't know what happened. I told him. He is also in shock and can't believe it. He asked me, "What happened to Frankie?"

I said I don't know. I tell him Joe is on the way and we'll find out everything. He says he's coming as soon as he can. I ask him if this is a good idea. "This is a murder case, and you're an ADA in the homicide bureau."

He says he doesn't give a flying fuck. He will be there as soon as he can. A couple of minutes later, one of my secretaries comes in and tells me Joe is outside waiting to see me. I tell her to bring him right into my office and hold all calls. I ask her if I have any appointments, and she said, "Yes, but the first one starts after one, so you're okay."

Joe comes into my office. He looks at me and asks me if I know everything. I tell him what I know and tell him, "If you're going to tell me something I don't know, then I would like you to give me a retainer to represent you and possibly Frankie. I need that retainer so that everything you say to me afterwards is confidential, protected by the attorney-client privilege; so, I cannot repeat what you tell me to anyone."

He asked me, "How much of a retainer?" I told him, "Twenty dollars."

He looks at me, takes twenty dollars out of his pocket, gives it to me, and then hugs me.

I ask him if he would like a coffee or something before we start. He says, yes. I call in one of my secretaries, and she gets him coffee with some cream and two sugars. (It's incredible the nonsensical, unimportant things I remember sometimes.) He tells me pretty much what I heard. I asked him how many people were in the bar, and if he knew any of them who witnessed it. He said from what he was told, the bar was pretty crowded, and so he believes it was witnessed by a lot of people. I ask him about Frankie. He says, "After the shooting, Frankie disappeared, and I don't know where he is."

I look at him, he looks at me, and nothing further is said. As we are talking, Ronnie shows up, comes in, sees Joe, and walks over to him. For the first time, Joe sees Ronnie, breaks down, and starts to cry, hugging Ronnie.

The three of us start to chat. Since everything that Joe can tell us is not confidential, it's okay for Ronnie to sit in with me and him. He asks me, "If I find my son, what should I do?"

That's a tough question. The obvious answer is that he should turn himself in. I tell him that and also say, "I'm almost legally obligated to tell you that, but if it was my son, although I would do it, it would be a difficult thing to do as I am sure it's going to be for you."

He asked me what I think will happen if Frankie turns himself in. I tell him that considering how it happened and with all the witnesses, this is a case that cannot be won, and Frankie will go to jail for a long time. I tell him I think the District Attorney's Office will charge him with murder one since he had time to think about it, go home, get a gun, and come back. It seems like premeditated murder, and I think that's what the District Attorney's Office is going to charge him with.

I'm saying this as the lead assistant district attorney in the Queens District Attorney's office is sitting there. It was an awkward moment. Ronnie said nothing. Sal looked at him. Ronnie said nothing, but the look he gave Sal I think confirmed what I was telling him. He looked at both of us and said, "I guess my son's life is over." We were all silent for a moment.

I asked Joe when he had spoken to the police. He said, "They came almost in the middle of the night, looking for Frankie." Joe had a beautiful big apartment above the shop and so was sleeping with his wife when they came. When he answered the door, they told him they were looking for Frankie and what had happened. He said the sad thing about it was that one of the two cops who came was a customer of Frankie's. "Can you believe that? They were courteous and polite and told me how sorry they were that this happened. I thanked them for letting me know and told them I did not know where Frankie was. They said if I heard from Frankie to tell him to turn himself in. I told them that before I did anything, I wanted to speak with my attorney. Both of the cops were in plain clothes and obviously detectives, and one of them handed me his card."

I told Joe to keep in touch with me, and if he heard from Frankie, and Frankie decided to turn himself in to let me know, and I would make the necessary arrangements. The funny thing about it was that a great number of cops and the detectives and ADAs were all customers of either Frankie or one of his brothers. There were going to be a lot of ADAs other than Ronnie who were going to have to recuse themselves because either Frankie or one of his brothers was their barber, and they knew them personally. I also told Joe if he heard from Frankie, and Frankie decided not to turn himself in, there was nothing further I could do for him, but if he had any questions, to either call me or come in. I told him to tell his wife, who was a wonderful woman and cancer survivor and whom I knew well, how sorry I was.

After Joe left, Ronnie and I spoke for a while. I asked him what he thought, and he said, "If it was me, I would be in the wind." Because the likelihood was that he would spend the rest of his life in jail, and not in a minimum or medium security jail but possibly in Attica or some other relatively unpleasant prison. In all honesty, I would probably make the same choice, but I certainly could not tell that to Joe.

No one ever heard from Frankie again. Life went on. I continued to go to the barbershop, but now Gino, Frankie's younger brother, cut my hair. He was good, but nobody was as good as Frankie. I saw Joe often; we never spoke about Frankie again; it was as if Frankie had never existed. I couldn't ask Joe about Frankie because supposedly, Joe didn't know where he was and never saw him again, and if he did know where he was, then he was withholding that evidence from the police. The easier thing to do was just not to ask about Frankie, and so I didn't. Frankie's two brothers, Gino and Sal, ran the shop; with Gino taking over Frankie's back room.

Over time, I became pretty close with Gino and Sal, having represented them in different civil matters. They also had the same customers that Frankie had and again formed close relationships with a lot of the wise guys, Gino, the older of the two, basically taking over for Frankie. Gino would also go to John Gotti's club to give haircuts to John and his crew. Over time, I heard that they were both getting involved in some shady deals with some drug guys.

I spoke to Gino and Sal, telling them I heard they were dealing with some really lowlife dangerous drug dealers, and I hoped it wasn't true. I asked them if their father knew because I knew if their father knew about it, there would be holy hell to pay. You didn't fuck around with Joe. They both got very anxious and asked if I had spoken to Joe about it. I said, "No, I don't want to start any trouble between you and your father, but you know what your father would do and say if what I heard is true."

They both denied being involved in any drug deals but mentioned to me they had friends who had gotten involved and made more with one large deal than they made working for one year. I read between the lines, and the feeling I got was that they were involved. I warned them I had represented drug dealers and knew the money involved is huge, but so are the risks. I told him what a horrible lowlife type of business it was and to please not get involved.

We spoke for a while, and the feeling I got was that they were involved but did not want to become drug dealers and were looking to make one big hit and get out. They didn't tell me that, but that's the feeling I got after speaking to them. Since I couldn't prove anything, I didn't want to start a family row by telling Joe, and so I just butted out.

A couple of months after I had that talk, I was at home, getting ready to go to work. I used to get a few newspapers delivered to my house every morning: *The Wall Street Journal*, *The Post*, and *Newsday*. So, there I am, having breakfast, sipping a cup of coffee, and I grab the first newspaper; on the front page, there was a big picture of a barber chair. Slumped over the chair, apparently shot dead, was Gino. I was in shock. Bonnie was sitting across from me and saw the expression on my face and asked me what happened and if I was all right?

I showed her the newspaper. It was in two of the three papers, I believe. I read the story. Basically, the story said that Gino Cantone was shot and killed. The story went on about the barbershop and its history, mentioning that several years back, another member of the Cantone family, namely Frankie Cantone, had been involved in a murder and the circumstances of that murder. Once again, I was in shock. I liked the whole family so much and had grown very fond of Gino. Of course, the first person I called after speaking to Bonnie about it was Ronnie. I woke him up. He had just finished trying a case and was taking the morning off before starting to work on a vicious rape case that Jimmy, the head ADA, wanted him to try.

I asked him if he had read the morning papers yet. He said no. I told him about Gino. There was silence on the phone for a moment. He couldn't believe it either. We talked about it for a while, and I told him I was not sure what to do, but when I got to the office, I would call Joe to extend my condolences and ask him if there was anything I could do. He told me to keep in touch, and if I needed his help in any way to let him know.

A couple of hours later, as I walked into my office, the place was abuzz with the news, and of course, a couple of the lawyers and secretaries came up to me to find out if I had heard. I told them that I had read about it this morning, and as I was chatting with them, one of my secretaries who had been in the back lunchroom came up to me with a note and telephone number in her hand. Joe had called the first thing in the morning and wanted to see me right away. Since I normally did not take appointments in the morning, I was free and immediately called him back.

The first thing I said was, "Joe, I'm so sorry, I don't know what to say." He said, "Thank you, Bobby, I have to see you."

I said, "Of course."

He said, "I'll be there in a couple of hours. Right now, I have to take my wife to the doctor to get her some medication. She is hysterical." We made an arrangement for him to be at the office after eleven.

At around eleven o'clock that morning, my secretary buzzed me that Mr. Joe Cantone was here. I tell her to bring him right back to my office and then get us a couple of cups of coffee with milk and sugar. Joe comes into my office, and I can tell that he's had a rough night. Always well-dressed and dapper, this morning, he was dressed with a suit and black tie and kind of looked the same as always, except his shoulders were sloped a little and he looked exhausted.

We hugged each other but didn't say anything. We walked over to the couch in my office, and JoAnn, one of my secretaries, brought us the coffee. This was one time I didn't want to sit at my desk with all my diplomas behind me and him sit in front of me as a client. It was too sad, too impersonal. I wanted him to feel at home as if he was sitting with a friend who cared, not an attorney.

After having a sip of coffee, he started to tell me what happened. Apparently, the night before, Gino had received a phone call, asking for an early morning haircut appointment with him and also with Sal. I asked Joe, "Who called?"

He looked at me and shrugged his shoulders; from that, I knew that he knew, and I asked nothing further.

To this day, I don't know, but my best guess is that the person or persons that shot Gino were drug guys who had a lot of money but were not connected to the mob and who at that time did not permit their guys to deal in drugs. They were probably the same guys I had warned Gino and Sal about and whose names I didn't know. This is just a guess on my part. I could be wrong.

Joe told me that as bad as this was, it could have been much worse because Sal was supposed to be there, too; fortunately, Sal overslept and came late, and he's the one who first found Gino. Apparently, the people who killed Gino didn't want to hang around and wait for Sal. And so, the reason Sal was alive was because he overslept.

Joe said, "I think that they will come back looking for Sal, and it's just a matter of someone getting to them before they get to Sal." That's when I knew that Joe was just more than a mere barber shop owner. Someone getting to them? I didn't have to ask who that someone was.

He then laid this bombshell on me. He told me he had a beautiful home in Sicily with beautiful land, part of which was a farm, and that he wanted to sell everything here and move to Sicily because he didn't want to take a chance on anything happening to Sal. He told me he had intended to retire there a few years from now, but because of what just happened, he decided to leave right after Gino's funeral. He wanted me, as his attorney, to take care of all his affairs, to sell the business, and anything else that needed to be taken care of, including some other properties he owned.

We would then make arrangements as to how the money would be transferred to him. It was a big undertaking. There was a lot of money involved, and when it comes to money, Sicilians don't trust anyone but family. So, the fact that I was not family and was asked to do this was a big honor, and I knew it, and Joe knew I knew. I told Joe that, of course, I would take care of it. He said, "Your fee is whatever you think it should be."

Gino's funeral was an overflowing affair. It seems that the family knew everyone. Between his coworkers and their families, plus, of course, Joe's friends and family, plus half of Ozone Park, who were customers of the barbershop, and of course, half of the wise guys in Queens, it was quite an affair. Anyone who was anyone in Ozone Park was there.

Within a week after the funeral, Joe and his family were gone. We made arrangements to keep in touch, and I promised that once everything was concluded, I would come to Sicily and visit with them. You don't make promises to a Sicilian if you don't intend to keep them. I intended to keep that promise. After all, I am Sicilian, and a lot of my own relatives still live in Sicily; and so, I thought I could kill two birds with one stone, visit with Joe, and also get to see my family, whom I had never met. I corresponded with them on occasion, and they had constantly invited us to come visit with them. More about them later.

It took me several months to take care of Joe's estate. When everything was in order and the proceeds from the sale of everything were turned over to his accountants, who were family members, I wrote Joe a letter. I described everything I had done, what the proceeds were, what my fee was, and that per his instructions, everything had been turned over to his family accountants. A short time after I sent that letter, I got a call from Joe. He thanked me for everything and then wanted to know, as I had promised, when I would be coming to Sicily.

I told him I would have to talk to Bonnie. She and I and he and his wife had gone out to dinner several times, and he had been a guest in my home. He and his wife really liked Bonnie, as everyone does, and was happy that she would be coming with me. I told him I would get back to him within a week or so. He said OK and thanked me once again for everything that I had done.

That night, when I got home, I told Bon everything that had happened and that I had promised to go to Sicily to see Joe and his family when I had concluded taking care of everything for him. She said, "I can't go to Sicily."

I said, "Why not?"

She said, "There are too many Italians."

Very funny, Bon. We discussed when we could go and for how long, and then Bonnie came up with the bright idea of asking Ronnie and his latest girl-friend to come with us. I thought that was a great idea, and so right on the spot, I called Ronnie at home.

At the time, Ronnie was seeing a beautiful Italian girl, Allegra. She had been to Catholic grammar school, Catholic high school, and Catholic college, just as Ron and I had been. She was beautiful, funny, and just delightful to be around. In addition, she was very bright. I thought this could be it for Ronnie, but alas, it wasn't to be. Why? Ron hesitated to tell me. He says to me, "Bobby, I think she may be a sexual deviant.

I said, "Are you kidding? This girl's been to Catholic grammar school, high school, and college, how could that be?"

He says, "I think that Catholic upbringing repressed her sexually, and now she's become somewhat of a nutjob." Now Ronnie wasn't one to kiss and tell, especially about his girlfriends. I was one of the few along with Bonnie whom he confided in when he wasn't sure on how to proceed with one of his girlfriends.

I tell him, "Bonnie and I are just getting used to her, and we really like her. Are you sure you can't work things out with her? If it's not too personal, what the hell are you talking about anyway?"

He says, "Okay, I'll tell you about it, but get Bonnie on an extension. I don't want to have to do this twice."

I say, "Okay" and call and tell her to get on the extension as Ronnie is having some second thoughts about Allegra.

Bonnie gets on the phone and says, "Hi, Ronnie, I'm here." She says, "What's cooking with Allegra?"

Ronnie, always one to be cautious, reminds us not to say anything to anyone else, and the reason he hasn't mentioned this before is because he did not want to have us judge Allegra.

I tell him, "Ronnie, stop with all the drama, what happened?"

He said, "It all started one night when they were making out and about to have sex. She said, 'Ronnie, let's make love outside on the balcony.'" At the time,

Ronnie had a beautiful penthouse apartment (which as I mentioned before I, on occasion, helped subsidize). It had a four-and-a-half-foot wall that was flat, and it was about a half foot and a half wide.

"She says to me, 'Let's make love on the ledge.' I tell her the ledge is only a foot or so wide, and if we fall, we would fall eight stories to our death. She looks at me and says, 'I know. That's what makes it so exciting!' I'm thinking, *where did this come from?* She was so normal for a while, but as we got more familiar with each other, she started wanting to do these crazy things."

Both Bonnie and I are a little speechless. I say, "Ronnie, even though the ledge is flat, it would be so uncomfortable."

And he said, "She had a beach towel to put on the ledge so it would be more comfortable."

I thought about it and said, "Perhaps you should consider calling Creedmoor (a mental hospital)."

Bonnie said, "Stop, Bobby, this isn't funny." Bonnie asked Ron, "Are there any other things as crazy as this that you feel comfortable telling us about?"

He said, "There are several more, but I don't want to go into all of them.

I'll tell you about one more that really bothered me." Bonnie says, "Ronnie, only if you feel comfortable."

He says, "This one is so strange I have to ask you guys what you think." We say, "Okay."

He says, "One night a couple of weeks ago, she was over, and I was already in bed. It was late, and she was in the bathroom, getting ready to go to bed. She calls out from the bathroom, 'Ronnie, turn out the lights.'

"I say, 'Allegra, why do you want me to turn out the lights before you get into bed?'

"She says, 'Oh, Ronnie, just turn out the lights, I have a surprise.'

I'm thinking what now. But I turn out the lights. I hear her coming out of the bathroom and climbing over me to get into bed, but I feel instead of her having her normal pajamas, she felt like she was wearing some kind of coat. I say, 'What the hell is going on?' and turn on the lights, and there she is, wearing a full nun's habit with the headpiece on and only her face showing.

"I didn't know what to say. She says, 'Don't ask me how I got it, it's a long story. What do you think?' I'm speechless. She says, 'Come on, Ronnie, you were taught by the nuns, didn't you ever think that you would like to have had sex with one of them?'

"I say, 'With a nun? No, I never thought of having sex with one of my nun teachers.'

"She said, 'I always thought that most guys at some point or another wanted to screw one of the nuns who taught them.' She said, 'Come on, let's make love with me wearing my nun's habit.'

"I said, 'Absolutely not! I never thought about screwing a nun, and the mere idea of it turns me off.' Is that sick or what?"

I tell him, "I've seen worse."

Bonnie says, "This isn't funny, Bobby, this girl has some serious problems." I say, "Yes, but exciting and erotic ones."

And Ronnie says, "See, Bonnie? I can't talk to him." I start to laugh.

I tell him, "Ronnie, she seems like a delightful traveling companion for a trip Bonnie and I are going to take and we would like you and the charming Allegra to join us."

He says, "What trip?"

I tell him that I have finally settled Joe's business affairs, and as I promised him, I would go to Sicily to see him for a visit. I thought I would also get in touch with all of our cousins in Sicily and make arrangements to visit with them also. Joe's house was in the outskirts of Palermo, and our relatives lived in Catania, which was a several hour drive from Palermo. I thought we would visit with Joe first, spend several days there, and then drive to see our relatives in Catania and spend the rest of our time there.

Without hesitation, Ronnie loved the idea and said, "Count me in."

I said, "Bonnie and I will start looking for dates and get back to you."

He said, "Great." Then he said, "I have an idea. Let's call up Franca and Carlo and see if they would like to join us on the trip." If you recall, my cousin Franca Duval was an opera singer who was presently the star of the Folies Bergere, the world-famous show in Paris. She is living with her husband, Carlo Nell, who was a movie actor and had his own television show which at the time was one of the most popular TV shows in France. He was a comedian and singer, and Ronnie and I loved him and treated him as a third brother. He was often taken for one of our brothers. He was the same height and build and had the same fun-loving, irreverent, nutty take on life as we did. He was exciting, crazy, and fun to be around.

I would be remiss without taking a moment to tell you a little bit about him. My cousin Franca met him when she was a guest on his television show. He had a variety show. I believe it was every Saturday night, and he would sing, entertain, tell jokes, and have various guests on his show. Since Franca was at that time the star of the Folies Bergere, he invited her to be a guest on his show, immediately fell in love with her, and started to pursue her.

She wanted no part of him because he was a notorious playboy who I believe tried out for the French Olympic ski team; plus, he belonged to a soccer team that was well-known. I had a picture of him on skis high up in the air, and below him is a small ski lodge with people having coffee. He literally flew right over the ski lodge. It's hard to believe he could do something like that. Anyway, after dodging him for a while, Franca got sick with pneumonia and was hospitalized for several days. Guess who came to the hospital every day, twice a day, with flowers? You guessed it: Carlo. She says, "He just broke me down, Bobby."

And I said, "It was meant to be to see how great it all turned out." This is when they were already happily married for several years.

He was such an unusual and interesting character that I have to tell you a little more about him. His real name was Carlo Bartolo. He was not French but Italian, having been born in Italy to an Italian mother and father. This was just before the second world war and Mussolini was in power. Although he was too young to go into the army, somehow, he was drafted into what could be called pre-army training school. His parents knew that there was going to be a war, and they had relatives in Switzerland. They decided to flee Italy and moved to Switzerland.

Since he was in some type of pre-army school, he was not allowed to go. His parents told him they would come back for him after they settled in Switzerland. He still remembered all the drills and salutes he learned in that Italian school, and on stage, when he started to perform later in Paris, used to do them and make fun of them. He would raise his arm in a Hitler salute and say in Italian, "*Il fascista vince sempre,*" which means in English, "The fascists always win," and then make a gesture that basically said: fuck you. The French audiences loved it; I know. I was there. He had records of some of Mussolini's speeches. I don't know how he got them, but he had them and he would quote some of them to his audiences when he was doing one of his nightclub acts.

I remember part of one speech, and in Italian, it went like this, "*Non dormo tranquillamente finché non arriviamo al porto di* New York," which translated says, "I will not sleep tranquilly until I arrive at the port of New York," meaning he and the Italian army were going to invade the United States and he would not sleep tranquilly until he did so and arrived at the port of New York. Carlo and then the whole audience would break into uproarious laughter. He would end by giving the last lines of that speech which went like this: "*E dopo, E dopo aver volute vedere la bandiera Italiana in cima alla* Casa Bianca" which translated to: "And then, and then I want to see the Italian flag on top of the White House." This last line got the biggest laughs of all.

So, getting back to Carlo and that Italian school. He was there for almost a year and found out that his parents could not come back into Italy without being arrested. The war was just starting. He decided to run away from the school and hitchhike, jump on freight trains, and do whatever else he had to do to get to Switzerland. He was thirteen years old. He told me how he did it. It took him over a month. By the time he arrived in Switzerland, he was almost a living skeleton because he had to scrounge for food; he thinks he must have walked half the way, but he did it. I would listen to him for hours while he told Ronnie, me, and Bonnie those adventures on the road and getting to Switzerland. What a book that would be, and I once told him he should write it, but it seemed he never had the time.

He said he when he finally arrived in Switzerland, he miraculously found his parents. When his mother opened the door, she didn't recognize him; he had gotten so thin and looked horrible. The family rode out the war in Switzerland, and after the war, Carlo decided that he wanted to be in show business and knew the real opportunities in Europe were in Paris; so, at nineteen, he left home and moved to Paris. He had various jobs, but it seemed he could not get a break as far as show business was concerned. He tried to figure out how he would be noticed and given a shot in show business; and along the way he decided to save his money.

He then rented a helicopter that flew over parts of Paris, dangling from it. It was in the newspapers, and he got interviewed and, when asked what he did for a living, told the reporter he wanted to be in show business. Someone read the papers and gave him a small acting job, and from there, he started getting bigger parts in movies; then, he started to do a nightclub act, and eventually got his own TV show. When I visited him in Paris, at first his being famous was fun, and then after a while, it was a real pain. What do I mean? I mean while walking around Paris with him, he was constantly stopped to take pictures and autographs; and he always complied with the request. I once asked Carlo, "How do you do it? This is a real pain in the ass, and after a while, the thrill is gone, and it's not fun anymore."

He said, "Bobby, this is my job. This is how I make a living. This is my audience, and I can never turn them down." He said, "I never forgot how I got here; I remember the difficult times, and I will always be grateful to these people."

Occasionally, when we were walking around Paris and people asked him for his autograph or to take a picture, he would say something to them in French which, of course, I don't understand, and they would come and start asking me for my autograph. I asked Carlo, "What's going on?"

He said, "Just give them an autograph," which I did. When they left, I asked Carlo, "What's going on?"

He said, "I told them you were a famous American actor and director, and so they wanted your autograph."

"Carlo, see what I mean? I always told Franca you were crazier than me."

While in Paris, I forced him to take me to all the tourist spots which was an absolute pain in the ass for him, but he did it. I remember being on top of the Arc de Triomphe, taking pictures from there, when several policemen came up to me and him and started to speak in French to him. I didn't know what was going on, but he said to me, "Bobby, I'll be right back" and left. It turns out that they all wanted to take pictures with him and get his autograph, and so there he was on top of the Arc de Triomphe, taking pictures with the policemen. I don't know why, but when I think of all the things we did in Paris, that's what I remember. He truly was Ronnie's and my soulmate. It was incredible how all three of us were so much alike.

I remember the first time I met him, when Franca brought him home to New York to meet the family because they had decided to get married. Most of the family was there. We were having a big dinner for him. Ronnie and I had been at work, and he stopped by the office, and together we went over to my Aunt Sara's house. My Aunt Sara was Franca's mother and my mother's sister and my favorite aunt. She only had one child, Franca, and therefore, Ronnie and I became like sons to her.

Sometimes while working, I would get a call from Aunt Sara, saying, "Bobby, do you have time to come over?" She had made this special dish she knew I loved. She worked in Manhattan as a pattern maker and dress designer and, at the time, was making over fifty thousand dollars a year, quite a lot of money for the time. She was quite a special lady. So, we arrived at Aunt Sara's, and everybody was already sitting at the dining room table (because we were a little late). My mother and Aunt Sara and Franca were serving the first course, which was pasta. They saved two places for me and Ron, and as we sat down, Franca introduced us to Carlo who was sitting across the table.

We both said hello. His English at the time was pretty good and, of course, got better over time. Well, we all dug in and started eating and, while eating, started to chat with him. The first thing Ronnie asked him was, "How do you say *seal* in French? You know, the animal, seal."

Ronnie and I both had this little bit of ridiculous, useless information that the pronunciation of the word seal in French sounds like the word fuck. Carlo looked at Ronnie and didn't understand the question.

Ronnie asked him again slowly, "How do you pronounce *seal*? You know, the animal seal, in French?"

Carlo now understands the question and says, "Fuck," not knowing or realizing the meaning of the word in English.

Everyone looks up. Franca, in French, says Carlo, "What are you doing?"

He explained what Ronnie just asked him. She looks at Ronnie and me and laughingly says, "Bobby, Ronnie, don't start with him."

She then looks at Carlo and tells him what we just did. He looks at us with this look I will never forget. Almost like Curly of the Three Stooges, looking at some guy who was giving him a hard time, and saying, "Wise guys, hah!"

We, of course, exploded laughing, and he didn't know at first whether to be mad or not, but our laughter must have been contagious because he started laughing too. My mother, seeing what was going on as she was putting some more food on the table, looked at both Ronnie and me and says, "My two sons, my two educated dopes." Which of course caused us more laughter. Since my mother is standing right next to Ronnie, he gets up and gives her a huge bear hug.

Carlo sees this, and for some reason, I think that was the beginning of an incredible bond between the three of us. Although we didn't know it at the time, he was the exact same way with his mother. They were staying with my Aunt Sara for the summer, and my Aunt Sara's house was only a ten-minute bicycle ride to my office. So, while I was working, for exercise, Carlo would bicycle over to my office around lunchtime, and we would have lunch together. You can imagine my secretaries' reactions when meeting him. He was tall, well-built, handsome, with this incredible French accent, and of course, he was the ultimate flirt. They all fell in love with him. I would take him on occasion to Café Geo for some coffee and desserts, and because he was with me, they allowed him in and served him. When he rode his bicycle, the jersey he wore by pure accident was that of the Italian soccer team.

You can imagine his reception the first time he entered Café Geo with that shirt. Speaking perfect Italian, his first language, and upon seeing the television sets going with the Italian soccer team, he went nuts, telling everybody in the place that this guy and that guy is my friend and on and on. He was an immediate big hit at Café Geo and subsequently went there quite often.

On occasion, usually on a Saturday, I would go over to Aunt Sara's with my bicycle, and Carlo and I would ride to different places to have lunch. Sometimes Ronnie came with us. On one occasion that I remember vividly, we rode our bikes to Bloomingdale's Department Store which was a forty-five-minute bike ride. We would shop around the department store and then have lunch. He loved Bloomingdale's because in a way, it reminded him of some of the French stores he used to go to.

Of course, he would always stop to chat with different people. One time, as we were walking around in the perfume/cologne section of the store, he saw this beautiful woman who was working behind the perfume counter. He went over to her and tells her how beautiful she is, and he thinks he has fallen in love with her. He's saying this with a French accent, and she tells her coworker, "My god, do you hear his accent?" as she flirts right back at him.

He gets on one knee, tells her that he thinks he loves her, and then starts singing this French song, "Louise." It went something like this: "Every little breeze seems to whisper Louise, birds in the trees seem to whisper Louise, could it be that I love you, Louise?"

Well, as he is singing this song, a crowd of women start to gather around him, and now he has an audience as he goes into his second verse. Boy, was he a showman! I never until that moment realized just how incredibly talented, he was. He had women eating out of his hand. When he finished the song, there was a round of applause.

I want to tell you one last story about Carlo before getting back to my story about Frankie Cantone. It's about how Carlo met Bonnie. At the time, we had just graduated from law school, and Bonnie had moved into an apartment in the city with a roommate, Amy. I was still living at home. On a Saturday morning, I had made plans with Bonnie to go into the city and play tennis with her. She had been giving me lessons, and I had been getting better. Bonnie, before she started college, had been a nationally ranked player, and the only reason she didn't turn pro was that in those days, there were only amateurs, and therefore, it was hard to make a living at it. (This was before the amazing Billie Jean King came on the scene and was instrumental in getting title 1X passed, rewarding equal prize money for men and women athletes; additionally, title 1X gave girls the same opportunities to participate in team sports in school as the boys had.)

It's early Saturday morning, around eight-thirty, and Carlo comes bicycling over to my mother's house from Aunt Sara's, which is only five blocks away. He tells me, "Let's go bicycling."

I tell him, "I can't, I'm going into the city to play tennis." He says, "Who are you going to play tennis with?"

I tell him, "There's this girl I went to law school with who I really like, and I'm going to play tennis with her."

He says, "Bobby, can I come along? I love to play tennis." I said, "Carlo, can you play?"

And he says, "I'm not that good, but I do play."

Being the incredible athlete that he was in soccer and skiing, I knew he could probably play anything, and I thought Bonnie would like him and it would be a lot of fun, so I said sure. I tell him, "Let me get my stuff together. Throw your bicycle in the back of the car. I'll take you to Aunt Sara's to get changed." And off we go.

He says, "Great."

I had made plans to meet her at a beautiful tennis park on the east side next to the water. She had reserved a court.

We get to the park, and Bonnie is already there. As we were walking toward her, Carlo asked me, "Is that her?"

I said, "Yes."

He said, "Oh my god, she's beautiful."

Bonnie was about five-eight, thin, and stunning. He said, "Now I know why you really like her."

I said, "Carlo, it's more than just looks. She is really smart, has good values, and is a lot of fun to be with, you'll see."

As we walk to her, I give her my usual hug and kiss, and then turn to introduce Carlo. As I am introducing him, he grabs her hand, bows, and kisses it. Bonnie is taken aback for a moment as I hadn't told her he was coming with me.

But as he kissed her hand and started to speak, she immediately noticed the French accent and then realized who it was because I had been talking about him. She immediately liked him; it was hard not to. We chatted for a minute or two. Bonnie welcomed him, and then we discussed how we were going to play. "Are we going to do a threesome, two on one side, one on the other? Or hit one-on-one, taking turns?"

Carlo, not knowing that Bonnie is a pro, says to me in Italian, "Let me play a couple of games with her. I'll make it quick, and then we can really play and have some fun." I guess he assumed that as a girl, she probably couldn't play well, and anything he did in athletics he was serious about and made sure he could play any sport well.

Bonnie is wondering why he is speaking to me in Italian. I told her very quickly in English because if you spoke really quickly, he had a hard time understanding. You had to speak to him in a regular tone, a little slowly, and he understood. I said, speaking quickly so he couldn't understand, "Let's have some fun. I want you to blow him off the court."

She said to me, "Bobby, I don't want to do that."

I said, "Well, he wants to blow you off the court so that we can have a real game of tennis, just he and I."

She said, "Okay."

I tell Carlo slowly so that he can understand, "You play with her first." And then I say in Italian, "Make it quick, blow her off the court, so we can have a real game."

He gives me a wink like, "Okay," and off he and Bonnie go to play. I am sitting on the bench, watching. They warm up, and Bonnie is hitting the ball very high and softly to him, but he, being an athlete, notices that she's pretty well coordinated and says to me in Italian, "You know, she's really not that bad."

I say to him in Italian, "Make it quick, I want to play." He nods. Bonnie says to Carlo, "Why don't you serve first?"

He says, "Okay." He serves and gets the ball in, and Bonnie hits it softly to his backend. He gets it, then she hits it to his forehand, and he runs to get it and, in fact, gets it back, then she hits it to his backhand again and, before you know it, she has him running back and forth. Because he is such a great athlete and playing lots of soccer, he naturally has good footwork, and because he was in such great shape, he kept on getting the ball back. Finally, Bonnie decides to put the ball away and crushes it. First point is hers.

He gives me a look, but I assume he thought it was just luck. At the fourth point, she had won the previous three and had him running back and forth and back and forth and finally again smashes the ball and puts it away. He is now on one knee, trying to catch his breath, looks at her, then looks at me, and says, "Bobby, you son of a bitch!" as I am rolling around laughing. He finally caught on.

That was it for Carlo. Besides being beautiful and smart, she was a great athlete; for him, that was the icing on the cake, and from that moment on, he adored her.

So now getting back to my phone call with Ronnie. We both decide it's a great idea to ask Franca and Carlo to meet us in Italy if they can. They both speak perfect Italian, and of course, it was always fun to be with them. Both of them were well known in Italy. Franca, an opera star who sang at La Scala, in Milan, the most famous opera house in the world, was known throughout Europe. We decide to make the call, and Ronnie says he'll do it and get back to me later that day as there is a six-hour time difference between New York and Paris. That evening, Ronnie calls and tells me he spoke to both Carlo and Franca, and they love the idea and ask to give them the dates when we intend to go.

We finally all agreed on a date, which was at the beginning of July. Ronnie, Bonnie, myself, and Allegra (yes, Allegra, as Ronnie has somehow come to terms with her unusual sexual proclivities as her sweetness, fun to be around, and incredible smarts have outweighed her mild deviant leanings). Besides, Bonnie and I just loved having her around. Our plan is to meet Carlo and Franca in Sicily on the third day of July. Our plane from the United States would be arriving at one o'clock, Italian time, and Carlo and Franca's plane would be arriving one hour before if all went well.

We notified Joe Cantone and our cousins in Sicily when we would be arriving. We were going to meet Joe at the airport because he insisted upon meeting us there. Our initial plan was to go to our hotel, check in, get comfortable, and then meet with him. He had other plans, and so we agreed to meet him at the airport. We were meeting him in Palermo, intending to spend several days there before going cross-country to Catania to visit with our cousins before returning home.

The day finally came, and off we went, excited and looking forward to our trip. There's a stopover in Rome, and we finally land in Palermo at almost exactly one o'clock, on time as scheduled. As we deplane and walk into the airport terminal, there waiting for us is Joe and his whole family. There must've been ten people. His brother, who was a college professor at the University of Palermo—at least I think it was the University of Palermo—spoke perfect

English and was an absolute delight to be around for the time we spent in Palermo.

When I first saw Joe, he looked concerned. He said there was a kidnapping at the airport, and he was concerned that maybe it could have been us as, we are, in some Italian eyes, rich, American tourists. I was touched by his concern. Everyone is chatting away as everyone knows each other; even Allegra has met Joe a couple of times. He, however, had never met Carlo and Franca. I had mentioned them to Joe when we were making arrangements to visit so he knew that my cousins were coming and asked me where they were. I told him I had no idea. They were supposed to arrive an hour or so from Paris before we did.

He said, "Let me search around and see if I can find them."

I said, "Their names are Carlo and Franca Nell."

He speaks to a couple of people in uniform who work at the airport, and off they go. About ten minutes later, as we were chatting, waiting around for Carlo and Franca, I heard in the distance a loud voice that could be none other than Carlo. He and Franca were walking toward us, chatting away with the people who Joe had sent to find them. We are happy to see them and are hugging and kissing each other when I realize I have not yet introduced them to Joe and his family and friends. After all the introductions were made, we discussed what to do next. We decided that first we should rent a car and then go to our hotel to unpack, maybe take a short nap, then freshen up as we were going to Joe's for dinner.

Around four o'clock that afternoon, after taking a nap and showering and shaving, I decided to go downstairs and look around. Bonnie was still napping. As I'm walking through the lobby, I see Carlo already up and about, chatting with some of the hotel employees. I tell Carlo, "Let's take a walk around." I had to go to the car we rented because I had left my sunglasses in it. The car was parked almost a block away as getting a parking space in Palermo was almost as bad as trying to find one in New York City.

As we were walking back toward the hotel, I noticed right in front of the hotel, there is a coffee stand that also sells cigarettes, magazines, newspapers, and the most delicious cappuccino and espresso coffee which they sell in small paper cups. There are two people behind the counter. One is an attractive woman in her forties, who is serving customers. The other is an older gentleman I would say in his fifties, who is sitting in the corner, reading the sports section of the newspaper. He was reading about the Italian soccer team, and Carlo, seeing this, immediately goes up to him. He tells him in Italian "I follow all the soccer teams from England's famous Manchester United to the Sicilian soccer team."

They start talking, and an immediate connection ensues. I can see right away that this gentleman likes Carlo. After chatting about soccer, he asks me where I'm from. He says, "I can tell you're American."

I tell them, "New York."

He says, "But you speak Italian."

I tell him my mother was born in Catania and my father was born in the United States, but his family came from Palermo. Before you know it, we were engrossed in conversation, drinking the delicious cappuccinos.

There is a reason I am telling you about this gentleman which I will get to shortly. As we're chatting, I start to complain about the parking and that it's worse than New York City and that we had to park almost a block away and we were lucky to get a parking spot. He asked me how long we are staying in Palermo, and I told them five days. He says, "Park your car right next to my newsstand, and nobody will bother you."

I tell him, "Next to your newsstand is a no parking zone." He says, "Don't worry about it, just park here."

I thank him and run and get the car and pull it into the no parking zone right next to his newsstand.

I noticed that the streets are blocked off, leaving only the main street fully open, and as I am wondering why, I hear this incredible sound like a shushing sound; it got louder and louder, and finally I looked down the street and I see the most incredible sight. There must be over one hundred bikes coming toward us. All the bicyclists were dressed in bright red and green and yellow racing uniforms with numbers on their sleeves and helmets. They were actually in a race going through downtown Palermo, and the race would finish about seven that evening.

They were bunched tightly together, and the sound they made was just unforgettable. They must have been going forty or fifty miles an hour, and within a minute, they passed us. I asked the owner of the newsstand, whose name I found out was Sal, what was going on, and he told me, "You have come during the Palermo Grand Touring Bicycle Race" as I remember it. The race ended at seven o'clock that evening, just as Joe was going to pick us up to take us to his place for dinner. I thought, *When I get back to the room, I'll call Joe*, whose phone number he gave me, *and tell him about the race*. And when he came at seven, I'd ask, "Could we hang out to see the end of the race before having dinner?"

He said, "Sure, I'll tell my wife that we will be eating at eight instead of seven-thirty." Joe told me, "It is something to see and that he forgot about, but was happy I reminded him he likes to see the end of the race also."

The race was something to see. There was a big stand set up with a band on it and several officials wearing ribbons, and as the winner and runners-up came up to receive their medals, the band played each time, and each one of them gave a little speech. It was really an incredible start to our stay in Sicily.

Then off we went, following Joe to his home, which was on the outskirts of town, I would say a couple of miles away. His home was like a mini mansion on a few of acres of land with all kinds of fruit trees and vegetables growing in the back. It was totally fenced in and was quite impressive. There was a big dining room table that seated about eighteen people, set up with the most beautiful China and crystal glasses

Besides the six of us, there was Joe, his family with his son and wife, his brother and his wife and daughters, and cousins made up the other twelve chairs. It was wonderful. The food was literally out of this world. Almost all the vegetables were grown right on his two acres. The tomatoes tasted like they were from another world, like when I was a child; they were simply indescribably delicious. Dinner lasted until almost one in the morning, and by the time we were leaving, we were so full we could hardly move, a typical Italian festive dinner.

We did a lot of touring around Palermo. Every morning, when we left the hotel, Sal, the owner of the coffee newsstand, would greet us, and we'd always have a coffee with him, read some of the local newspapers, and chat for a while before Bonnie and the girls came down. It was great to have our car parked right in front of our hotel every day, and we always thanked Sal who waved us off with a, "no problem".

When Ronnie and I were small, my father would take us to Manhattan from Ozone Park to this little Italian restaurant that he loved on Second Avenue, downtown. I don't recall the name of it, but my father loved it. Now my father was a typical American, born in Manhattan, and lived there until he married my mother and moved to Ozone Park. This little Italian restaurant was famous for a sandwich that was called a "Wastell," which both Ronnie and I loved. It was made on this delicious Italian bun with a couple of different kinds of Italian cheese, including ricotta, and some meat, not hamburger meat but sliced meat that we thought was steak. We later found out it was not.

The sandwich was sticky, juicy, and just delicious. One time, when we were at the restaurant, my father ordered something he had never ordered before. Our sandwiches were delivered first, and as we were eating, they brought out this big covered tray. They put it on the table, removed the cover, and what we saw was so horrible that we dropped our sandwiches and ran out of the store. My father had to come running after us to bring us back. We said we would not go in; we were too frightened. My father said, "Okay I'll return the *testa di agnello cotta*," the translation of which is the cooked lamb's head.

The eyes were still in its head and the tongue was hanging out. Apparently, it was an Italian delicacy. My father, being an American, we never thought he would eat something like that, but both his parents were from Italy, and they cooked it at home, and he got used to it. My mother never cooked it, so this was a first for us.

The reason I'm telling you about this sandwich, the "Wastell," is because it came from Palermo. In fact, it was invented in Palermo and was over a hundred years old. The reason it did not become a sensation in the United States, like pizza, was because we later found out that the meat used was cooked lamb's lung. The simple thing to have done was to change the meat to something else like beef, and perhaps it would've been a sensation like pizza, but the old Italians were traditionalists, and they said changing the meat would not make the sandwich taste the same, and they wouldn't do it.

When we finally found out about the meat, we continued to eat it as we were so used to it that it didn't matter. I now understood how my father could eat lamb's head. You get used to something, it's delicious, and you just don't get grossed out. And now here in Sicily, we were looking for the store that actually invented it over a hundred years ago; and it was famous and still in business.

The first three days, we looked for it and couldn't find it. Finally, we decided to start asking around. It turns out that everyone knew about it, but the name of the restaurant was different, and when we finally described the sandwich, the clerk behind the desk in our hotel told us where it was, which was right around the corner at the end of the block. I don't remember its name. I do remember running there with Ronnie as the girls were not interested in the sandwich after we told them what was in it, so it was just Ronnie and I. Carlo did not come with us because the sandwich had cheese in it, and Carlo was deathly allergic to cheese. The sandwich was delicious but not as good as they made it in New York City.

Speaking of cheese, I want to tell you about a little incident that happened as we were walking around Palermo, going in and out of different stores. Ron, I, and Carlo would walk into a store, browse around, and then leave. As we are walking down the street, Ron sees a food store and opens the door and walks in, followed by me and Carlo, Carlo the last one to enter the store. It turns out to be a cheese store. Cheese or just the smell of it made Carlo nauseous.

Ronnie and I smell the cheese and quickly turn around and walk out. Carlo, the last one in, smells the cheese and turns to make a quick dash out of the store. The problem is that Ronnie and I are outside of the store, holding the door so he can't go out. He's pushing to get out, and the two of us are pushing to keep him in, and he looks like he's in a gas chamber. Finally, after a moment or two, we relent and let him out. He is pissed off at us at the same time that we are convulsing with laughter. We literally fell to the ground, laughing so hard, and he stands over us, and as we continue to laugh, he finally starts to laugh also. It was just one of those moments that I'll never forget.

Our stay in Palermo was finally coming to an end, and the day before we were ready to leave, Joe comes by and picks me up, just me, as we are going to see the Italian attorney who is handling all of Joe's legal affairs here in Sicily, and he has some questions for me regarding the sales of some of his property and the estate in general.

As we are walking to his lawyer's office, I get a funny sense of what is going on because as we are walking down the street toward the office, everyone seems to know him, bows their heads, and greets him. A couple of the men who he seems to know come up to him and grab his hand and bow so low they are almost kissing his hand. As we walk on, I look at him, and I notice he glances over at me, but nothing is said. Finally, the moment is so obvious that as we are walking, he says, "These are poor people, and I have helped a lot of them out in different ways, and that's why they're so respectful."

I nod and say nothing. What I think is it is more than just paying their respects to a generous man. I say nothing more to him as we enter his attorney's office.

The lawyer's office is very impressive with a big mahogany desk, leather chairs, lots of Italian law books on the wall, and several people coming and going. Two of them have desks in the outer office with diplomas behind them, indicating they are notary publics, which in Sicily is a big deal. The others, I assume, are his secretaries. As we walk in, the lawyer comes up to me very respectfully, shakes my hand, and says, "Doctor, I am so happy to meet you. I've heard so much about you." In Italy, if you are an attorney, you are referred to as a "Doctor." In America, when you graduate from law school, you get what is called a Juris Doctor, which basically means a doctor of law, but are not referred to or called Doctor but are called Counselor or lawyer or attorney, even though you have a doctor's degree. In Italy, if you have any kind of doctor's degree, you're called Doctor.

We start to chat in English as his English is better than my Italian, although every day that I am in Italy, my Italian is getting better and better. He tells me he is so surprised that for such an accomplished lawyer (Joe must've told him I was a pretty good lawyer), I was so young. I thanked him for the compliment, and he goes on to tell me, "I hear you come from an accomplished family as your wife and brothers are also attorneys and that your twin brother is an ADA in the homicide bureau in New York City." To him, that was quite impressive. Joe must have given him a rundown about me and my family as in Sicily, it's very important who you are and where you come from and who your family is. They are very self-conscious of family and heritage and background.

In Italy, at least as far as I could ascertain, there appeared to be a class system. There is the upper class, consisting of the educated and wealthy, and then the middle class consisting of most working people, and the lower class consisting of unskilled workers such as laborers. But, in Italy, as far as I could determine, the poor or underprivileged were deferential to the educated and the wealthy. I didn't know the reason…

I thanked him for his compliments, and we got down to business. I told him exactly what I had done and what was left to be done, which was very little. He asked me pointed questions. This guy was sharp and knew his stuff. I answered them, I guess to his satisfaction, because the next thing I knew, we were going to a café for coffee and some delicious pastries. Oh my god, how could they make such delicious baked goods? I tasted nothing like this in America and told Joe that. He told me, "Bobby, it's the ingredients. The fruit which is grown with this rich soil just makes everything taste different and better." He was right.

The night before leaving, we had another fantastic dinner at Joe's home with his family. Nothing was ever mentioned of Frankie. I knew better than to ask, and he knew better than to tell me. We all said our tearful goodbyes, although I knew I would still be dealing with Joe to settle up the final little things regarding the estate. I told him I would be speaking to him in a couple of weeks after I returned home. We all hugged and kissed each other and said farewell. It was kind of tearful because we all knew we would probably never see each other again.

The next morning, we all packed and got into our big car which fit six comfortably, with luggage. I don't remember what kind of car it was; just that it was like a huge station wagon. Carlo and I were the first one's downstairs, and as we walked over to the coffee, cigarette, and magazine stand, Sal the owner was there. We thanked him so much for being so kind to us and watching our car and offered to give him a hundred dollars; we would have had to pay a lot more than that if we had to park in a garage.

He raised his hand and thanked us for the offer but said, "No, thank you, that isn't necessary."

We thanked him again, and he said the coffee that we were now drinking was on him. We thanked him again for his kindness and said that if we were ever back in Italy, we would insist that he let us take him out to dinner. He said, "That's a deal." He knew we were headed toward Catania and said, "Drive safely, and God bless you all."

Now before I describe our trip to see my relatives in Catania, let me tell you a little bit about Sal. What I'm about to tell you happened about six months after we were back from Italy during Christmas time, when Carlo and Franca came from Paris as they did every year, to spend the Christmas holidays with us, their family.

We are all at Aunt Sara's. It was a Wednesday night when Carlo and Franca flew in from Paris. My mother and Aunts Sara and Mary and my cousins Olga and Cora had prepared, I think, a five-course meal. The Christmas tree was up, Christmas music was playing, and we were all in great spirits. Franca and Carlo finally arrived, and after all the hugs and kissing and greetings, Carlo had something very exciting he wanted to tell Ronnie and me. So, we go to the kitchen table, and Carlo takes out a French newspaper from his carry-on bag.

As we we're looking at it, he opened it to the middle page, and there, on both sides of the page in color, are several different pictures; pictures of lots of policemen surrounding someone, pictures of a coffee/newsstand, pictures of different people, but the main picture was a picture of this man in handcuffs. Ronnie and I are looking and looking, but all the writing is in French. We can't read it and can only look at the pictures. We tell Carlo, "What's going on? What is this?"

He says, "Look closely."

Ronnie and I look really closely. We tell Carlo we still don't get it. He says, "The man they are leading away with all the policemen around him is the head of the Italian Mafia in Sicily."

We're looking. "He looks familiar." Carlo says, "Look closely at him."

Ron and I are looking closely, still not sure who this guy was. Suddenly, Ronnie says, "Wait a minute, wait a minute, I know that coffee/cigarettes stand."

Carlo says, "Now you're getting it. Now look closely at the man again."

I looked really closely, and then I was in total shock. I said, "Carlo, is that guy Sal from the coffee stand?"

Ronnie looks again and says, "Yeah, that's him."

We still don't get the connection. Then Carlo tells us that Sal, the owner of the cigarette/coffee stand that we became friendly with, the guy who told us to park our car next to his stand, the guy we offered the one hundred dollars to when we left for being so great with us—that guy was actually the head of the entire, Italian Mafia in Italy. They finally got him. "They are taking him to a special island surrounded by two hundred guards just for him. That's how dangerous they consider him."

Ronnie and I are in total shock. We can't believe it, but the more we look at him, the more we recognize him. Whenever we spoke with him at the coffee/ newsstand, he had glasses on and was dressed with an old shirt and a pair of trousers, nothing fancy. He was so nice to us. He said, "God bless you" when we left. How could this guy be the head of the Italian Mafia?

Carlo says, "Apparently, he was at that stand for a long time, and nobody ever recognized him. Or if they did, they didn't say anything because I think their life wouldn't be worth much if they did."

Carlo starts to read the article, and it says the reason he was able to work out of that coffee/newsstand for all that time was because he was not frequently photographed and known only by a select group of people. He had never been in jail, and he ran the Mafia very quietly and was not photographed often. "And you're right, he doesn't quite look the same as when he was at that coffee stand. At the stand, he kind of slouched around. In these pictures, he is walking upright, looking straight ahead." But the more we looked, the more we realized it was our Sal from the coffee/newspaper stand.

Carlo now starts to read the newspaper, going slowly as he has to convert it from French to English. "It says he was captured at his cousin's house late one evening from a tip. The man who gave the tip received a big reward and has since left the country under a new name." He continues to read the article. "It says they took him to the courthouse with around two hundred policemen guarding him. He had a lawyer. No bail was set for him, and they were bringing him to a special island where he would be the only prisoner until his trial and would have a contingent of a couple of hundred guards as they were concerned that the Mafia might try to storm the place where he was incarcerated and get him out.

"Apparently, he was respected by the whole Mafia. He was known as a just man who treated all those who worked with him fairly. It seemed he had no bad habits, didn't gamble, cared little for money, and so all those who worked for him shared in all the money the Mafia was making to a greater degree than ever before, and the article says that was one of the main reasons why everyone was so loyal to him. While he was head of the Mafia everybody was making money.

He kept an extremely low profile, kept out of the news, and therefore, there was no great urgency to get him. Things had quieted down in Sicily, although it was said that he was responsible for over fifty murders. The police were not actively looking for him as things were quiet for a while, but when he fell into their laps with this tip, of course, they pounced."

Carlo continued to read, and he would read it in French first and then start to laugh, and we would say, "Carlo, what happened?

Why are you laughing?" And then he would translate for us to English.

It seems when they started to question him before his attorneys arrived, he answered the questions. So, Carlo starts reading the questions that were asked and his answers. Some of the question and answers that I recall went like this:

Q. Are you the head of the Italian Mafia?

A. Me? I'm a simple farmer.

Q. We searched your farm and found machine guns and all types of rifles and handguns. Why do you need all of these guns?

A. I like to go hunting and shoot a lot of birds.

Q. We have searched your home and found bank accounts and records from several different countries, including Switzerland, where the amounts are in the millions of dollars. How do you explain that?

A. Really? Thank God, who was so kind as to leave me all this money?

Carlo read on and on. I don't remember all the questions and answers, but I do remember that as he read them, we were laughing. I remember telling Carlo, "He had all this money all over the place, and yet he was known for generously sharing the wealth with his people." Some parts of the article that Carlo read to us mentioned that he had these incredible accountants who took care of all his money, and he probably really wasn't aware of how much money he actually had.

The man had a farm with over a hundred acres of land, but the farm was very modest, and in taste and appearance, so was he. Carlo said, "Can you imagine the amount of money that the Mafia makes if this guy can accumulate that kind of wealth and still give away so much of it? He was a hero and a legend to his men."

I remember that news of his arrest made it to the papers in the United States, but the articles were not front-page news as they were in France and Italy, and I eventually lost track of what happened to him.

So now to our trip from Palermo to Catania to visit my relatives. As we are traveling along the main highway from one city to the other, there are some stops where you can purchase food and use the bathroom facilities. There were also some stops where you could pull your car over to rest, and those stops had these little restaurants that were legendary. They were very small affairs with only outdoor seating. So, basically, the restaurant itself was just the kitchen where they cooked. You walked up and ordered your food, and then the food was brought to your table. Kind of like the food trucks we have in America, except instead of it being a truck, it was a small building that basically was the kitchen.

It was mom and pop run, with a couple of kids who would bring the food you ordered. The reason I'm telling you about this is because we did stop to eat at one of these small places, and the food was wonderful, as good as any of the best Italian restaurants I've ever eaten in New York. I couldn't believe it. Even Carlo was raving about it. The menu was written in Italian on a board that hung on the building. There were a couple of pasta dishes, a couple of meat dishes, and a couple of salads. There was also one soup of the day. I remember I ordered a pasta dish that was served simply with a little pasta sauce, ricotta, and some grated cheese on top. It was incredible.

Something else that I specifically recall was that as we traveled along the roadway, which was beautiful and well-maintained, we would get this incredible smell of lemons, and if you looked at both sides of the road, there were lemon trees literally up to the sky; then you traveled further and were among orange trees with the same incredible smell of oranges. It was just remarkable how they cultivated every inch of land and made it so beautiful.

We finally arrived midafternoon, checked into our hotel, freshened up, and then decided to meet downstairs and go for a walk around the city. The stores were just opening up. Apparently, they close from one to four, at which time they have their main meal of the day and then take a nap. Just like in Spain, where they have the siesta. At four o'clock, they go back to work and generally work until seven.

They then go home to freshen up and have a very light dinner, if you could call it that. Generally, it consisted of fruit, some pastries, and coffee, similar to a dessert. After that, they generally went out to the cafés where music and musicians were always playing and sat around and listened to the music and talked and had a drink or some coffee. This usually lasted until about eleven in the evening when they slowly started to leave.

I thought it was an incredible way to spend your life. They didn't come home from work, eat dinner, watch TV, and go to bed. In my judgment, their life was much richer and more fulfilling. Of course, they had the advantage of beautiful weather all year long that's just me and my way of thinking.

Before going out to shop, we called our cousins who were waiting for a phone call. They knew where our hotel was and told us they would be there at around seven. At around six, we all took a nap; it had been a long day, and made plans to meet at our hotel at seven that evening.

At a little after seven, my cousins arrived. There were seven or eight of them, men and women. They were all unusually tall for Italians as at that time, I think the average height of an Italian male was about five-eight or nine. My cousins were at least six feet tall, elegant, thin, and bilingual. Their wives were also tall, pretty, and for the most part, bilingual. It was like a storm coming through the lobby. They had been looking forward to meeting us for so long and were warm and gracious, hugging and kissing all of us. It was really heartwarming. I was almost in tears by their warmth and good spirit.

Of course, they knew Carlo and Franca as they had been to Paris to see Carlo do his TV show and also to one of his nightclubs shows. They had gone to the Follies to see Franca and, of course, were blown away by her as most people were. She was beautiful and she had the most incredible voice you've ever heard.

I was surprised by how sophisticated they were. They had an air about them that I couldn't put my finger on at first, but as I got to know them, I realized this air came because they were well traveled, were all wealthy, educated, and either owned successful businesses or were professionals.

The richest of all was my cousin Gintina. She and her husband, Sergio (who was my actual blood relative), owned the company that owned the water rights for the city of Catania. Talk about being rich. They had several homes but mostly lived in this duplex apartment that was located on a magnificent street that had special street lights, kind of like the Fifth Avenue of New York. It was the most beautiful and biggest apartment I had ever been in.

The two floors together must have been over six thousand feet. We had dinner there that evening, and it was magical. They had servants coming and going, all of whom were wearing clothes you would see waiters and waitresses wear at a fancy restaurant. For the several days we were there, we had dinner every night instead of midday because we were on vacation, and they were taking us sightseeing every day. The six of us met for breakfast in the morning, with Franca always being late and Carlo giving her a hard time for being late. Ron and I would tell Carlo to leave her alone. We always defended her, telling him after all, "Il sangue e sangue," which translated means blood is blood, and Franca was our blood cousin. He would say with all the fancy education and big shot lawyer stuff, "In the end, you're both Sicilian." In truth, we loved him as much as her.

After breakfast, we would usually hang around and get some sun, then go swimming. In the afternoon, my cousins would pick us up, and off we go to a place or site we've never seen before. One of my cousins, Nino, was a well known doctor who had a love of sports cars and had several Ferraris. At the time, I had a couple of cars, and one of them was a Porsche Turbo, and so we would argue over which was the better car. He said to me, "Bobby, let me take you for a ride in one of my Ferraris, and you tell me what you think."

He took me down these narrow streets where you could barely stick your arms out of both windows without touching the buildings, going eighty miles an hour. I thought, *this rather ritzy doctor is truly nuts*, and I told him so. He laughed, then pulled over and jumped out of the car and said, "You drive."

I had never driven a Ferrari before; it was a manual six speed. My god, what fun! I had the car up to 105 miles an hour on an open roadway, and Nino was bored and said, "Open her up already, Bobby!"

That's when I knew I would never be a racecar driver. One of my other cousins was an attorney, and I asked him if he was in private practice or worked for a law firm. He said no the attorney general. I didn't get it. While we were having this conversation, we were interrupted by another cousin, so I asked my other cousins where Sergio practices law. "Does he work in the attorney general's office?"

He said, "No, he doesn't work for the Attorney General, he is the Attorney General."

I said, "He's the Attorney General of Sicily?"

He said, "No, he is the Attorney General for all of Italy."

He was only in his late thirties; I couldn't believe it. And so all of my cousins were somewhat nuts, like Ronnie and me; all tall like Ronnie and me; and all quite accomplished and sophisticated, unlike Ronnie and me. Sergio spent half the night speaking with Ronnie as he knew Ronnie was a trial lawyer and tried murder cases in New York City, which to him was the pinnacle of practicing law the major leagues. He was just so interested in everything Ronnie had to say. Our last night in Catania was one of the most magical nights

I've ever had in my life. My cousins picked us up around eight o'clock. There were twelve of them, and off we went. We drove for about twenty-five minutes when we came to this small little fishing town. I don't remember its name.

All the stores were closed. Basically, this was one of those towns where everything shut down at closing. My cousins parked the cars on the street and then walked over to this closed fish store. They knocked on the front door, and after a moment, the back door opened in the store, and we could see the lights on in the kitchen with several people working. Someone came to the front door and opened it and turned on all the lights in the restaurant and greeted my cousin warmly with a kiss on both cheeks. They were speaking Italian so rapidly that I couldn't really understand what they were saying.

A few moments later, people started coming out of the restaurant with long tables and chairs, and in a few more minutes, in the middle of the street, there was this long table that would probably accommodate twenty people; it was set with tablecloths and silverware and candles. It was unbelievable. And then a three-piece band came out and started playing these beautiful Italian songs.

The six of us were in total shock. We had never seen anything like this. This street we were on was closed down, and as we were all chatting, a couple of my cousins started dancing, and shortly thereafter, the food started coming out.

Apparently, they had been preparing for hours for this dinner. Well, we had dinner on the street in this most beautiful town on the water. Between dining and dancing in the beautiful summer Italian night, it was truly magical. How in the world did my cousins plan this? I have no idea. The next morning, at around eleven o'clock, we had to leave to go to Palermo where we would be catching a flight to Rome and then New York.

My cousins showed up at our hotel shortly before we were to leave. We didn't know what to do or how to thank them. In the five days we had been there, we all felt such a close connection to them. They were our family, they were our blood relatives, and I felt there was something special about that. I don't think there was a dry eye in the crowd as we hugged and kissed each other. I think part of it was that everyone knew there was a chance we would never see each other again, although they promised to come to New York and be our guest, and we promised to come back and visit them again.

When we got to Rome, there was another tearful parting as Franca and Carlo were catching a plane from Rome to Paris, and we were catching a plane from Rome to New York. As usual, Franca, who was such a soft touch, started to hug Ronnie and Bonnie and me and crying. Carlo looked at her, almost annoyed, but not really, and said, "Are you going to start?" He knew her. He knew how important we were to her. We were her family.

In Paris, she was very well known and had lots of friends, but we were her family. It was different. I remember when we were eight or nine years old. Franca was like a big sister to me and Ronnie. I remember her taking us to a show in Manhattan, and as she walked down the street, all these people, especially men, would look at her, literally stare at her. Ronnie would say, "Franca, do you know these people?"

And she would smile and say no. We would ask, "Why are they all staring at you?"

And she would say, "I don't know. You got me."

Little did we understand that they were staring at her because she was incredibly beautiful. You would never know it from her. I guess she just accepted it as part of her life and didn't think about it too much.

Bonnie, of course, had been a big hit with my cousins. They knew she was an accomplished tennis player, and they all loved sports; and of course, her being an attorney was the icing on the cake because as I said before, they were a little class conscious. That was just the way it was in Italy, different from America.

I remember one incident with Bonnie and my cousins as we were walking down this beautiful street in a small Italian village. There were three churches on that street alone, all being repaired. Bonnie remarked to one of my cousins, this does not look like a prosperous town, and yet there are three churches within two blocks, all being repaired. He looked at her and said, "You're not Catholic, are you?"

I said, "Bonnie, don't start." But he looked at her once again, and he, being a university student, agreed with her. She said, "Basically, I think that they should stop spending money fixing churches and help the people."

A couple of days after I got home, I called Joe Cantone and told him that I had completed everything and had sent everything to his lawyer in Palermo. I thanked him once again for being such a generous host. He thanked me for everything I had done for him and promised to call me when he visited New York. I never saw him again. He never came back to New York, but every Christmas, I would get a lovely card from him and his wife.

Donald-Tommi-Stephen

After Bonnie and I were married, we moved into a great apartment in an area of Queens, New York, called Jamaica Estates. The street was Wexford Terrace. I had just begun my law practice, and Bonnie was working in Queens County criminal court for the Legal Aid Society. I was already starting to do okay, and Bon was making a decent salary. We made big plans. That summer, we were going to Europe, and in the winter, we were going on a vacation to the Caribbean.

We were married in February of that year and went to the Bahamas for our honeymoon. While in the Bahamas, our first day there, we discussed having a family sometime in the future. Bonnie said to me, "Bobby, do you think it's so easy to have a child? My best friend, Amy, has been trying for three years. I am already twenty-eight years old. It could take years. I'm not going to get pregnant so quickly.

I said, "You're probably right." So, we decided to leave it in the hands of God. Nine months from our honeymoon night, Alison was born. In the hands of God all right. You know that saying, "We make plans, and God laughs"? Well, he must have had a really good laugh on us. When we found out she was pregnant, we asked the doctor for a due date. I told Bonnie, "You better not have this baby before nine months; my mother and aunts will be counting."

She looked at me with that look that said, "You're as crazy as ever."

The apartment we rented was great. It was spacious with two large bedrooms, two full baths and a large living room and dining room area. We could hardly afford it, but now that we knew we were going to have a baby, we were happy we took it. Alison was born nine months and three hours from our honeymoon night. I figured it out. The night Bonnie went into labor, I rushed her to the hospital and called Ronnie.

He met me at the hospital, and Bonnie's doctor came in to tell Ronnie and me that it could be several hours before she gave birth and that we should go home and he would call us. It was different then. Husbands didn't stay in the labor room with their wives when they gave birth. To tell the truth, I kind of liked it that way. The last thing I wanted to do was to see Bonnie in pain or agony. The doctor called at around five in the morning to tell me that Bonnie had a baby girl and that both mother and daughter were fine, and we could come whenever we wanted to see the baby. We were overjoyed, mostly because it was a girl, and I'll tell you why.

My mother always wanted a daughter. Her first child was a boy, my brother Vincent. My father was very happy with just one child he could easily support. My mother wanted another child because she wanted a daughter. It took my mother almost eleven years to convince my father to have another child. He finally relented and agreed, and after she became pregnant, she went to church for the full time she was pregnant, praying for a baby girl.

So, what did God give her? Two more boys. As Ronnie and I got older, we found out about this, and we used to tease her. We would say, "Ma, is it really true that you went to church because you didn't want us, you wanted a girl?"

She said, "Yes, it's true, but I didn't know what I was doing. Look what God gave me, my two beautiful sons." She was our mother, and simply put, we adored her.

So, when my mother found out that Bonnie was pregnant, and so far, she had no grandchildren, she was overjoyed but never mentioned to us that she hoped Bonnie would have a girl. The only telltale sign was that she told me, "If it's a boy, call me first thing in the morning and come and get me, I want to see my first grandchild. If it's a girl, call me immediately when she's born and come and get me."

So, when Alison was born, I knew that my mother would be over the moon. The relationship they had from day one was just special. I will give you an example. Years later, when Alison was thirteen years old, my mother needed heart surgery. We all were around her, and the doctor said only one can come downstairs with her until she goes in for surgery. Without hesitation, she grabbed Alison's hand.

After Alison was born, we would take her to the park, which was just across the street from our apartment. Bonnie or I would carry her in our arms in the elevator, and when we got downstairs, put her in the stroller. After living there a while, we found out that the building had several judges who also lived there. I guess it was kind of a ritzy building. It had a doorman twenty-four hours a day and birds in cages in the lobby downstairs. There was an older couple who lived on the same floor as we did who we would often meet in the elevator going downstairs. The woman thought Alison was so cute and would always put her finger under Alison's chin and talk to her.

The first time she did it, Alison was eight or nine months old, and as soon as the woman touched Alison's chin, Alison reached out, put both her arms around the woman's neck, and went to her. Alison was raised with such love and affection that she would go to anybody. The woman was shocked, but I think at that moment, Alison stole her heart because whenever we met on the elevator and I was holding Alison and she saw the woman, she would always go to her.

One day, while we were in the elevator, the woman was there with her husband and said to him, "Oh Jim, you must do something nice for this young couple." I had no clue what she was talking about.

He said, "Sure."

A couple of weeks later, I received a letter from the Queens County Supreme Court Surrogates division. It seems Jim, one half of the older couple we always met in the elevator, was a judge and the Surrogate of Queens County. This was a very powerful position as he handled all the wills and trusts in Queens County which involved millions and millions of dollars. I had no idea he held this position or that he knew Bonnie and I were lawyers. The letter stated that I had been appointed the guardian of an elderly woman who was in the hospital, and I would have to represent her in court in a competency hearing. I had never represented anyone in this type of matter. I found out I first had to go to the hospital to interview her to determine whether or not she was competent to take care of herself and her affairs.

At the hospital, it was clear she was incompetent; she could not hold a conversation with me, and all the medical reports I read confirmed this. There was also a psychiatrist who had been appointed to this case whose report I read which confirmed what I believed. Still, I had to go to court, pick a jury, and then call as my only witness the state-appointed psychiatrist to confirm my findings.

Now at this point in my story, I have to digress for a moment. Bonnie's mother and father lived in a lovely home in Forest Hills, New York. We had dinner there often, and Bonnie's father, who was a well-known patent lawyer, often spoke about his next-door neighbor whom he nicknamed Curly. Curly, it seemed, was as crazy as a bedbug, according to my father-in-law, and he would have me cracking up with some of the silly things that this neighbor did. He said, "Can you believe that this nutjob is a psychiatrist who treats people? Most shrinks are crazy anyway, and he fits the bill." I never met the man, but I knew that his nickname was Curly.

Fast-forward, I am now in court after having picked a jury in this incompetency hearing. The psychiatrist whose report I read previously but whom I never met was sitting in the courtroom. I had not questioned him before his testimony since I knew his report and would just ask him to read it as to the woman's competency.

I called the psychiatrist to the witness stand. He was well-dressed, looked bright, and classy, I thought almost regal in his demeanor. After he was sworn in, I asked for his name and address and for his academic credentials. He gave his name which I was not familiar with, and then gave his address which was— Ingram Street in Forest Hills, right next door to my in-laws.

I looked at him and suddenly realized it was Curly. The man was totally bald, and I guess that's why my father-in-law called him Curly. I lost all train of thought and was speechless, just staring at him, thinking, *my god, this is Curly, this is really Curly, the shrink next-door to my father-in-law who is crazy as a bedbug.*

The judge, Jim, my neighbor, who had given me the case, asked, "Mr.

Aliazzo, are you all right?"

I snapped back to reality and said, "Yes, Judge, I just lost my train of thought for a moment." I was just so surprised that Curly appeared normal.

He went on to give his testimony in a clear and concise manner, and I thanked him, and the judge discharged him. Summation by me took just a couple of minutes; the jury was out for about forty-five minutes, and came back with the desired results that indeed the woman was incompetent and would be placed in a facility that could care for her.

The fee I made, which I had no control over, was what I believe the judge had ordered and was the customary fee for this type of case. It paid my rent for the whole year that we lived in our apartment. I had no idea how lucrative it would be working in wills and estates, but was not interested in doing it. Although I could help people, it was just too sad for me to do every day.

Later on, when I saw Judge Jim at home with his wife, I thanked him. He said, "Bob, you did a great job, and I can assign more of these types of cases to you."

I thanked him but told him my feelings about it. He understood and said, "If you ever change your mind, let me know."

I thanked him again and I thanked his wife. A couple of months after this, we found a home in West Hempstead, a beautiful brick colonial that Bonnie and I loved. I was doing well enough to put the down payment on it, and so we moved. Before we moved, I saw Jim and his wife and told him we were moving. They were very sorry to see us go. I understood, especially since his wife had become attached to Alison.

A couple of months later, we were in our new house which was a center hall brick colonial. There was only one other house on my block which was to the right of me and two houses across the street so that our block consisted of four houses. The day we moved in, and as the movers were bringing in our furniture, our next-door neighbors, Hal and Elaine Warren, knocked on our door and came in and introduced themselves.

Little did I know then how special they were and how close we would become to them, especially to Hal. When they came into our house to introduce themselves, I was holding Alison who was nine months old. Hal came over to her and said, "Oh what a cute little girl!"

And, you guessed it, Alison went right into his arms, and that was it, love at first sight. As she got older and started school, when she came home on the bus, if we were both outside, she would run to him first.

For almost the rest of his life, Hal had a small picture of Alison on his night table next to his bed. His real name was Harold Weissberg. When I got to know him, I asked him why he changed his name to Warren. He said, "Bobby, I am not religious, but I faced so much prejudice because I'm Jewish and thought, *why do my kids have to go through the same bullshit?* So, I changed my name to Warren. It made it easy on all of us."

He didn't care what anyone thought he was. He owned a trucking company, a very big one, and as I got to know him, I sometimes called him Sluggo. Why? Because if any of the big truck drivers gave him a hard time or threatened him, he would remove his glasses, walk up to them, and knock them on their asses. After a while, he got a reputation of "Don't fuck with Hal Warren." He was really a kind, gentle soul, who was so smart and who became one of my closest friends. I really loved the guy, and he trusted no one to represent him but me, unless I recommended another lawyer.

He went into the army during the second world war as a private and came out a caption or major I don't remember which. Need I say more? That's the kind of guy he was. That he eventually considered me his best friend was an honor.

The neighbors directly across the street from us were a married couple. He was a podiatrist who had an office close by. His name was Neil Brancy, and his wife was Beryl. She was an artist who became pretty well known. They were an odd couple but one of the most beautiful, handsome couples I had ever met. He was incredibly handsome, and she was absolutely beautiful, but they were nuts. At one time, they had several pets, including a monkey and an alligator (they kept in a pit.)

We did not get to meet them the first couple of months we were living there. Neil Brancy, besides keeping unusual pets, didn't believe in material things and used to drive a Volkswagen bus that his kids had painted with psychedelic signs, and because it didn't always start, he liked to park it in front of our house. Then if it didn't start, he would push it, and as our house had a slight incline going forward, he could jump in and start it.

Hal told us that the man made a fortune as a podiatrist, yet he refused to get a new battery for his Volkswagen bus. Well, he parked it in front of our house one day as we were going to have a party. I couldn't believe it. I told Bonnie I was going to go speak to him. She said, "Don't, I'll go." She knew I was a little hot and didn't want me to get off on the wrong foot with him the first time I spoke to him. As she was walking across the street, he happened to be coming out of his house, I guess intending to go to work.

She met him in front of his bus and started to chat with him. It seemed like a very friendly chat, and they were talking for a couple of minutes. Finally, she comes back into the house, and I said, "Well, did you tell him?"

And she says, "Tell him what?"

I said, "About parking his car in front of our house." She said, "Oh no, I forgot."

I said, "You forgot?"

She said, "Bobby, he was so handsome with beautiful blue eyes and so charming that I forgot everything as he spoke to me."

I said, "Are you kidding?"

She said, "No, no, wait, I almost forgot, but I did tell him we were having a party and could he park his car across the street."

He said, "Of course."

I said, "What the hell is going on?"

She said, "Bobby, he was so good looking and so charming it was impossible to concentrate." We later found out that he was the Romeo of the neighborhood, had several girlfriends, and was quite the man about town in his psychedelic Volkswagen bus (if you can believe it).

I got to know him, and Bonnie was right, it was hard not to like him. His wife, Beryl, was a pretty well-known artist who had one of her large paintings hanging in Bloomingdale's Department Store in New York City for several years. It was through Beryl I finally got to meet Donald Cameron and Tommy Parzinger, two of the people this chapter is about. We'll get to them in a little while.

The last couple on our block was Buddy Beano and his wife, Helen. They had both been professional dancers and met while working on a cruise ship, fell in love, got married, and for several years worked on cruise ships, entertaining with their professional ballroom act. He was Italian, and she was Jewish. They were very close with Hal and Elaine and, in fact, had been on many vacations together. He later retired and started a vending machine company and was very successful.

Of course, they all got to know Ronnie who was around our house a lot with his various girlfriends. Buddy had three daughters. The oldest one was in her mid-twenties, and upon meeting Ronnie for the first time, I think she fell in love. The problem was that she was really pretty, with a great figure, and Ronnie liked her too. Of course, everyone loved Ronnie, and Buddy wanted me to tell Ronnie to ask his daughter out. He thought it would be a great match. I told him, "Buddy, he's not ready to get into a serious relationship. He has girls com-ing and going from his penthouse apartment. It's not a good idea."

He said, "I really like your brother, and I know Ellie (his daughter) likes Ronnie."

I said to Buddy I would talk to him about it. I spoke to Ronnie about it, and he said, "Are you kidding me? She's beautiful, of course I'll take her out."

I said, "Ronnie, unless you're ready to walk down the aisle, you cannot fuck around with this girl. You cannot even think about bringing her to your penthouse apartment unless you're ready to propose."

He said, "Bobby, you're serious?"

I said, "I'm as serious as a heart attack. I love these people, and you cannot fuck around with their daughter."

He said, "Okay, okay, I'll leave it alone for now."

I told Buddy that I had asked Ronnie about dating Ellie, and he said although he thought she was beautiful and would love to take her out, he was dating somebody he liked, and if it didn't work out, he would love to ask Ellie out. I had to lie. I couldn't tell Buddy the real discussion I had with Ronnie. Ronnie just wasn't ready.

Buddy also became a client, and on occasion, I would tell him I was not going to do the legal thing he wanted me to do unless he did a dance routine for me. He would say, "Bobby, you're the craziest lawyer I've ever known, but what can I do? I've become very fond of you." So, he would perform his dance, which was magical. He danced like Fred Astaire, I swear it. So, these were my neighbors who would become lifelong friends.

Now let me tell you about Donald Cameron and Tommi Parzinger, the two men who this chapter is mostly about. First, I'll tell you how I met them. Beryl Brancy, my new neighbor, a fabulous painter who lived across the street, was having a Japanese dinner party. She was making all the food herself. I had represented her in a legal matter. This was about a year after I had moved into my house. I would not charge her a fee, but she insisted, and so kidding around, I said, "I would like to have that five-by-six-foot painting of the naked lady you have hanging in Bloomingdale's." I was kidding, it was far too valuable.

A couple of days after I had jokingly asked her for the painting, it arrived at my front door, a packaged work of art delivered by two men carrying it very carefully. I've had it ever since, and as I write this, it is hanging in my living room. It's the painting of a beautiful naked lady sitting on a carpet in a living room, playing Tarot cards. It's one of the things I treasure most in the world.

Now Beryl's house on the outside was lovely with a nice garden, like many of the other houses in the neighborhood. However, when you went inside, it was decorated in the most incredible way. The furniture was very modern and sleek. Everything about the inside I thought belonged in a ritzy, million-dollar apartment in Manhattan, and yet here it was. The first time I saw it, I was amazed and said to Beryl, "If I ever buy another house (which I wanted to do someday because my dream house was a house on the water), I would decorate it exactly how you decorated your house."

She laughed and said, "Bobby, I did not decorate this house or buy one stick of furniture. The furniture was made and designed by two of my friends, Tommy Parzinger and Donald Cameron."

"You're kidding, who are they?"

She said, "They have been my friends for many years. They are artists, both of them paint, and I met them through my painting exhibits that they came to visit years ago. They loved my paintings, and so we became very good friends."

I asked, "What does painting have to do with the furniture that you have here?"

She said, "Painting is their hobby, well, really only Tommi. It's Tommi's hobby presently, but when he retires, he wants to become a full-time painter. Donald just paints in his free time because he enjoys it. Their profession, for which they are very well known, is that of furniture makers and interior home designers. They come to your home and will basically redesign it. They're very well-known already, and of course, there's a waiting list for their designs and services. They have a beautiful showroom on 57th Street and have loads of famous clients who they designed furniture for.

"A while ago, Lucille Ball and Desi Arnaz came into their showroom to have a special table designed. Tommy spent some time designing the table, which if I recall correctly was going to be a long Mikasa ebony table. After he showed them the designs, he started to discuss price as the furniture was made at a special place in Long Island City by his old time, German, furniture makers.

"Lucille Ball told him that she didn't expect to have to pay for it as just having the table at her home would be free advertising; all her friends would know who designed it, and she was sure he would get further business from famous people. Tommi, who was born in Germany, told her in no uncertain terms, he expected to get paid for his design, for the time he put into it, and for the actual furniture which would be delivered to her. She declined and basically said if she could not get the furniture for nothing, she would go elsewhere.

"He told her by all means try someone else and even recommended a couple of other famous furniture designers, knowing they would give her the boot just as he was about to. He was going to send her a bill for the work done in designing the furniture, but that would entail him having to give her the furniture design and drawings; and he was afraid that someone else would try to make his furniture, screw it up, and have his name on it. So, he decided not to send her a bill and forgot the whole matter."

After hearing this story, I said, "Well, that lets me out as there is no way I'm going to be able to afford to have custom-made furniture in the house I'm going to build someday and have them also decorate it. But Beryl, wow, is this place special."

Beryl said, "When the time comes and if you like their work, they will do it for you."

I said to Beryl, "I don't think so."

She said, "You have a special advantage." I said, "What's that?"

She said to me, "I would do anything for them as they would for me. If I asked them to and told them you were my close friends, they would do it for their cost. They are brilliant men, but when it comes to finances, they are a disaster and could really use someone like you to help manage their affairs and represent them legally so they don't get screwed, which has happened to them in the past, too many times

I told Beryl if I could help them in any way, of course I would. I told Beryl I was going to start looking for property on the water in the coming year and would love to meet them before I actually bought a property and hired an architect.

She said, "Consider it done. Next week, we are having a party at a friend's house. There will be dining and dancing and lots of fun, and Tommi and Donald will both be there. Donald has been my dancing partner for years because Neil hates to dance, and we have become quite good."

I said, "I can't wait to see you guys' dance." She said, "Tango is our specialty."

I said, "Are they partners in the business?"

She said, "Yes, but Tommi is the name on the door; the business is called Parzinger Originals. He's several years older than Donald and met Donald after he had already been in business several years and was well known."

I asked if either one was married and had children, and she said, "No, they're gay. They have been together for years but still maintain separate apartments two blocks from each other. The party is going to be next Saturday night, can you make it?"

I said, "I'll ask Bonnie, but I'm sure we will be there." I go home and tell Bonnie of my conversation with Beryl and that next Saturday; we're going to a party to meet them.

She said, "Fine, sounds like fun."

The following Saturday night, Bonnie and I arrived at the party about a half hour after it started. It was at this beautiful home that must have been on a couple of acres of land somewhere in Roslyn Harbor, as I recall. The backyard was lit up, and there was a walkway leading there, also lit up. We followed the path to the back where there was a band playing and people were dancing on this large wooden deck that was about a foot off the ground. The music that they were playing was an Argentine tango, and there were only a couple of people dancing to it. I immediately notice Beryl dancing with this very good-looking man about six feet tall with dirty blond hair and a very thin handlebar mustache. I would guess he was in his late forties at the time. He was wearing a bolero outfit with sleeves that puffed out at the wrists. I had never seen anything like it, and that was my first look at Donald Cameron, who was to become one of my dear-est and closest friends.

As they were dancing, holding each other, they did a step where they both went forward, turned, and went the other way. They were laughing and having a great time, and as they turned to go the other way, she lost her balance and fell over the railing with Donald, and into the bushes.

I said to myself, "Oh my god, do I love this guy or what?" I, along with Bonnie and several other people, ran over to see if they were okay. They both got up laughing and brushed themselves off. It was then I realized they were both drunk. As Beryl got steady on her feet, she looked up, and saw Bonnie and me and came running over to us with hugs and brought over Donald and introduced us. He was immediately taken with Bonnie and how beautiful she was. He was always hugging and kissing her. Bonnie used to say, "He's slobbering all over me." Usually, when he was doing this, he was drunk. Yes, she cared for him; it was hard not to.

Tommi was sitting at a table with some people and seemed very reserved. My first impression of him was that he was incredibly good-looking and must have had "movie star looks" when he was young. (If you want to get a look at him, go online, type his name in, and you will see him.) Upon meeting us, he was still somewhat ridged as he had been born in Germany, left in his twenties but, always maintained a certain formality.

He looked at Bonnie and immediately was also smitten, I could tell. I'm thinking about what it is about these two gay guys that they are so attracted to Bonnie. I asked Tommi later on about it, and he said when he first met her, he just thought she was beautiful; she had great facial structure, and an artist could see that. Donald, when I asked him, said, "Obviously, she's beautiful, but I sensed a goodness in her, a kindness that just drove me to her."

I said, "Donald, she's a very tough criminal defense lawyer."

He said, "Say what you want, I see her." He was right.

We had a great night. We laughed and danced and ate and got a little drunk. You could not help but get a little drunk hanging out with Donald and Beryl. Tommi was not a big drinker and as I said before, he was very reserved with a dry sense of humor. So, he was great to be around. As I got to know Tommi and Donald, they would tell me such great stories, especially Tommi who had been born in Germany and left in his twenties. He knew being gay, especially with Hitler coming into power, would eventually be a dangerous place to be, even if his family and father were very wealthy. There were many stories over the years that Tommi told me about his early life in Germany, and I could go on and on with those stories. But I'll just tell you about one that really rings out and I'll never forget.

Tommi was born into a very wealthy family. His father was concerned about Germany and where it was going. Tommy told me when it happened, but it was a while ago, and I don't remember the exact date. It seems Tommi's father was having a dinner party with over twenty guests. He wanted his son, Tommi, to be part of the dinner party despite Tommi's objections. He said he didn't want to attend a dinner party with so many stuffy people. His father insisted.

Tommi was smart, looked older than his age, was handsome, and as his mother would say, a prize at any social gathering. His mother had no idea that he was gay and was always looking for a suitable socially acceptable mate for him. There were to be several beautiful women at this gathering, and so she seated him strategically next to a very beautiful, available, single woman. He was seated at a long table with the other twenty guests. This was in a very large dining room with several servants in attendance, taking care of the guests.

Tommi, always had an eye for beauty. Although gay, he appreciated beautiful women. This woman, besides being beautiful, was educated and very bright, and he was enjoying chatting with her. At one point, she said to Tommi that she felt sorry for the man sitting to his right as he was pretty quiet and wasn't conversing much with anyone. Tommi turned to him and apologized for not introducing himself sooner, and so they started to chat. The man had piercing blue eyes, and he could tell after speaking with him for a while that he was uneducated and felt slightly intimidated by his surroundings.

He was among the very wealthy, educated people from well-known families, and Tommi could tell by his speech, demeanor, and the way he was dressed that he came from a humble background. When the conversation turned to art, Tommi could tell that he was an art lover and knew quite a lot about art and paintings, which surprised him. After speaking to him for a while, Tommi found him very interesting and, despite his appearance and demeanor, very bright. Tommy asked him how he knew his father, and he said, "I don't know him very well. I only met him a couple of times, but he has been very supportive of me and the movement which I have begun." Then he went on to speak about how dangerous the Communists were and if we weren't careful, they would be taking over our country, and then on and on about Germany and the trouble it was in.

Tommi found him very interesting and some of the points he made compelling, and as they were chatting, someone else started to speak to him, and so Tommi turned back to the beautiful young lady to his left and resumed chatting with her. The rest of the evening was uneventful.

The next morning, at breakfast with his father and mother his mother asked if he liked the young lady whom he had been seated with the evening before. She emphasized to him what a special lady she was, from such a good family, and on and on. Then she asked Tommi if he would be calling her and seeing her, to which Tommi replied, "I think so, yes, Mother," just to satisfy and pacify his eternal matchmaker mother.

He then asked his father about the gentleman that he was seated next to that evening. His father asked what he thought of him, and Tommi said, "Despite his discomfort among wealthy, educated people, he seemed very bright and was interesting, but he went on and on about politics." Which Tommi basically had no interest in. Tommi said, "I didn't catch his name."

His father said, "He is one of the up-and-coming politicians." And his father thought he may have a future in politics, and of course, he was looking for money from his father and friends to support his new party. "His name is Adolf Hitler."

Tommi said, "Good luck to him, but I don't think he'll ever make it in politics. He's too ill at ease among the people who can give him money and support him the most, but he seems like a pleasant fellow."

I said, "Tommi, are you telling me that you sat next to Adolf Hitler and had dinner with him?"

He laughed and said yes. He said, "Of course, at the time, I had no idea what a monster he would become later on, and he was one of the reasons I fled Germany. But at the time, he seemed benign, and I guess I just misjudged him."

I said, "Tommi, you have to tell me every word of the entire conversation you had with Hitler that evening."

He said, "Bobby, I really don't remember. I know it was about politics and art, but in the end, I didn't give it much thought. It was really just chitchat with one of my father's boring political friends."

A couple of days after the party, Donald called me up at my office and said that Beryl had given him my phone number and if he wouldn't mind, he had been having discussions with Tommi for some time, about writing their wills. "Then, when we met you the other evening, Beryl told us you were both lawyers, and we thought now is the time. Tommi and I have met lots of lawyers through our business, but after spending the evening with you and Bonnie, we feel very comfortable with you guys, and if in fact you do wills and estates, we would love for you to do our wills."

He went on to say he and Tommi had been together for over thirty years, and Tommi only had some long-lost relatives in Germany that he hadn't seen in years, and I don't remember whether Donald had any family left in Canada, which is where he came from, but in any event, he wanted to leave everything to Tommi.

I told him yes, I do wills and estate planning, but only a limited amount and only for friends and family. I said since, "Beryl and Neil are good friends, and since I have a feeling that you and Tommi are going to become good friends of ours also, of course, I would be happy to do it." I made an appointment for them to come see me at my office and in fact did Tommi's will first. Donald kept on putting off getting his will done, so I don't remember whether we got around to doing it or not.

As Donald and I were on the phone, he seemed a little upset. I could tell by the tone of his voice. I asked Donald, "Is everything okay?"

He said, "Not really, you just can't believe what Beryl did."

I said, "Beryl? What could Beryl possibly have done to upset you so much?

You guys have been friends for over twenty years."

He said, "What I'm about to tell you is hard to believe, but here's what happened. Years ago, Tommi designed a beautiful dining room table and chairs for her; the table was made of a very rare rosewood, and he had the actual rosewood tree shipped to our furniture makers in Long Island City, it took them over a month to make that table. It was and is a work of art, signed personally by Tommi underneath (today, that table, if it still exists, is worth a fortune). You know, she's having a Japanese dinner this Saturday night and you and Bonnie are invited. Tommi and I will also be there."

I said, "Yes, Donald, I'm looking forward to seeing you guys' Saturday night and having a delicious Japanese dinner. So why are you so upset?"

He said, "I'm afraid to tell Tommi, he's going to go apoplectic. In order to make it feel like an authentic Japanese party, you're supposed to sit on the floor, so Beryl decided to cut the legs off the table so that the table would almost be on the floor, except we could put our legs under the table with our legs crossed. She figured out mathematically how she should cut all the legs off. She did that to our beautifully designed table. She told me that when the party was over that she would glue the legs back together, and no one would be the wiser. Can you believe it?"

I tried not to, but I started laughing, and he heard me, and after a moment, he started to laugh too. He said, "God knows I love that lady, but she's really nuts."

I said, "That's probably why you love her."

And after another moment of silence, he said, "Yeah, you're probably right."

The following Saturday night, we had our Japanese dinner party. Since we lived across the street from Beryl, it was an easy trip. The place looked great. The table, even without the legs, looked magical, kind of like a magnificent looking woman buried in the sand up to her waist. I never realized what a beautiful work of art it was. Of course, as soon as we walked in, we were greeted by Neil and Beryl, who already were on their way to inebriation, and I wondered how Beryl was going to finish cooking this meal. It turns out she was smart enough to get help. In the kitchen was a Japanese woman who was helping her prepare the meal and would serve it.

Of course, drinks were immediately put into our hands, and off we went. I told Bonnie, "If worse comes to worse, we could always stagger across the street." There were several of Beryl's friends there whom we didn't know. All were artists with their better halves. We started chatting, and since they were already one sheet to the wind, they were extra friendly, and Bonnie and I liked them immediately. The last guests Beryl was waiting for and finally arrived were Tommi and Donald.

Since neither one of them drove, they had a car service take them to Beryl's and would have one pick them up at the end of the evening. Good thing because there would be no way that Donald would be able to drive after the party, even if he could.

Tommi never learned to drive, he always lived in the city and took cabs and city transportation. I heard the car pull up and looked out the window and saw the car come to a stop, and Donald got out. They had both been sitting in the back of the car, but only Donald got out. Tommi stayed seated and did not exit.

As Donald was walking up to the front door, I opened it and came out to greet him. He was such an elegant, handsome looking guy, always dressed impeccably, but what always got to me was the beautifully waxed, very thin handlebar mustache.

He always said the same thing when he saw me. A big "Bobby," and then a hug.

I said to Donald, "It's so good to see you, so happy you're here." I looked at the cab and said, "Why isn't Tommi getting out of the cab? Is he okay?"

He said, "Before Tommi comes in, he wants to know that the alligator is safely put away in the pit and that the monkey is locked up." I looked at him and then Tommi sitting in the car, and the insanity of it sent me into instant laughter. I looked at him. I looked at Tommi in the car. I turned and looked at the house and thought, *these people are all truly wacky. What am I doing here?*

Then I realized they were all very smart and truly gifted. I really liked them a lot, and rather frighteningly realized I would be lucky to be here with them, if they would have me, because I was not as incredibly smart or truly gifted as they were. I said, "Wait a minute, let me go ask Beryl."

I went inside and said, "Beryl, before Tommi comes in, he wanted to make sure that the monkey and the alligator were safely put away."

She said, "Oh that Tommi, what a big baby. Tell him yes, come in."

So, I walked back outside and told Donald, and together we got Tommi and went in.

As we walked in, everyone came up to greet Donald and Tommi. Apparently, they knew everyone and, of course, were quickly handed drinks. Everyone knew that Donald's favorite drink was vodka and tonic, which he could polish off in astronomical amounts, laughing and smiling as if he were drinking orange soda. It always amazed me, his ability to drink large amounts of alcohol, and still remain standing. The good thing about Donald's drinking was that as he drank, he became very happy, funny, and affectionate. Tommi, on the other hand, liked an occasional drink and was always in full control. I never saw him, even slightly inebriated. He would look at Donald as he carried on when he was drinking with affection as we all did when Donald was on a roll.

As we were chatting, the crowd kind of loosened up, and for the first time, Donald and Tommi saw what Beryl had done to their beautifully designed, handmade, one-of-a-kind dining room table. Everyone looked at Donald and Tommi in total silence as they stared at the dining room table that was now on the floor, waiting for their reaction. They studied the table in silence for what seemed like an hour, when in fact, it was just a few seconds, and then Tommi, in his rather elegant style and with the slightest of German accents, said, "I didn't intend that my beautifully designed and hand-built dining room table would be suitable for midgets."

Of course, everyone laughed. Donald came up to Tommi and put his arm around his shoulder and said, "It's not so bad."

I said, "Tommi just think it's low enough now so that Beryl's alligator can climb on top of it and take a snooze."

Everyone laughed again, and Tommi already had his thinking cap on. He said, "Beryl, I will have one of my furniture makers come to your house next week, and I think he can put screws in the table legs, and we can screw the legs back on so that should you ever want to have another Japanese dinner, we can unscrew the legs and then screw them back together so that you will never notice they were sawed off in the first place. He looked at Beryl with that twinkle, and he said, "Beryl, what do you think?"

She came over and gave him a big hug, then turned to Neil and said, "See, I told you he would fix it." Everyone started clapping. Then, of course, some of the guests wanted to visit the monkey who was in his cage and see the alligator in his pit.

When everybody was well-lit, we sat down to this sumptuous Japanese dinner. There were several courses, and I must say each one was delicious. Bonnie is not a big Japanese food person, but even she, I think, enjoyed the food. We drank sake, which I had never had before. It was warm, and I thought it was very good. Discussions during dinner with Beryl's guests were spirited, funny, informative, and never boring. The points of view expressed by Beryl's dinner guests varied from, I believe, in socialism to the views to the right of Donald Trump. But everybody respected each other's opinions.

The stories told by some of the artists and by Donald and Tommi were sometimes funny, sometimes sad, but always interesting to listen to. Bon and I had a great time and managed to walk home under our own power. I made an appointment to see Donald and

Tommi the following week since I had completed Tommi's Will and Testament, and since Bonnie and I were going into the city in the afternoon to attend an angel party (I'll tell you about that in a little while), we would drop by after.

Tommi suggested that instead of coming to the showroom, we meet at his apartment and he was going to prepare a dinner for us. Tommi was quite a gourmet cook, and so we made plans to meet at his apartment for dinner.

That Friday morning, I was at my office, doing some work, planning to meet Bonnie at around one o'clock to head into the city when I got a call from Ronnie. We're chatting for a while, and he says, "Wait, before you go, I've got to tell you an interesting little story that involves the day before."

At around twelve-thirty, Herbie comes into the courtroom. He walks up to the front of the courtroom, not down the middle but on the side of the courtroom and motions to me. Ronnie is at the bench with the other attorney, speaking to the judge. The courtroom is pretty full. Ronnie sees Herbie motioning him. Ronnie says, "Your Honor, would you please excuse me for just a second" and goes over to Herbie and says, "What's going on?"

Herbie says, "I have to speak to you."

Ronnie says, "We're going to have a break in about thirty minutes."

Herbie says, "Okay, I'll meet you outside the courtroom at one." They agree, Herbie leaves, and Ronnie goes back before the judge.

Ronnie says, "The court breaks at one, I go outside, and Herbie is very excited. I say to Herbie, 'What's going on?' He says, 'Follow me, you can't believe what I'm about to show you.'"

Now before I go on about Herbie, let me give you a little bit of his background. Herbie was born in Brooklyn to working-class parents. He had a younger brother who became a cop. Herbie decided to become a lawyer, went to Brooklyn law school, graduated, I think, with honors, and then got a job with a very famous, well-known big New York medical malpractice firm. They represented doctors and hospitals who were being sued for medical malpractice.

Within three years or so, Herbie was trying all the firm's major medical malpractice cases and became a partner. Their cases were worth millions of dollars, and of course, he had a major winning record.

Herbie was about six-foot-one, thin, and handsome. He had gotten married very young and had three children and, by the time he was in his mid-thirties, had gotten divorced. Bonnie represented his wife in that divorce case as both Herbie and his wife agreed on the terms and conditions of the divorce. It probably was a mismatch from the beginning. They were both wonderful people but not just wonderful together. Now that Herbie was on the loose, he was quite the ladies' man. Women adored him. Besides being tall, thin, and good-looking, he was making a lot of money, had a flashy, beautiful green Jaguar, and had an incredible gift of gab with the ladies.

After several years working with his large law firm, he decided to go out on his own and opened up his own office. From that day on, he did all my medical malpractice cases as a plaintiff's attorney. I don't think he ever lost a case for me, and my clients adored him. He had the type of personality that jurors just related to. When he finally was ready to try a case, he knew more about the malpractice and how it had occurred than the doctor who committed the malpractice. He was simply brilliant. For as sophisticated as he appeared, he was basically a Brooklyn guy with the best sense of humor, and I always had the most fun with him, trying cases.

One other thing I want to say. People think that lawyers love to sue doctors in medical malpractice cases. I found just the opposite. For every medical malpractice case I took, I must've turned away five. It always amazed me how ready, willing, and able people were to sue their doctors if they thought they had committed malpractice. It's extremely difficult to prove a medical malpractice case.

To explain in the simplest terms; first you have to prove that the doctor deviated from medical procedures and that's just the beginning; then you have to get other doctors who are willing to testify that a doctor committed medical malpractice, (also extremely difficult to do); and then you're suing a doctor who had every good intention and just screwed up as we all do. Some of the medical malpractice cases I had were heartbreaking. I had one client, a young man in his thirties, who went in for a simple back procedure and wound up a paraplegic.

So, getting back to Herbie and Ronnie. Herbie is with Ronnie and is walking toward the civil court building which is right next door to the criminal court building. Ronnie says, "What are we doing and where are we going?"

Herbie says, "Just be patient and you will be there in a minute." They enter the building and make a right turn and are walking toward the elevators. They took an elevator, I believe, down to the basement, which had a very large room that accommodated a couple of hundred people, and it was where all prospective jurors waited to be called.

They walk into the jury room and are at the front, and Herbie says, "Okay, Ronnie, look around."

Ronnie says, "Herbie, are you nuts? This is the jury pool, why are we here?"

Herbie says, "Ronnie, stop for a second, listen to me, just look around."

Ronnie starts looking around very slowly. He takes about a minute and then says, "Okay, Herbie, I give up. What are we doing here?"

Herbie says, "Ronald, your powers of observation in this particular instance suck." So, Herbie says, "Okay, I will help you. Look at the last row all the way to the right."

Ronnie looks and notices there are two really nice-looking women sitting together, chatting. Now Herbie says, "Go up three rows all the way to the left."

Ronnie does that, and he notices there's another very attractive woman sitting there, reading a newspaper. He started to get the hint. Then Herbie says, "Look four rows up to the right in the middle, take a look."

He does so, and there's another very attractive young woman sitting there, waiting to be called.

Herbie looks at Ronnie and says, "We've found a gold mine in this room. There must be twenty or thirty attractive women that are possible dating material."

Ronnie looks at Herbie and says, "Herbert, you've finally gone nuts."

Herbie says, "I can't tell you how many women I've met here in the last couple of months."

Ronnie looks at him and says, "Are you kidding me? How do you do it?"

Herbie says quite simply, "What I do is I go up to them, sit down next to them, and start a conversation. Of course, I am always dressed in a suit, shirt, and tie and look my best. Then I usually start by saying I'm an attorney, and I am trying a civil case, and I'm having difficulty getting a juror's point of view on what I'm trying to prove. Since you're a prospective juror, would you mind if I asked you a couple of questions? And would you give me your point of view which would be helpful to me in picking a jury? I never had one woman turn me down when I was asking for her help.

"Then we start to chat, and if we're getting along and I can tell that she likes me and doesn't have a wedding ring on, what I usually do is say I have so many more questions to ask, maybe when you break for lunch today, I can take you to lunch and you can kind of be my guinea pig as I'm trying to do my research to find out the best type of juror to pick for my case. I can tell when we're having lunch if we connect and if she likes me or is attracted to me. By that time, we're finished with lunch, most of the women can tell I'm attracted to them and flirting a little bit. Then I tell them I've had such a good time maybe we can meet for drinks or coffee or dinner sometime, and if they feel the same way about me, they generally will give me their number, and we're off to the races."

Ronnie looks at Herbie and says, "Herbert, although this is quite unusual, I think your idea is brilliant."

Herbie says, "See, I told you so."

Ronnie says, "I do not, however, have the need to search the jury pool for suitable women since I meet lots of attractive women just being in court every day. Besides, I am presently dating two different very beautiful ladies, and there's no way I have time for another."

Herbie says, "Speaking of attractive women, my present girlfriend has a very good-looking friend, and I told her all about you, and she would love to meet you."

Ronnie says, "Herbie, I just told you I have more than I can handle right now, and besides, the last time you set me up, it was a disaster."

Herbie says, "So it didn't work out, but the girl was good-looking."

Ronnie tells Herbie, "She worked in a bar as a go-go dancer. She had the IQ of a turtle, she chewed gum the whole night, and I had nothing to say to her, and your girl, the head go-go dancer, was even worse."

Herbie says, "I didn't bring her to meet you to talk."

Ronnie says, "I'm beyond that, Herbie, I just can't take out a girl to get laid. I have to have some feeling. I have to be able to communicate with her."

Herbie says, "I've been communicating and living with one girl for the last fifteen years, and I'm tired of communicating and talking. I just want to have fun and get laid."

Ronnie tells him, "You know, I think you regressed backward to your teen years."

And Herbie says, "Yes, I have, and I'm loving it."

Ronnie says, "I'm happy for you, but no more blind dates. Thank you, Herbie."

I said, "Then, Ron, if this was the conversation between two suave, sophisticated, experienced New York State trial lawyers? God help the rest of us."

Ronnie says, "You're right. I'm telling you, ever since his divorce, the man has gone crazy and reverted back to his teen years."

I say to Ron, "How could you not love the guy?"

And Ronnie says, "You're right, that's why I put up with his craziness." Ronnie says, "By the way, where are you headed?"

I said, "Bonnie and I are going into the city this afternoon at two. We're going to an angel party."

Ronnie says, "What the hell is an angel party?"

I tell him, "An angel party is a get together of investors, and what they are going to invest in is a Broadway play, if they like it. The people who put up money for the Broadway play, I found out, are called angels, so this is an angel party. It's usually held in someone's apartment or house or, in some cases, on a Broadway stage when there are no performances."

He says, "How the hell did you get into this?"

I said, "Irving Casey called me and told me about it. It's in this fancy apartment on Fifth Avenue. Sounds like fun, something to do, and then from there, we're going to meet Donald and Tommi. I finally got his will done. Tommi is making us dinner after the angel party. I hear he's quite the gourmet chef. I'll let you know how it all turns out."

It's a little after one when Bonnie finally gets to the office. She took a car service to the office since we only wanted to have one car to go back and forth into the city.

After saying hello to most of the secretaries and some of the lawyers, all of whom are complaining about how crazy I am—she is shaking her head. She sees how happy they are that she's getting me away from the office, so, off to the city we go. The apartment we are going to is located on Fifth Avenue, a few blocks down from the Plaza Hotel. It's a very ritzy place with doormen in a general's uniform; and, you could just smell money. We give the name of the party we are there to see to the general, and he tells us, the fifth floor.

Walking down the hallway to the apartment was impressive. The hallway was extra wide, the carpets were beautiful, and the lights on the wall must have cost a thousand bucks each. I look at Bonnie and say, "Who the hell lives here?"

We knock on the door, and a man dressed formally and very elegantly answers the door. We introduce ourselves and tell him we are here for the angel party. He greets us and takes us down a long hallway lined with paintings and shows us into a very spacious living room with chairs lined up in rows. The walls have several paintings. The first painting I notice is an original Grandma Moses. Next to it is a large Picasso.

I tell Bonnie, "Whoever the hell owns this apartment, I am going to follow the missus around in case she is wearing any jewelry; if it's priceless like the paintings, it could be worth a fortune. If she happens to lose it, and I happen to pick it up, we will be really rich."

Bonnie gives me one of her, "There he goes again" looks.

As we enter this large room, we see Irving with his wife. We go over and greet them and start to chat. I say, "Irv, are you kidding me with this apartment? Who the hell owns it?"

He says, "I'll be damned if I know. The guy who invited me to this get together is a garment guy on Seventh Avenue; he's a major player."

As we were chatting, someone came by with glasses filled with champagne, and we grabbed a couple and continued the chat. The room filled up with lots of people, and almost all the chairs were taken. The people, for the most part, are all formally dressed, men with shirts and ties and jackets, and the women in beautiful dresses. The jewelry in the place, from what I can tell and from what I know about jewelry, could feed a family of ten for the next hundred years. At least that's what I thought. There were, however, a couple of hippie types with hippie type clothing, but one hippie type guy was wearing a very simple watch with a black leather strap. I looked at the watch closely since I know a lot about men's wristwatches. Why? Because when I was a kid, about nine years old, I already had an interest in wristwatches, I don't know why, I had saved some money and wanted to buy a nice wristwatch.

Ronnie had no interest. So, one day, my father took just me into the city to a very nice watch place to buy a wristwatch. I think it was the first time I was ever alone with my father, without Ronnie.

As I looked around in the store, I saw a watch that I loved but couldn't afford, but my father winked at the guy and made up the difference, and I bought my first wristwatch. After that, my dad took me for lunch, and we hung out, and it was just a special day.

I continued buying wrist watches for many years, always thinking back to the day in New York City, being alone with my father when he bought me my first watch.

Getting back to that angel party and the hippie with the black leather strap. I noticed the watch attached to that black leather strap was a gold Breguet, one of the most expensive watches you could buy, more expensive than a Rolex. I had, after saving for a couple of years, actually bought and owned a Breguet. One of the reasons I bought it, besides the fact that I loved watches, was an ad I saw in the *New York Times*.

The ad had a picture of a beautiful Breguet watch, and it said the following: "When Napoleon surrendered to the Duke of Wellington at the battle of Waterloo, they were both wearing Breguet watches." The ad also mentioned that President Roosevelt and Winston Churchill both wore Breguet watches. And to top it off, it mentioned that in the book, *The Count of Monte Cristo*, the hero of the book, the Count of Montecristo, while in prison, was allowed to keep his watch.

The watch was a Breguet, and he looked at it every day; and it helped maintain his sanity; I speculated that if the watch was good enough for the Duke of Wellington, Napoleon, the Count of Monte Cristo, President Roosevelt, and Winston Churchill, it certainly would be good enough for me. After two years of saving, I bought one. What an ad. It was the best ad I have ever seen, and it certainly got to me. When I told Bonnie about the ad and my intention of saving to buy that watch, she said to me, "Oh, so now you think you're in the same class with Napoleon, the Duke of Wellington, President Roosevelt, and Winston Churchill, not to mention the Count of Monte Cristo?"

I said, "I certainly am, and I intend to own that watch."

Again, she gave me one of her long looks, like, "There he goes again." Maybe it sounds crazy, but it's lots of fun to own it and wear it and to tell people about its history and the famous people who owned one, and here I am, writing about it in this book.

So, getting back to our angel party, at the front of the room, there was a large baby grand piano, and there were several people milling about, chatting. There was sheet music on the piano, and it appeared that they were looking at it, chatting about it. There were several people next to us who were chatting who had British accents. I thought how elegant it would be if only I could speak with a British accent, and I told that to Bonnie. She looked at me and said, "Why couldn't I marry someone normal?"

I gave her a hug—Bonnie, another lady I was crazy about (after my mother) who me and my brothers absolutely adored. I mean, my mother is my mother, but after my mother, I was just crazy about that lady. She always kept me down to earth, and I couldn't get away with anything with her. She was just too damn smart. Marry a lawyer? What was I thinking? I should've known better. I've won very few arguments in all the years we've been married.

So, getting back to the angel party once again. After several minutes, one of the men at the front turned to all the people milling about, sitting, and chatting, and said, "May I have your attention, please? Will everyone now please take a seat?"

Everyone obediently obeyed, and within a couple of moments, we were all waiting to see what would happen next. The guy who asked us to be seated then spoke for a few minutes. He told us his name, which unfortunately I do not recall. He then went on to tell us what an angel party was.

Angels (a show business term) were people who put up money for a production they believed in. "Basically, you people (angels, investors, shareholders) will put up the money for the play we intend to produce. If the play is successful, we will all share in the profits."

I thought, *it sounds reasonable enough to me. If the play is a success, we make money. If it fails, we lose our money, which sounds pretty standard to me.* There is a business principle I always followed, and that is, it's not the money you put up, it's the money you put up chasing the money you put up that gets you into trouble. Here's an example. Let's say you put up $25,000 for a business venture. The business is doing okay but requires some more money, so you as an investor put up another $5,000 because if you don't, you may lose your initial investment of $25,000. Now you're into it for $30,000, and they tell you, "Listen, we need another $5,000 or you will lose it all." So now you put up another $5,000. Now that $25,000 initial investment has gone up to $35,000. That's what I mean by chasing the money you put up; that is, the original $25,000.

Now the people who are asking you for the extra money could be good, honest people who didn't correctly calculate the actual amount needed for the investment to succeed. That happens in most of the cases I see. So, a good rule of thumb I would tell my clients who are looking to invest was to make sure after the initial investment was made that no other funds would be necessary, and if necessary, the people who brought you into the business venture in the first place would put up the same amount of money that they were asking you to put up.

If they are not able to or unwilling to, then for the most part, I recommend against going into the initial investment. I would tell my clients, "There's an old rule of thumb I learned from a lawyer friend of mine, a brilliant guy who went to Harvard law school. The rule of thumb goes something like this: 'If we bleed, we all bleed together.' That means the people who are asking you to invest also put up some of their money so that they have a vested interest in succeeding and will lose money the same as you will if the venture fails."

So as this guy is speaking to us, these are the thoughts that are going around in my head, but I figured, *Let's hear what he has to say, and at the end, if I'm interested, I'll ask him those questions.*

He starts to tell us about the play which is based on a comic book series and now is going to be a musical; they have already written several numbers for the play. After telling us about the play, which took about twenty minutes, he says, "We would like to play one of the songs we've written. It will be the lead song in the play." Then he sits down at the piano, and a woman walks up next to him who obviously is going to sing, and he starts to play the song. The song, as I remember, went exactly like this:

The sun will come out tomorrow

Bet your bottom dollar That tomorrow There'll be sun

Just thinking about tomorrow

Clears away the cobwebs And the sorrow

Til there's none

I'm listening to the song and thinking, *oh my god, that is really a catchy tune.* I turned to Bon, and she gave me a wink of approval, and then I turned to Irv and his wife, and they both gave me a thumbs up. The song, when completed, was absolutely wonderful. The whole audience stood up and applauded. He tells us the name of the play is *Annie*. He spoke for another couple of minutes and then asked if there were any questions.

Someone asked, "How much for a share and when is the money due?"

I don't remember the exact amount, but I think it was something like

$25,000 a share which back in 1976, I believe the year was, was a lot of money. He went on to say that those people that were interested in investing should leave their name, address, and phone number with the two people at the desk in the back who were prepared to take that information. I didn't want to get into all the questions I had for him at that time regarding putting up more money if necessary, thinking that when the time actually came to put up the money, I would find out.

Everyone seemed to be very excited, and there were two lines waiting to give their name, address, and phone number. Irving and I got in line and gave that information. I said, "What do you think, Irv?"

He said, "I really like it and so did Meg, and we'll see what happens when we get the info from them." They told us that we would be getting all the information we needed to sign up in about two weeks, when checks would then be required to secure a share.

I said, "Let's see what happens."

About a month went by, and we didn't receive the information required for us to sign up. After about six weeks, I had one of my secretaries call to find out when we could expect to receive the info regarding the purchasing of our shares. She comes back a couple of minutes later and tells me that the offer to purchase shares has been rescinded and that one person was going to produce the show. His name was Mike Nichols.

In the end, Mike Nichols did produce the show, which was a tremendous hit and shown worldwide, plus a movie was made of it, plus dolls and toys of Little Orphan Annie were made, and on and on and on. I believe the purchase of one share if the ancillary rights were included would probably return $1 million. That's just a guess on my part, but that's what Irv and I thought. Well, we gave it a shot. It was a lot of fun, and I was happy for the success of the play. It was wonderful.

After the angel party, Bon and I went on to see Tommi and Donald at Tommi's apartment. His apartment was on 53rd Street off First Avenue. It was a lovely apartment and the furnishings were all Tommi's designs, which were absolutely modern and magnificent. At the time, Tommi was not doing much furniture designing but was concentrating on his paintings. He was semiretired, and Donald was running the showroom and the business. His paintings were beautiful. I am fortunate to have several of them.

One of them is a painting that's four feet wide by five feet high, a large painting of a Saint George holding a lantern with his foot on a serpent's neck. I have a few others also. They are unusual, very modernistic, and Bon and I love them; and since they were painted by our dear friend Tommi, they are really special to us.

When we got there, Donald and Tommi were already preparing dinner and, of course, had cocktails galore. By the time we sat down, we were already slightly high just as Donald had intended.

Dinner was a four-course meal. I don't recall what we ate, but I remember it was elegantly served and delicious. After dinner, I went over Tommi's will and had him execute it. We then settle down for a long conversation with the two of them. Donald started telling us some stories which were just amazing. He told us that he and Tommi had many famous people come to their store to purchase furniture and, in some cases, Tommi's paintings.

Donald told us about the time Gary Cooper and his wife, Maria, came into their showroom to purchase some furniture. Donald said that Gary Cooper sat down in a chair and did not say one word other than hello and goodbye. His wife, Maria, did all the talking. Donald said he was surprised at how thin and good-looking he was in person, which reminds me of a story my cousin Carlo Nell, who had the TV show in Paris, once told me.

Apparently, Gary Cooper was on his TV show, promoting a film, and after the show was over, Carlo took him to a beautiful French restaurant for dinner. Carlo recommended the steak which was made with peppercorns and was delicious at this restaurant. Gary Cooper ordered the steak, and then Carlo told me he had maybe half of it, although he still appeared to be quite hungry. It turns out the man was constantly on a diet because he had to maintain his weight for the films he was making. Carlo remarked, "What a way to live. You can't eat and you're perpetually hungry."

Anyway, getting back to Donald and Tommi and their stories. The best story Donald told me was the story of Mrs. Miller.

Mrs. Miller came into his showroom recommended by someone and wanted several pieces of furniture made. Tommi and Donald showed her several designs, and she approved of a couple of them; they agreed upon the price and started to have the furniture made. They would take pictures of the furniture as it was being made in Long Island City by German furniture makers, and she would come by to look at the pictures and to chat.

Donald said she was a very pretty lady who always wore a scarf and sunglasses but, appeared to be lonely. Several times, Donald and Mrs. Miller went out for drinks as she usually came by around five o'clock, closing time. They got along famously. Donald really liked her, and she apparently really liked him. They mostly discussed furniture and design and kind of artistic things. The furniture she was buying was very expensive, and Donald assumed that either she was very wealthy on her own or her husband was wealthy.

One day, they were walking along First Avenue to a place they both liked called the Mayfair, a bar/restaurant type establishment, which had mostly booths with lights directly hanging over the table so it had a great dark type atmosphere, very private and just special. Bon and I went there often with Donald and Tommi. It was one of our favorite places, nothing very fancy, but the hamburgers were really good. The coffee was great, I think mostly because they served it with heavy cream. Try it sometimes. Coffee and heavy cream will blow your socks off.

Donald noticed lots of people stared at her, both men and women. This had happened before, but he never paid attention to it. Now, although she was a very attractive woman, Donald thought the stares were unusual. Donald was not a moviegoer and did not have a television in his apartment and so wasn't acquainted with a lot of the movie stars of the day, although he knew who some of the more famous ones were.

He asked Mrs. Miller, which is what he always called her, if she knew any of the people who stared at her. She said, "No, I don't,

Donald." As I said before, she always wore a scarf and big sunglasses.

He said to her, "Why are these people on the street staring at you? I know you're attractive, Mrs. Miller, but this is unusual."

She said, "Well, Donald, I'm an actress and I've made several movies. Mrs.

Miller is my married name, but my real name is Marilyn Monroe."

Donald looked at her and said, "I've seen pictures of Marilyn Monroe, you're not Marilyn Monroe."

She said, "Yes, I am, Donald, would you like to see Marilyn Monroe?"

Not really understanding what was going on, he said yes. She took off her scarf, removed her glasses and jacket, and just stood up and started to walk so differently, and he looked at her, startled, and said, "Oh my god, Marilyn Monroe!" And she laughed.

I said, "Donald, how could you not know it was Marilyn Monroe?"

He said, "Bobby, it just never dawned on me, she was always Mrs. Miller. You know I'm not a big movie buff, so the only time I ever saw her was maybe pictures of her in the news."

I said, "At the time, she must've been married to the very famous playwright, Arthur Miller." And so, the evening went with these great stories by Tommi and Donald.

As Bonnie and I were leaving, I reminded Donald that the following Monday afternoon, we had a meeting and were going to a little town called Malverne, which was located on Long Island, very close to the Queens, New York, border. I said, "Donald, you're going to come to my office and we're going to meet with my new partner, Stephen, have a bite to eat at this great place in Malverne called Ickle Bickel, and then we will go to the space we want to rent." Donald, who along with Tommi had done many complete interior designs for very famous people and millionaires, had agreed to do my little new haircutting salon. I love those guys, they were special.

He said, "I've never done a haircutting salon before, and it's going to be fun doing it. I can't believe Tommi agreed to help me with it. It's only because he loves you and Bonnie that he's agreed to it, and besides, you're his lawyer, he can't say no."

Now let me back up a minute and tell you a little bit about my new venture with my new partner, Stephen. It all started with my daughter, Alison, who was three years old at the time. We were living in West Hempstead in this beautiful brick colonial house that I think I mentioned before, and we were lucky enough to find a babysitter for Alison. Before we hired her to babysit, we wanted to meet her parents who lived around the corner from us. The name of our new babysitter was Lori. I think at the time she was sixteen years old and an absolutely beautiful girl with great warmth; most importantly, we felt she was very responsible.

We met her parents, Barbara and Everett, who we liked immediately and who we became very friendly with. After Lori had been babysitting Alison for a month or so, I got a call from her father, Everett, who invited us the following Saturday to a barbecue that he was having at his house. I asked Bonnie, and she felt as I did about Barbara and Everett and said yes. I called Everett back and told him we were looking forward to coming.

The following Saturday afternoon, we went to the barbecue, taking Alison with us. It was a lovely day, and we were having a good time, chatting with Barbara and Everett and some of the friends they introduced us to, and then something happened that basically would change our life a little bit in a very incredibly good way. Lori came over to us as we were chatting and said she would like us to meet her boyfriend, Stephen. The first thing that struck us upon meeting him was how handsome he was, unusually good-looking.

We said hello, shook hands, and chatted for a while. He was exceptionally polite, very bright and interesting, and I'm sure aware of his good looks, yet seemingly unaffected by them. I think at the time, he was seventeen years old. Somehow, we got to chatting about cars, and he said he had just bought one. "Would you like to see it?"

I said, "Sure," and followed him out to the front of the house, and parked next to the curb was an absolutely sparkling English car called a Morris Minor. When I was in England with Bonnie, we saw lots of great Morris Minor automobiles. They were small and very beautiful in an English sort of way. They were so rare I had never seen another one in the U.S. It was unusual because it had the steering on the left-hand side, that is, on the American side, as compared to the British automobiles which had steering on the right-hand side.

The car was gleaming. There wasn't a speck of dust on the car, the carpets were immaculate, and the first thing I thought was, *this kid standing next to me must be obsessive-compulsive to have an automobile that is so rare and so incredibly perfect.* Of all the cars a kid could get, when I saw this car, I knew Stephen was special. Most kids his age would want a hot rod, a fast car; not Stephen. His sense of aesthetics was unique. Right then and there, I knew he was an old soul in a handsome kid's body, and as I got to know him, I found out I was right. I asked him how he found the car, and since he was in high school, how could he afford it.?

He told me he worked after school and sometimes on the weekends in a printing shop right here in West Hempstead and that he had saved for a long time and finally found this Morris Minor which, at the time, was the car of his dreams. He told us he lived in Franklin Square, which was the next town over from West Hempstead and was a senior in West Hempstead High School. We chatted for a while, went back to the barbecue, and then kind of mingled with the rest of the crowd. I asked Bonnie, "What do you think, is that kid special or what?"

She said, "Yes, I think he is very special."

I told Bon, "Hopefully, I will run into him again."

About a month later, I think it was on a Saturday morning, Bonnie and I were having breakfast when the doorbell rang. At the door was Stephen, looking very uncomfortable and nervous. Bonnie answered the door and said to Stephen, "What a surprise! It's so good to see you."

He said, "I hope I'm not bothering you guys, but I think I'm in trouble, and I know you guys are lawyers, and I was wondering if I could ask you some questions."

We said, "Of course, come in, sit down and have a cup of coffee with us."

He was so nervous he couldn't or wouldn't have a cup of coffee. Bonnie said, "Let me get you a glass of water. You look upset."

He finally agreed to accept the glass of water. We chatted for a minute or two about the party and Lori, and then Bonnie asked him, "What's cooking?"

He said he was in trouble and had to go to criminal court because he had been issued a summons. Bonnie asked him to tell us what happened. He said he and his friend, Frankie Vinci, were at a Fair in Franklin Square with a bunch of friends, and Frankie was leaning on a car. Turns out the car was a police car, and the cop who was next to it told Frankie not to lean on his car. Frankie said sorry and moved away from the car. And a little while later, while chatting again with his friends, he forgot and leaned on the car again.

The cop came over to him and said, "I told you not to lean on my car, and he started to remove his policeman's club."

Stephen got upset, got in between the policeman and Frankie, and said, "You're going to hit my friend because he leaned on your car?"

With that, the policeman issued both of them summonses for obstruction of governmental administration. Stephen said, "What does that mean?" He didn't know what to do. He said he didn't tell his mother or father.

Bonnie said, "Calm down, Stephen, this is not a big deal. I will represent you."

Stephen said, "How much will this cost? I don't have a lot of savings." Bonnie said, "Don't worry about it, I'm not going to charge you." Stephen said, "I can't ask you to do this for free."

Bonnie said, "Let's take care of it, and we'll worry about that later." He said, "Okay, thanks, Bonnie."

The following week, Bonnie met both Stephen and Frankie in criminal court, represented them both, and got the matter dismissed.

Now let me tell you a little bit about Frankie Vinci, who lived around the corner from Bonnie and me. He, like Stephen was in high school. He was also a musician and had a band. He, I think, was also seventeen years old at the time. He was tall, thin, with blond hair, and also very good-looking. He, like Stephen, was also a kind and gentle soul. I told Bonnie, "These kids are really special. Where the hell do they come from?"

Bonnie and I liked Frankie immediately. He used to practice with his band in his garage around the corner from us and we always enjoyed listening to their music. Alison had a tricycle; she was three years old and would ride her tricycle on the sidewalk and stop across the street from his band to listen to them.

They were really good. Frankie was and is to this day so talented. He wound up going to Nashville, Tennessee, to write songs for some pretty famous country music stars. He also made a living writing jingles and presently, among other things, has become an artist and has been selling some of his paintings for thousands of dollars. I'm so happy and proud of him to this day. Sometimes you're just lucky to run across special people and maintain lifelong friendships with them.

Frankie's older brother, Johnny, was also a musician and very talented. He formed a band called The Illusion, and they had a very popular song called "Did You See Her Eyes." At the time, Johnny was a rock star, and I thought Frankie was every bit as talented as Johnny. Now let me tell you one or two things about Johnny Vinci.

Johnny took up golf, became a fanatic about it, even made his own golf clubs. One morning, while I was at home, reading the newspapers, I see an article in the sports section, saying this golfer just broke the course record at Bethpage State Park, which is in Farmingdale, Long Island, New York, and where the US Open has been played. He shot somewhere in the sixties. I wondered how that happened.

I never knew Johnny was such a great golfer, but then I found out all these things about him, He was a scratch golfer to start with, and I guess he just had a real good day when he broke the course record. The last thing I heard about him was that he was a golf pro at a club somewhere in the Carolinas. Life is funny, isn't it?

So now getting back to Stephen. After Bonnie represented him, he asked about her fee, and of course, she told him she was not going to charge him. He thanked her. A couple of weeks later, there's a knock on our door, I think on a Sunday morning, and it was Stephen. He has two packages, beautifully wrapped, which he gave to Bonnie. Bonnie asked Stephen, "What's this?"

He said, "Since you wouldn't charge me, I wanted to get you something. I thought you might like this."

Bonnie said, "That's so thoughtful of you, Stephen, but you shouldn't have."

She opened the first package, and it was a beautiful set of personalized stationery. She opened the second box, and it was a beautifully engraved oval sterling silver pin. Bonnie loved it, thanked Stephen, and to this day, she has it and wears it often; it is one of her prized possessions. We said, "We were just having breakfast, please join us." And he actually agreed. He was still maybe a little shy around us.

After breakfast, as he was leaving, I went into my garage to get my English racer bicycle since I was going for a bike ride. Stephen saw the bike and said, "I have an English racer, too, and I love to go riding, but I never have anyone to go with me." At the time, I was thirty-three years old and in good shape. I wasn't sure that Steve could keep up with me. Little did I know that I would have to try to keep up with him. We would go bicycling for hours. We would find a destination to go to. Most of the time, it would be for lunch as we would go biking in the morning. Our favorite place to go was Bloomingdale's, which is in Garden City. The restaurant there was very fancy, and we would park our bikes outside, lock them up, and then go to this fancy restaurant in our bicycle gear. I guess it was acceptable as no one ever told us we couldn't have lunch there because of the way we were dressed.

Bloomingdale's, especially on a Saturday, was always crowded, and half the time, we were the only guys in the restaurant. The place was crowded with women who had been shopping and were stopping for lunch. I think we were big hits at that restaurant. As I mentioned before, Stephen was good-looking, and the women would stare at him, especially the teenage girls. I could see them staring at him and then turning to their girlfriends and nodding toward him. It never seemed to affect Stephen; he was almost oblivious to it.

I, of course, was not oblivious to it and would, on occasion, flirt with some of the women. I would walk up to a woman I found attractive and look right into her eyes and say, "May I ask you a question?"

Most women looked at me curiously and said yes, and then I would say, "Do you believe in love at first sight?"

Most of them would smile and laugh as it was obvious, I was flirting with them. Some of them did not respond immediately, and then in a second or two caught on and would laugh. It was fun. Most of the women I flirted with were flattered by the attention. It helped that I was six feet tall, in good shape, and polite.

I don't recall anyone ever getting offended by it. I wonder what would happen in today's day and age. I remember Bonnie getting hit upon constantly by the police and the court officers and the lawyers when she was in Legal Aid. I would say, "Bon, what do you say to them?"

She would say, "I'm happily married now, but try me in six months." I said, "Bon, you must be kidding."

She said, "No, in that way, I never offend anybody or make them feel rejected."

I said, "Bonnie, smart as a whip."

So, Stephen and I became regular bike riders, and then he would just pop over the house all the time and hang out with us for a while. Bonnie and I got to meet his parents and sisters. Stephen got to meet a lot of my friends and my family, and of course, Ronnie took an immediate liking to Stephen. It was hard not to. I remember Ronnie going away for one weekend to his Cathedral in the Sky in New Hampshire with one of his new girl-friends. Stephen had a hot girl he was taking out and really couldn't afford fancy restaurants or places to take her. By that time, Ronnie was so close to him, as we all were, that he said, "Stephen, I'm going away and using my girlfriend's car, so you can use my new Cadillac convertible. Here are the keys to my apartment. Have fun."

Stephen could not believe it. Anyway, he tools around with Ronnie's Cadillac and spends the weekend at Ronnie's apartment with his girlfriend. I spoke to Ronnie the following Monday when he came back and asked him if he had seen Stephen. He said, "No, he left before I got back. Bobby, you can't believe my place."

I said, "Ronnie, he's not the kind of kid to make a mess and not clean up after himself. I can't believe it."

He said, "Bobby, it's just the opposite, the apartment is cleaner than when I left. It's spotless. I think he vacuumed the rug before he left." I knew that Stephen was a little bit of a neurotic/compulsive, which was definitely part of his charm.

So as Stephen started to become part of our family, we would ask him what he was going to do with his life. Was he planning on going to college? He said he hated school and wasn't sure what he wanted to do. He was obviously bright enough to go to college if that's what he wanted to do, but it appeared he had no interest in doing so. We started thinking, Ronnie and I and Bonnie, what the hell could Stephen do. I was convinced that anything he did, he would be successful as he was that type of kid.

Bonnie hit on what I thought was a great idea. She said, "Listen, one thing about Stephen, there's always a line of girls following him around. He worked for a while at a luncheonette, and the girls would line up at the counter, just looking at and staring at Stephen. Why don't we ask him what he thinks of the idea of becoming a hairdresser?"

I said, "I think it's a natural. Girls would line up for him, and if he decided later on, he wanted to go to college, he could always go and pay for his college with the money he made from hairdressing; even if he only did hairdressing part-time."

We all agreed it was a good idea, and so one day, we got together with Stephen and we broached the idea to him. He said, "Let me think about it."

After pondering the idea for a week or so, he said, "I think I would like to give it a try." Upon graduating from high school, he applied to beauty school and became a student at a New York State accredited school.

I remember Stephen telling me that one day, as he was learning to cut hair, in walked Ronnie for a haircut; and, he only wanted Stephen. Stephen was stunned and was afraid to give Ronnie a haircut. He never got over the fact that Ronnie was kind enough to come to that school and trust Stephen to give him a haircut. Well, Stephen finished beauty school and looked around for a job and got one with a guy named Tony in a hair salon in Lynbrook, New York. He started working for Tony and, of course, within a very short period of time, was booked with all the young girls who adored him. He started to tell me that he really liked his boss, Tony. He was a great guy but thought that the place could be run better and started to make suggestions which Tony was smart enough to take.

One night, when we were having dinner—Bonnie, Ronnie, me, and Stephen—I suggested that he should consider opening up his own place. I was sure he would be an immediate success. I knew he didn't have the money to open up a nice haircutting salon, the cost of just building one, plus the cost of rent, equipment, hiring people, and all the other costs that he would incur would probably take a couple years of savings, and so I said, "Stephen, if you think you would like to do it, I'll go partners with you and put up all the money."

I think at first, he was frightened. He didn't want me to risk my money in case it didn't work out. If I was ever sure that an investment would succeed, I was sure of Stephen. So now we come to Donald and Tommi. I told Stephen these were two world-class artists, interior designers, and furniture makers who were my good friends and clients, and I think if I asked them, they would build a shop for us. Stephen agreed.

Now for a suitable place to open up a new salon. I think we had been looking for a few weeks when Stephen called me and said he thought he found a great place in the town next to Lynbrook, called Malverne. We went, looked at the place, and the size was perfect for what we wanted to do. We met with the landlord and agreed to rent the place. Stephen signed the lease with a shaky hand, and I understood it was a big undertaking for him and a whole bunch of money for me. The space had a basement which Stephen told me could be used for hair coloring, facial massages, and other stuff. I had a friend of mine, Tommy, to build the place.

Friday night eventually comes around, and at around 5:00 p.m., one of my secretaries, Ann Marie, comes in to tell me that there was a gentleman waiting to see me by the name of Donald Cameron. She says, "My god, where did this guy come from?"

I said, "Why do you ask?"

She said, "Bobby, I never saw a guy dressed like him. He's wearing a cream-colored fedora. He's a good-looking guy but has a very thin handlebar mustache and has this camel hair coat with a belt around it which he is wearing over his shoulders, and he has some kind of sketchpad."

I said, "That gentleman happens to be a dear friend of mine, and among other things, he's an interior designer who is going to design the haircutting salon that I am going to open with my friend Stephen." By this time, she had met Stephen several times, as had most of my secretaries.

She comes back with Donald who was dressed exactly as she said. I gave him a big hug, but I knew better than to offer him a cup of coffee. I had a full bar in my office and made his favorite drink, a vodka and tonic. He said, "Well, Bobby, I'm anxious to see the space."

And I said, "And I'm anxious for you not only to see the space but to meet my dear friend Stephen who I'm sure you're going to get along marvelously with. We chatted for a while longer, and by five-thirty, we jumped into my car and headed to Malverne and to a little restaurant called Eckel Bickel. When we arrived, Stephen was already there since he was very punctual, always early compared to me, who was perpetually late but not by much. I always would say, "Fashionably late, maybe five or ten minutes."

I introduced Donald to Stephen and knew immediately that they would like each other. Donald was taken as most people were with Stephen's good looks, and he looked at me as we were approaching Stephen, and I said, "No, Donald, he's not gay."

Donald said, "Most men that are that good-looking generally are." I said, "Well, not Stephen."

They hit it off immediately. They were both very gentle, sensitive people, both with exquisite taste which Donald was to find out about Stephen as we proceeded with the buildup of the salon. I made sure during dinner that Donald didn't drink too much since I wanted him sober when he looked at the place. Little did I realize that when he worked, he drank very little, and other than the drink he had at my place, he had just a glass of wine with dinner.

After dinner, we went over to the space we rented which was within walking distance of Eckel Bickel. The landlord who had one of the stores in the complex that Stephen was in, a few doors down from Stephen, was an undertaker. I immediately gave him the nickname of Digger from an old radio comedy series that contained an undertaker who was called Digger O'Dell. We had already rented the place and had given him the down payment and security. He was here because Stephen had called him prior to our meeting to go over some stuff, like where the heating, air-conditioning, and plumbing was located and how to turn it on and off. It was then I first realized how incredibly responsible Stephen was. He was always one step ahead of me, anticipating what was needed and scheduling it or getting it done before I even thought of it. I didn't realize how competent he really was until he took on the responsibility of building that salon along with Tommy, our contractor, and Donald.

After Digger left, Donald took off his coat, took out his pad, and started to sketch. Stephen and I walked around the place for the first time, realizing the large undertaking we had just embarked upon. I asked Donald how long he thought it would take to sketch out the place and do his thing. He said, "Not too long, this isn't that difficult, probably two hours."

Two hours? I thought it was going to take him ten or fifteen minutes. Just goes to show you what happens when you deal with real pros. He would sketch for a while and then he would get up with a long tape measure and measure, and then he would sketch for a while, then measure again, and it went on and on like that, never saying a word, just concentrating on what he was doing.

We tell him that since it's going to take a couple of hours, we're going to get some coffee and donuts. He says, "Fine, take your time, I'll be here."

We went to Dunkin' Donuts, got some donuts and hot coffee, and came back and basically just watched Donald sketch and do his thing. After about two hours, he was done and started to pack up his things. We asked if we could take a look at some of the sketches that he had drawn, and he said, "Generally, I don't like to show my work until it's in better shape and I can explain what I'm trying to do, but if you'd like, you can take a quick look at it."

He opened the first page, and what we saw was an incredible vision. It just looked beautiful the way he had positioned the chairs in the waiting area with a step up and a step down, and the kind of material he was using was like a light blond wood. We were stunned. We had no idea that he could do something so beautiful. It was as if Frank Lloyd Wright had designed a beauty salon. It was like no other salon I had ever seen.

It was built exactly as he had sketched it. Our contractor told us it was a pleasure to build because the measurements were so exact there was really nothing to it. He just followed Donald's instructions and measurements and couldn't believe how beautiful it turned out. Twenty years later, it still looked exactly the same—beautiful, elegant, sleek, simple, and timeless.

We had our grand opening on July 29, 1979. I remember it well because Bonnie was nine months pregnant with our second daughter, Amy, and was due to give birth any day. We went to the grand opening, and Bonnie looked like a Sherman tank. She must've gained thirty or forty pounds. I said, "Bon, is it healthy to gain so much weight?"

She said, "Weight? What weight? I think I look fine." She told me the doctor said it was normal and she would lose it after the baby was born, which she did.

The grand opening was a night to remember. The place was jam-packed. We had champagne and hors d'oeuvres while music played, but not too loud, which was at my insistence. I wanted to have people talk to each other without screaming, and it was just a great night. Stephen had already hired, I think, three different hairstylists, one more beautiful than the other, all in their early twenties. I said to Stephen, "How do you do it? And where did you find them?"

He said, "Bobby, it's more than just that they're beautiful, they're talented.

Or I would never hire them. Every one of them is just special."

I remember one was nicer than the other and all incredibly pretty. Stephen's friends were all there, and I guess I can write another book just about some of the special friends he had. They all grew up in West Hempstead or Franklin Square or the surrounding towns, but all of them grew up on Long Island. It's amazing how many of these friends became millionaires and, in two instances, billionaires.

But as rich as they were and are, they are still very close to each other and to Stephen. When I see this, it always warms my heart.

I'm always amazed how they managed to maintain their friendships, even though some of them have moved to Florida and California. I'll give you one example. Stephen had a friend named

Barney who I met, I guess, when he was still a teenager. He was a wonderful tennis player and somehow found out that Bonnie was also a tennis player and a good one; a match was arranged between the two of them with several friends in attendance. It was a great match, which if I remember correctly Bonnie won. It was so much fun. He started working with this company called Music Command with another one of his close friends, Robert.

I incorporated the company initially for Robert, never dreaming that it would become as successful as it eventually became. Barney eventually moved to California to open up a Music Command center there which, of course, became very successful and is still operating successfully. Music Command has had many famous clients, too numerous to mention; but the one that comes to mind, is Madonna. Barney eventually met a lovely gal and got married. The gal he married came from a very wealthy California family who was involved with real estate. Barney, while running Music Command in California, started to help run his wife's family's real estate business. They do very well.

I'll give you an example that just happened recently. Stephen sent me a picture of the yacht that Barney was renting for a three-week vacation. The cost of renting the yacht for three weeks was several hundred thousand dollars. He never took himself too seriously and was also one of the funniest of all of Stephen's friends.

Stephen called one day and said, "Barney wants to build a beam." I said, "A beam? What kind of beam?"

He said, "A strong wooden beam that would go across the top of the ceiling and that could hold a couple of hundred pounds."

I said, "Why?"

He said, "So if things really get bad, he could throw a rope over the beam and hang himself." Ever since then, whenever things go bad for me or for Stephen, we always say, "Get the beam ready," all because of Barney and his sense of humor.

A couple of years after that, he told me, "Barney is thinking of growing the toenail on his foot."

And I said, "What the hell for?"

"So that he can reach and pull the trigger of a rifle with his toenail, when he wants to kill himself. I guess the beam would be too slow."

Now I know obviously, he had no intention of killing himself, but Stephen used to have me rolling, laughing. They would get stoned on occasion and were so much fun to be around. One of his friends eventually started a hedge fund; another one became a partner in one of the biggest law firms in New York City and became a millionaire. On and on it went, incredible success stories. Yet with all their successes, they never have seemed to lose their humanity. They still all were very down to earth. I sometimes wonder if it was something they were drinking or smoking that made them all so bright and successful.

There are times in life when you meet someone and they have a profound influence on you and you never forget them. I'll tell you about one. Barney had an uncle that lived in England. His name was Uncle Bernie. I met him just once. I spent the afternoon with him and his wife. His wife was Barney's mother's sister. Barney's mother had been born in England and met Barney's father, in New York after the war. I remember the whole afternoon, and all I did was laugh. He was funny, bright, and also a little nuts.

He was a socialist, and so we discussed socialism and the benefits and the reasons why I thought it couldn't succeed. I remember Uncle Bernie saying why is it necessary for a man to have two cars when he only needs one; I guess suggesting that if you can afford two, you should consider giving the other one away to someone who was less fortunate than you. His ideas were crazy, but he was such a kind and generous soul, and he and his intentions were so pure, magnanimous, and loving that you couldn't help but just love him.

During the course of our conversation, I read him a saying that I had saved. I have over a hundred sayings that I keep on my iPhone, some of them political, some of them spiritual, some of them social, but all to remind me of what's important in life and to try to be the best person I can be. I obviously always don't succeed, but dammit, I try. So, as he was speaking about the virtues of socialism, I pulled out one of my sayings (I don't remember where I got it from) and read it to him. He listened in silence. The saying went as follows:

"A feature of a free society is that some are more gifted than others and, therefore, have more than others. Therefore, a free society ensures intellectual and financial inequality. Such are the risks and rewards of capitalism."

He listened intently and made me repeat it twice, then he thought about it and said, "Bobby, do you see what I mean? Those who are smarter and have more must share it with those who are not smart and have less."

I said, "But what about those people who have less not because they're less smart but because they don't care to work as hard?" I told him that socialism and communism will always fail because it goes against man's human nature. A man works for himself and for his family. He doesn't work for the greater good of all humanity. That's just pie in the sky. I'm not saying that there aren't special people who work for the good of all mankind, but those very special people are not in the majority. They are not the rule but the exception to the rule.

So, the argument went on and on, but always with him throwing in a thought that just cracked me up. What a generous man, what a kind soul, what a pure soul. Delusional, I thought, but boy, I just couldn't help but love that guy. His arguments remain with me to this day because although not practical, I thought, *wouldn't it be wonderful if everyone had the pureness of heart and the soul of an Uncle Bernie?*

Within a couple of months of the opening of our salon, we realized it was going to be a huge success. Stephen ran it with an iron fist. You would never think that someone like Stephen, who up to that point had a carefree life with not many responsibilities, could step up to the plate and run a business the way he did. The place hummed; it was sparkling at all times. After that, we all got together for dinner one night. There was me, Ronnie, Bonnie, Stephen, Donald, and Tommi. As I sat there among them as they were chatting and laughing and toasting to the success of our salon, I thought, *what a lucky person I am to have such wonderfully talented people who are my family and friends.* I looked at them, and for a moment thought I really didn't belong here. They are all so special and talented; I'm just an average person.

Then I thought; *wait a second, I'm the one who put all these people together. I'm the one who asked Beryl to put me in touch with her designer. I'm the one who first met Donald and Tommi and hired them. I'm the one who encouraged Stephen to open up a hair salon. I'm the one who got Donald and Tommi to design it. I'm the one who put up all the money for the salon.* I realize, *I'll be damned. I think I really do deserve to be here among these incredible people.*

I once read that a true friend was worth more than gold. My first thought was, *how many ounces?* which is my natural bent to make light of things at first. Now it was time to move on to other things. I had other fish to fry, other things to do.

One of the great things about having your own law practice was that you never knew who was going to walk through the door the next day. Were you going to get a case that was worth a million dollars and strike it rich? Or were you going to get somebody in desperate need of help who had no money, but you knew you could help. It was exciting. I loved it.

A Week in the Life

Bonnie Linda Mencher, Esq. "Bonnie Aliazzo"

THERE WAS ONE WEEK DURING all the years I practiced that I thought I would end my little story by telling you about it. There were lots of crazy weeks, but for some reason, I remember this one. It all began on a Monday morning. I was having breakfast with Bonnie, reading the newspapers and chatting, when suddenly I mentioned something that she disagreed with. I said, "Well, I think you're wrong."

And she said, "Well, I think you're wrong," and an argument ensued.

I guess we're a reasonably normal couple and at times disagree, but it never really gets out of hand. We disagree, then either I admit I was wrong or she admits she was (that is after a careful discussion and presentation of our arguments; after all, we are lawyers) or we just drop it since we can't agree. This time, the argument became heated, and I don't remember what it was about, but here's what I do remember.

As we are arguing, she became a little heated which is unusual for her as she's always relatively level-headed, and she said to me, "Do you know what I think? I think you're a pedantic blowhard."

I said, "A pedantic blowhard?" I thought, *I'll be damned. I don't know what the hell that means.* I left the room and went upstairs to look up the words *pedantic* and *blowhard*. Here's what I found.

Pedantic is an insulting word used to describe someone who annoys others by correcting small errors, caring too much about minor details, or emphasizing their own expertise, especially in some narrow or boring subject matter.

A *blowhard* is a person who blusters and boasts in an unpleasant way.

Now I have had my share of insults. Anywhere from "Go fuck yourself" to "Shithead." But I have never been called a pedantic blowhard. What a spectacular insult. If you're going to be insulted, at least be insulted with some style and class. That was the best insult that has ever been bestowed upon me. I couldn't believe it, a pedantic blowhard. My god, what style.

I went downstairs, looked at Bonnie, who was still a little hot under the collar, and said to her, "So you think I'm a pedantic blowhard?"

And she said, "That's right."

And I said, "What style, what class. I have never been insulted so elegantly in my life."

And as she started to say, "You're crazy," I walked up to her and just grabbed her and hugged her, and at first, she resisted, but I started laughing, and then she started laughing, and so to this day, a pedantic blowhard has been one of my all-time favorite insults.

An hour or so later, I'm in my Bentley Flying Spur, driving to the office. Now why am I driving a Bentley Flying Spur? Simple, there are three reasons. One, I happen to hit on a big case. Two, I'm somewhat insecure, and it makes me feel better and less insecure driving that Bentley. Lastly, it really is a fine car and fun to drive.

I told Bonnie, "When I check out, I want to be buried in my Bentley, sitting at the steering wheel."

She said, "If you check out, I'm going to wrap you up and slip you under the pool cover into that fucking swimming pool that you had built and never go into."

I enter my office, greeting everyone a cheery good morning as I am generally peppy, especially in the mornings. One of my secretaries tells me that there is a message from Big Mike. Now who is Big Mike? Simply put, he is one of my favorite people in the world. Now you may think I have a lot of favorite people, and you would be right. One of my favorite movies is a movie called *Frankie and Johnny* with Al Pacino and Michelle Pfeiffer. One of the actresses in that movie was Kate Nelligan.

Well, there is a scene in that movie when Kate Nelligan looks at Al Pacino and says, "He's kind 'a cute, what do you think?"

Michelle Pfeiffer says, "You think everybody's cute."

And Kate Nelligan says, "You're right, I'm lucky that way."

Well, that's kind of like how I am. During the course of my practice and in my life, I have met hundreds and hundreds of people, and I always find something interesting about them. I guess, like Kate Nelligan's character in the movie, I'm lucky that way.

So now getting back to Big Mike. Who is Big Mike? And why is he one of my favorite people? Well, to start with, I've known him longer than I know Bonnie. He tells me the story of when he first met Ronnie and me, which as you will see I could have no memory of.

Big Mike was my older brother Vin's best friend and, therefore, is almost thirteen years older than Ronnie and me. He tells me the first time he saw Ronnie and me was December 14. He remembers it as a cold but nice day.

He said he was playing stoop ball with my brother Vin, waiting for my mother and father to come home from the hospital with Vinnie's new twin brothers. We were born on December 7, which in later life, Mike would always remind us we were born on a day of infamy as President Roosevelt said at the start of World War II.

So, my father pulls up to the curb with my mother and me and Ronnie. He and Vinnie ran up to the car to see Vin's new brothers. My mother and father get out of the car, each holding one of us. They walked over to the stoop and bent down and took the blanket covers off our faces. He said, "I looked down at you two guys and I knew you were going to be trouble, so I asked your mother and father if it was too late to take them back." So right off, you can see he's a little crazy but very smart with a great sense of humor.

Now my brother Vin had lots of friends, but there were three especially close ones to him. They were Big Mike, Louie, and Allie Pang, which was not his real name but a nickname given to him. When my daughter Alison was small, my brother Ron, whom she adored, used to call her Alison, then Al, then Allie, then Allie Pang, and on occasion, Pangulet. Growing up, those three guys were in my house constantly; they were all twelve and thirteen years older than Ronnie and me and were our heroes.

They always listened to us and, of course, dispensed their incredible wisdom and knowledge to us, like when at Belmont Race Track always bet the longest horse in a small field. They were irreverent, they were funny, they were incredibly smart, and above all, the four of them were really handsome. I once was driving with Bonnie in Ozone Park to pick up a paycheck from a bar I had been working at during law school, called the Post, and as I'm driving there, I see Louie walking down the street.

I pull over and yell, "Lou, what's cooking?" He looks up and yells, "Where are you going?"

I said, "I'm going to pick up a paycheck at the Post!"

He jumps into the car in the front seat, next to Bonnie, and I introduced him. She looked at him, and they chatted for a minute or two, and then I dropped him off. Bonnie was speechless for a while. I said to Bonnie, "Why so quiet?"

She said, "Oh my God, he is so handsome." Let me tell you a little bit about Louie and Allie Pang before I tell you about big Mike.

Louie was a major athlete. He could do anything. He boxed for a short time—won, of course—but didn't like it and stopped. He played baseball for a while and made the minor leagues going up to triple A, and we all thought he had a shot at the majors. Then, one day, in the middle of the summer and in the middle of the season, while he was away with the triple A club he showed up at home. He was very lonely and missed his girlfriend, his friends and family; so, he left the team and came home. He wound up running a construction company, got married to a wonderful, beautiful girl, and had several kids.

Allie Pang was altogether another story. Although also extremely good-looking, Bonnie never took to him. She thought he was too slick, which he was.

He ran a labor union and did quite well. He had the most girlfriends of all my brothers' friends. Big Mike was telling me one time they were going to this nightclub, and as they were entering, Allie said, "I'll be with you in a little while" as they walked in.

They found out later on that he saw a beautiful girl walking into the nightclub, he walked up to her before she got to the door, introduced himself, and talked her into leaving with him before they even entered the nightclub. As I said, he was very handsome, very smooth, but not Bonnie's cup of tea. I loved him.

Now getting back to Big Mike. He was like one of my brothers. He was always there, just like one of my brothers. He had a tortured life for a while but, in the end, came around. I remember when I was sixteen and needed some clothes for school. My father gave me some money and told me to go to Montgomery Ward in Jamaica, where Big Mike was working at the time as a salesman, and he would set me up with what I needed. I went into Montgomery Ward, and there is Big Mike in a suit and tie, looking like a million bucks, and I go over to him and give him a hug.

We chat for a while, and then I tell him the reason I came by is because I need some clothes when I to go back to Mount Assumption. I tell him what I need and the sizes, and after he helps me pick out everything, he puts the clothes in boxes. There was over a hundred dollars' worth of clothes, and I counted the money. I had just enough to pay for it, and I asked Big Mike for the bill. He looked at me. He said, "Forget about it."

I looked at him. With him at the cash register, no wonder Montgomery Ward went out of business.

Here it is several years later. I'm sitting at my desk with a lot of clients to see that morning and think I better call Big Mike before I get started. He picks up on the second ring. I said, "Mike, what's shaken'?"

And he said, "Bobby, I have a horse in the fourth race at Aqueduct who cannot lose, and I am a little short, and I'm going to be in Ozone Park later on, and I was hoping that you could front me a couple of bucks."

I said, "Mike, how long have you been going to Gamblers Anonymous now?" Big Mike had been going to Gamblers Anonymous for several years and he had been going to Alcoholics Anonymous for even longer. If there was any kind of anonymous, Big Mike should be and would be going to it.

He eased up on the drinking, but on the gambling, every once in a while, he would slip when he thought he had a sure thing as he did today. I said, "Mike, I am not going to contribute to your addiction by giving you money."

He said, "Bobby, don't break my balls. You are not going to start hassling me over a couple of measly bucks. You already forgot Cassius Clay."

What is Big Mike referring to? I'll tell you. The night of Cassius Clay cost me literally thousands of bucks; treating Big Mike, taking him to different places, dining in the finest places and just hanging out with him over the years. Was worth it; I don't regret one penny spent, and I would do it again a hundred times over.

Now let me tell you about Cassius Clay. Years before, while I was in law school, studying for final exams on a Friday night, I got a call from Big Mike. My mother answers and says, "Bobby, Michael is on the phone."

I pick up the phone, and he says, "Bobby, get ready. I'll be over to your house in twenty minutes. I'm taking you to Johnny's Steakhouse for a steak dinner, and after that, I have tickets to the fights at Madison Square Garden front row seats."

I said, "Who's fighting?" He says, "Cassius Clay."

I said "Mike, I can't go. I'm studying for final exams and I just can't take the time."

He said, "Are you crazy? A fight like this doesn't come along that often. I'm picking you up in twenty minutes, be ready." And he hangs up.

Twenty minutes later, he picks me up and takes me to Johnny's Steakhouse, one of the best steakhouses in Queens at the time. We have a great steak dinner, and as always, I have such a good time hanging out with Big Mike. He has so many stories to tell and he is so smart. From there, we head out to Madison Square Garden. We park and go in, and an usher takes us to our seats.

He's walking and walking toward the ring, and finally, I told Mike he was getting really close to the ring. He said Bobby the tickets say one row off the ring apron and sure as hell we are one row behind the reporters and the announcers. I couldn't believe the seats. We sit down, and there is a fight that just started between two lightweights, and as we're watching it, the crowd really starts coming in, and what a sight. There is nothing like going to Madison Square Garden to see the fights on a Friday night. The people you see there are a cross between Damon Runyan characters and Ripley's Believe it or Not.

There were lots of celebrities. I don't remember them all, but what I do remember most are the Black pimps who would walk in, dressed to the nines, with cream-colored hats and diamond rings and mink coats draped over their shoulders and four girls, two on each arm. What a sight. It was worth going just to see this show. Finally, I asked Big Mike, "Who's Clay fighting?"

He says, "A guy named Doug Jones." The main event finally comes around, and out comes Cassius Clay. I think he must've been in his early twenties. He stepped into the ring, and just the way he danced around and off the ropes was magical. The only other fighter that I thought was as good as him or maybe even better was my all-time favorite fighter, Sugar Ray Robinson. The difference between the two of them was that Cassius Clay/Muhammad Ali was more than just a fighter. He was a national and/or international celebrity.

He was the best promoter, not only in the boxing industry but the best promoter of his views and his causes. And the public took to him and loved him for the courage of his convictions and, of course, for his great boxing skills.

If you want to see the greatest performance by a boxer in history, in my opinion, go to YouTube and watch the fight between Muhammad Ali and Cleveland "Big Cat" Williams. It was more than just a boxing match; Ali was so light on his feet. To me, he was a cross between a boxer, a dancer, and a ballerina. He moved so fast that he made his opponent, Cleveland Williams, look like an amateur. Williams had an impressive knockout record. The man could punch and fight. Before the fight, I thought he posed a serious threat to Ali. Was I wrong?

He looked helpless against Muhammad Ali, like an amateur. It was an incredible fight, probably the best display of boxing I have ever seen, surpassing even Sugar Ray Robinson.

He had predicted that he would knock out Doug Jones, I think in the sixth or seventh round. I don't remember, but when that round came around, he went after Jones with a fury he had not displayed in the earlier rounds and almost knocked him out but didn't. The fight went on to be a decision in favor of Ali. It was a night I'll always remember; it was special and all because of Big Mike.

So here he is, asking me to lend him some money to bet on the horses. I asked Mike, "What happened to Gamblers Anonymous? I thought you stopped gambling." I was breaking his balls. I said, "After that great interview on the *Barry Gray Show*, you're back to gambling."

He said, "Bobby, are you going to start or are you going to lend me the money?"

I said, "Of course I'll lend you the money, or more specifically, I'm going to give you the money. Why? Because the horses that you follow unfortunately like to follow other horses."

Now let me tell you about the *Barry Gray Show* that I just mentioned a moment ago. The *Barry Gray Show* was a very popular radio show that was on late at night. One night, just after I had started practicing, I was coming home late from New York City, listening to the radio, and to the Barry Gray show. After Barry Gray was introduced, he says, "Tonight, ladies and gentlemen, we have a special guest, Mr. Mike Forella, the secretary of Gamblers Anonymous here in New York City."

I said, "Oh my god, that's Big Mike, can it really be?"

Suddenly, I hear Big Mike's voice talking to Barry Gray, and they had a discussion for probably a half hour or so. Big Mike telling Barry Gray and the audience about gambling and the problems it presents, and the people who are gamblers and cannot stop and on and on—it was quite an entertaining show, and I thought Big Mike was great.

About a week later, I'm leaving my office to go for lunch, and who comes walking toward the office but Big Mike. I tell him, "Mike, I heard you on the *Barry Gray Show*, you were great."

He said, "Yeah, a lot of people heard me."

I said, "How the hell did you get on the show?"

He said, "One of the show's producers is an alcoholic and gambler and wanted somebody from Gamblers Anonymous because they thought it would be a good topic for a broadcast, and the people at Gamblers Anonymous asked me, and I agreed to go."

I said to Mike, "What a program, it was really great. I really enjoyed it.

How's it going at GA?"

He said, "Really not that great, Bobby." I said, "What happened?"

He said, "Last week, the treasurer slipped." "What do you mean slipped?"

He said, "He had the money for our yearly party and took the money and went to the track and blew it all, several thousand dollars."

I said, "Mike, are you kidding me?"

He said, "No." You have to understand in GA the most important office is not the president or the vice president, it's the treasurer because he controls all the money.

I almost fell to the floor, laughing. He looks at me, and sadly, he says, "Yeah, it's a shame." In order to be the treasurer, you have to have been in Gamblers Anonymous for several years and not have gambled.

I can't believe it. It just goes to show, you never know. You have to be alert and conscious of your failings and always be on your guard. This is the same Big Mike who is now asking me to front him some money for a horse that can't lose. Turns out the horse was running that Friday afternoon, and so I agreed to join him for lunch at the track and to make our score of a lifetime.

About an hour after my talk with Big Mike, as I am seeing clients and discussing their cases, my secretary buzzes me to tell me that Jake Boland is on the phone and has to talk to me now, it can't wait. I say, "Fine. I'll take it in the other room." I hang up the phone and excuse myself, telling the clients I'll be back in a moment.

I go into the conference room, which is empty, pick up the phone, and say, "Jake, what is so important that it can't wait? I'm in the middle of seeing clients."

He says, "Bobby, I got an offer on the Valorous case. I think it's a great offer, but I have to say yes or no right now or the offer is going to be withdrawn." He tells me what the offer is. It's more than I told the client when I initially took the case. He says, "The court just broke for an early lunch, and the client has gone to a Greek diner for lunch."

I ask him if he knows where the diner is. He says yes. I tell him to go to the diner and tell our client that we have a settlement offer and that he is to come to the office now to see me, and I will discuss the offer with him. We both agree it's more than the case is worth. I told him to take it. He knows the client is crazy, and no matter what we get him, he's going to say it's not enough, but I tell Jake I'll handle him.

During the course of my practice, our office handles several different kinds of cases. We handle matrimonial cases, medical malpractice cases, real estate cases, of course criminal cases and personal injury cases, but only if we estimated that they had a certain value. At first, when we started out, we took anything, even if the cases were bad just to get the experience. Then as our practice grew, we started to get choosy and only took cases that we thought we could win.

Peter Valorous was just one of over a thousand cases that our office handled during the years I practiced. Let me tell you a little bit about him because he was unusual and not the typical type of client. When I took the case, I thought the liability was shaky. In order to win a personal injury case, you generally needed three things we used to call the Holy Trinity. You needed:

Liability—meaning that you did not contribute to the cause of the accident or injury. When I first started practicing law, the standard was called contributory negligence, meaning if you contributed even 1 percent to the cause of the accident, you could not sue or collect any money. That was changed to comparative negligence, meaning if you contributed to the accident, then you could collect money based on the amount you contributed to the accident. So, if you contributed 5 or 10 percent to the cause of the accident, you could collect 80 to 90 percent of the value of the injury.

Injury—there was a statutory requirement, regarding the severity of the injury before you could maintain a case; in other words, it had to be considered a serious injury.

Insurance coverage—meaning if you had a case that was worth half a million dollars, but the person who caused the accident only had

$25,000 worth of coverage and had no other money, you were screwed. The most you collected from that person was $25,000, unless you wanted to go after the person personally, but what would be the point if the person had no money? On the other hand, if there were lots of insurance, like let's say the accident occurred and the defendant was a city bus driver, well, now you're suing the city of New York and they have unlimited coverage. I hope I didn't confuse you, but that's kind of the way things worked.

One day, Peter Valorous makes an appointment to see me. I don't recall who referred him. He had an accident several months ago, was severely injured, and came walking in with a cane, limping. This is after several months. He tells me how the accident occurred, and I think the injuries are severe, the insurance coverage is unlimited, but the liability (how the accident occurred) was shaky. I think I'll take a shot with the case on a contingency basis, our fee being one third of whatever we get for him if we win and no fee if we lose. I also tell him if I find he has not been truthful with me and the liability is not as he said, I will discontinue the case.

If I discontinue the case, I will give it back to him before the statute of limitations runs out, which is three years, so that he can take it to another lawyer. He reluctantly agrees and signs a retainer. I tell him what I think the case is worth if we win. To make a long story short, we put it into suit, go through all the preliminary legal proceedings, including examinations before trial; and just as we get ready for trial, and in the process of picking a jury, for some reason, which to this day, I don't know, the insurance company attorneys, fold. They give us an offer for settlement that is more than I thought the case is worth, and more than they had told me when we first took the case.

I am beside myself with joy. I cannot believe the settlement we got. The thing that made this case so unusual was that while we were proceeding with motions and hearings, I found out that Mr. Volorous had taken the case to three other lawyers before me, who had all turned him down. He never told me about it. I think their loss is my gain. That's happened many times in the past when I took cases that other lawyers had turned down and won them. It was not so unusual. Some of the cases I accepted that were turned down by other lawyers involved lots of time and money, but I either thought the case had merit where they did not or I simply really liked the client and thought I would take a shot or I had hired some new young lawyer and thought I would give him experience by letting him handle a losing case.

To my surprise, sometimes these losing cases that were being handled by young lawyers turned out to be winners. But I had a feeling about Mr. Volorous. I had a feeling that no matter what I told him, when I got an offer on the case, he was not going to accept it unless I lowered my fee. The reason I had this feeling was because when I initially told him what my fee was, he objected. I said I understood his objection, but I was not going to take the case with a lower fee.

There were mountains of work to be done to put this case into suit and thousands of dollars in expenses, including fees for doctor's testimony when we got to trial, and if we lost, we would suffer all the expenses and time. He would have lost nothing. He then reluctantly agreed to the fee. The fee was a standard fee and was regulated by the New York State Bar Association. All lawyers charged the same fee.

Whenever I saw Mr. Volorous, from the first time he came into my office, he always walked with a pronounced limp and a cane. One of the reasons I took the case was because he walked with such a pronounced limp which I thought was a permanent injury. That's part of what gave this case in my view such value.

Several months before that trial, while I was driving to my office, I took a back way off the Southern State Parkway and passed a big park. It was on a Saturday morning, and I was meeting some clients at the office. In the park, there was a soccer game going on between what I assume was an Italian team because they had Italian uniforms and the Italian flag, and another team which I believe was a Ukrainian team because they had blue and yellow uniforms.

The whole thing was so colorful with all the colors and everybody running around, screaming, that I stopped my car for a moment, pulled over, and got out to watch the game as I was early for my appointment. And who do I see as one of the soccer players kicking a ball toward the goal? Mr. Volorous.

I was shocked. I couldn't believe it. I walk around to the sidelines, mixing with all the fans. Mr. Volorous, as he is running, sees me, and I'm staring at him. This is the man who comes to my office all the time with a cane and a severe limp. He had real fractures from his accident, but I guess recovered way better then he let on. He just stops and starts to walk toward the sideline, limping. I can't believe this guy. He comes limping up to me and looks at me, and I look him straight in the eye for what seemed like two minutes but was only a moment, and I walk away. This is the same guy whose case we are all working feverishly on.

Fast-forward now, almost a year later, and Jake has just told him we had a settlement offer, and he comes to my office to find out what the offer is. My secretary shows him to my office, and he comes in, of course with the cane and the pronounced limp. I get right to the point and tell him what the offer is, which again is more than what I told him the case was worth when I first took it.

His reaction, as I expected, was not one of joy but one of thoughtfulness, thinking about whether or not he should accept the offer. He says he thinks we can get more if we proceed to trial. I expected this reaction from him, and calling his bluff said he was the final word on whether or not we accepted the offer, even though it was more than we had anticipated. I told him that we would notify the court today that he had rejected the offer. Since he wanted to go to trial, then pursuant to our retainer agreement, which stated in part if we got an offer that we thought was acceptable, and he did not and he wished to proceed to trial, then from that moment forward, he would have to pay all further court costs and fees for medical specialists to testify which could be in the thousands.

Of course, upon hearing this and realizing his bluff was called, he agreed to accept the settlement offer but with the provision that when the check came, we would still discuss how much money I would get as he expected me to lower my fees. I agreed to discuss my fee once again when the check arrived.

Approximately three weeks later, we received the settlement check from the insurance company which was over $100,000, and I asked my secretary to contact Mr. Volorous. She called him and made an appointment for him to come in the following day to sign the settlement check and receive his portion of the settlement proceeds.

Now I had a little game I played on occasion, relatively infrequently, with clients that I knew to be unreasonable and prone to giving me a difficult time regarding settlement checks. When my secretary came back to tell me that she had contacted Mr. Volorous and had set up an appointment for the following day, she asked, "Are we going to play the old bait and switch game, and can I be there when you do it?"

Now all my secretaries and some of the lawyers knew I did this on occasion, and they tried to talk me into setting up a camera secretly so they could sit in another room and watch as I played my bait and switch game. I said, "No, of course not, that's ridiculous, absolutely not." I would allow whatever secretary who worked on the case to stay in the room with me as long as she did not laugh when I did it.

Now what was the bait and switch game? When the check arrived, I would make a colored copy of the check so that the copy looked like the real check.

Then I would take the real check and put it in my desk drawer and take out the fake check and put it in the file in the envelope in which the check came.

Now when Mr. Volorous showed up the next day, the following occurred. I welcomed him into the office, we chatted nicely for a moment, then I opened his folder and took out the fake check and showed it to him. He looked at the check very carefully, put it on my desk, and then said, "Can we discuss what your fee will be?"

I told him my fee would be what we had agreed to when he signed the retainer, and I would not take a penny less. He said, "I thought we were going to discuss this."

And I said, "Yes, we are going to discuss it. My fee is one-third of what I collect for you, minus expenses which were minimal since we didn't have to try the case. That is what I'm legally entitled to and that's what we agreed to."

He said there was no way that he was going to sign the check. He would rather give the check back to the insurance company. I reminded him that three other lawyers had turned this case down, which he failed to tell me. I took the case and wound up settling for more than we thought was possible, and his thanks to me was that I didn't deserve my fee. I looked at him and said, "Are you sure that's the way you feel and that's the way you want to do it?"

And he said, "Yes."

I looked at him and said, "Okay, I want to tell you something, Mr. Volorous. I'm going to get into my Silver Blue Rolls-Royce (which he knew I had and commented on it and loved it) and go home tonight and let the insurance company have all the money, I really don't care. As a matter of fact, I'll show you how little I care. I picked up the check while he was looking at me and ripped it in two.

He jumped up. I thought he was going to have a heart attack, and he said, "No, no, whatever you want! Can we get another check?" He was saying this as he was almost in tears and in shock.

I said, "Are you sure that you're not going to give me a hard time and you are going to give me the fee that we agreed upon?"

And he said, "Yes, yes."

I said, "Okay." Then I opened my desk drawer and showed him the real check, telling him, "This is the real check."

And he looked at me, dumbfounded for a moment, and then smiled and said, "I knew you were a good lawyer." My secretary, standing behind him, tried to stifle her laughter, and I gave her a stern look, and rather than start laughing out loud, she rushed out of the office. This I had done several times when I had clients who were just unreasonable and difficult. It always worked like a charm, and none of the clients I did it to ever got angry with me. They were just so relieved that I hadn't ripped up the real check.

Now getting back to the lawyer who settled this case, Jake Boland, let me tell you a little bit about him. At the time I knew him, he owned over twenty exotic cars. At least half of them were Rolls-Royces. He was a lawyer who had a special talent for settling cases with insurance companies, all kinds of cases. I realized his talent early on, and so for several years, I hired him to settle all my cases since I was a terrible negotiator; sometimes, one must acknowledge their weaknesses. In the end, I really had no great interest in money or haggling over it. I liked what money could do but realized my heart wasn't into negotiating for it. When one likes something, they tend to be good at it, and when they do not, they tend not to be so good at it.

I wanted my clients to have the best representation possible and therefore decided to hire someone that was better at it than me and liked it more. It worked out better for all three of us. The clients benefited from having someone like Jake (although they didn't know he existed; I paid him out of my fee). Jake made an incredible living doing something he loved and was great at, and I was relieved of a burden that I did not enjoy doing.

I made less than I could have, but I did the right thing and felt good about it. Jake, on the other hand, lived to negotiate and had over twenty lawyers who he negotiated for. His wife, a lovely lady, was a surgeon, a very talented one, and so together, they did very well. I knew and liked her a lot. She had blonde hair and blue eyes; her name was Marianne, and I would say, "Marianne, if I ever need surgery, promise you will operate on me."

She would say, "Yes, Bobby, I promise I will operate on you if you need surgery," humoring me.

Jake told me of all the vehicles he had, the one that he loved the most was an ice-cream wagon, like a Good Humor truck that sold ice cream to children. He saw one somewhere and decided to buy one, and so he did. On occasions when he felt in the mood, he would fill up the truck with ice cream and go around to different neighborhoods, mostly poor neighborhoods, ring the bell, and give all the ice cream away for nothing. How could you not love the guy?

When Alison was small, I think four years old, she wanted a dog. We stalled for as long as we could and finally agreed to get her one. A neighbor of ours had a litter with several dogs and asked if we wanted one, and so Henry (I don't remember how we came up with the name Henry, but Alison loved it, so Henry it was) fell into our laps. When we told Alison we would be picking up Henry that Saturday morning, she was overjoyed and couldn't wait. I was telling Jake about it a day or two before we were to pick up the dog.

That Saturday morning, at eight o'clock, when we were scheduled to pick up Henry, I heard a car pull up in front of our house, and the person in it was tooting his horn. Who was it? It was Jake in a long limousine that was custom-made that he bought from the owners of Manischevitz Wine company. It was the most luxurious limousine I had ever seen, and there was Jake, driving it. I ran outside in my pajamas as Jake was getting out of the car and said, "Jake, what the hell are you doing here?"

He said, "If we're going to pick up the dog, let's do it in style. Get Alison, let's go get the dog." Can you believe him? This was Jake. Ali was thrilled.

So, getting back to the week I remember, I finished out the day on Monday, and on Tuesday morning, I had to be in court for a settlement conference. When I finished, I stopped to see Ronnie who was on trial with a case that he didn't want but was forced to take. I popped into the courtroom, walked up to the front when there was a break, and asked Ronnie if he had time for lunch. He said no, he was jammed. I said, "Okay, I'll talk to you tonight" and left. I get back to my office, and who is waiting for me with a new client but Richie Branden?

Richie was a Black guy from Harlem who was quite the man about town. He was exceptionally handsome and had a bevy of beautiful women. He worked at Harlem Hospital on some executive committee. He was arrested just one time for selling heroin. It was the only time he ever did it, and unfortunately, he got caught. He never did it again. Let me tell you how it all went down. He was talked into selling several pounds of heroin. It was supposed to be a one-time deal. It was all set up by the New York City police department.

The way it went down, he was to meet a guy on a corner in Harlem, around 8:00 a.m., and the transfer of the drugs would be made to this guy, and in return, he would receive the money which was over a hundred thousand dollars. Prior to the meeting, the police set up a van with a camera crew to record and videotape the whole transaction. On the appointed morning, Richie showed up in his car with the drugs. The switch was made on the street corner very quickly with the police recording the whole transaction. As soon as the switch was made and duly recorded, the police arrested him.

Now who was his lawyer? His name was Alan Campo. The first time I ever heard of Alan was when Bonnie came back from court after working for the day and told me there was a new lawyer that had just arrived from Manhattan Legal Aid, who is probably one of the best lawyers she's ever seen at work. She said he was brilliant. She saw him cross-examining a policeman, and the thing was that he could go from the first question to the last question, back to the middle question, then to the third question, and within fifteen minutes, he had the policeman totally confused. She said she never saw anything like it; he was brilliant.

Ronnie and I got to meet him a short time later, and he became a really close friend of ours. The problem was that in addition to Alan being brilliant, he was also somewhat crazy, irresponsible, and unreliable. He would start work on a case, and then he would disappear, then he would show up again. Whenever he made a big fee on a case, the first thing he would do was go to a supermarket and load up his car with food until the freezer and the refrigerator was stuffed, then fill up the cabinets. This way, he felt if he did not make any more money on cases in the foreseeable future, he would always be able to eat; yes, he was a little nuts. He drove everyone crazy, but we put up with it because when he was in court, he was just amazing. I don't remember how it happened, but Richie got Alan for his lawyer.

Alan tried to take a plea with the District Attorney's Office, asking to reduce the charges to a lower-class felony. The District Attorney's Office refused to drop the case, even one felony count since they had him so dead. Since they had nothing to lose, Alan said, "Screw it, let's break their balls and try the case, you never know what can happen with a jury."

Richie, of course, trusted Alan with his life and agreed since he had nothing to lose.

To make a long story short and again keeping in mind the brilliance of Alan, Richie, with all the evidence against him, was acquitted. The judge was so outraged by the not guilty verdict he sequestered the jury, questioning the jurors as to how they arrived at the verdict. The foreman got up and explained their thinking and their acquittal. They told the judge that they believed some of the policemen lied about a telephone number that was exchanged prior to the arrest and lied another time and that one of the other witnesses they believed was untruthful about minor things. "And you, Judge, told us that if you believed the person or persons testifying was not truthful, then you should throw out his entire testimony. So, we threw out their entire testimony, which included how the meeting was set up, and if we threw out that testimony, then we had to throw out the videotape, and without that, they had no case, and that's why we acquitted."

It didn't hurt that half of the jurors were Black women and, of course, fell in love with Richie, and they adored Alan as most jurors did. So, Richie was acquitted of selling drugs on a street corner, which was videotaped; unbelievable, but true.

From then on, Richie was attached to Alan because he saved his life and would investigate for Alan and help in whatever Alan needed. Of course, Alan paid him, but Richie did it because he loved Alan. The two became close friends from the day of acquittal.

I'll tell you one quick story about Alan and Richie. First let me mention that both Richie and Alan were exactly the same height, six-foot-one, and I believe about the same weight. Richie comes into the office, and he's dressed in jeans and a T-shirt. I had never seen Richie without a suit, shirt, and tie. He had an executive position at the hospital that he kept, even while working for Alan part-time, and that type of dress, I believe, was required. He was quite the dresser and always impeccably attired.

I said, "Richie, what's the deal? I never saw you without a suit." He said, "Alan is driving me crazy."

I asked, "What happened?"

He said, "They got this new tailor in Harlem an Italian guy named Guido. He makes these most incredible suits. I ordered five suits from him in different colors and waited almost three months for them. After I picked up the suits, I put them in my car and went to meet Alan before coming here for my appointment with you. Clarence was with me the whole time. I was wearing one of the suits I had just purchased."

Alan saw the suit and said to Richie, "That it is the most beautiful suit I've ever seen. Let me try on the jacket. I want to see how it looks on me." He tried on the jacket, and it fit him perfectly.

So, what happened? Richie had to give Alan all his five suits which, of course, Alan paid for, and said, "Richie, you can order another five."

In the meantime, Richie is complaining to me. I said, "Richie, why didn't you just tell him to fuck off? You're not giving him the suits."

He looks at me sheepishly and says, "You know I can't say no to the man."

Anyway, that's a little bit of Richie Branden. Because he was so close to Alan, I got to know Richie really well, and we became good friends. Richie once asked me if he could borrow my Rolls-Royce for his daughter's wedding. I loved Richie and said, "Sure."

He never borrowed it. He told me he wouldn't be able to enjoy his daughter's wedding because he would be worried about the car.

Alan only handled criminal cases while my office handled several different types of cases, including medical malpractice cases. Richie worked at Harlem Hospital, and the number of malpractices that occurred there were, I guess, the normal amount that occurred in any hospital; except that Richie found out about all the medical malpractice cases since he was well known, and people complained to him about being treated improperly. He asked me if I would be interested in handling any of the medical malpractice cases that came across his desk all the time, and I said, "Of course, if it would help people who were getting screwed over."

I wasn't being altogether altruistic. I realized the financial implications involved for me. I also realized that all of these cases would have to be contingency cases, which meant I would only get paid if I won the case, and it would mean a substantial outlay of time and money for me and my firm, but I genuinely liked helping people who got screwed over. And the fact that I could make a living from it sweetened the pie. For every case I accepted, I rejected five. It's incredible how willing people are to sue hospitals and doctors, lots of times unjustly. Still, I was overloaded with these cases, but fortunately, I had Herbie and lots of help.

This morning, Richie came in with a young man who would become a client of mine. Let me tell you, his story. His name was Clarence Willow. Before he came into my office for the interview, I had one of my lawyers who would most likely handle the case with Herbie come in as I wanted him to hear Mr. Willow's case firsthand. His name was Tom McDonald. He was an experienced trial lawyer who had been in the District Attorney's Office for several years, trying mostly murder cases, and then had gone into the special prosecutor's office, trying cases for them, when I found out about him through Ronnie.

I was in real need of an experienced trial lawyer, and he seemed to fit the bill. After trying felony murder cases, civil cases in my judgment were much easier to try because the rules of evidence weren't as strict, and the stakes weren't as high. In criminal cases, a man's life and liberty were involved which, of course, were much more important than money, which most civil cases were about. Of course, he would have to catch up on medical terminology and medical malpractice, but he was bright, really bright, and I knew he would be able to handle it. He was in his early thirties at the time—tall, thin, in good shape, with blond hair and blue eyes.

When Ronnie first told me about him, he thought he couldn't miss. He had a great personality, didn't take himself too seriously, wasn't a pompous ass as a lot of these trial lawyers tended to be, and would fit right in with the people in our office. I immediately found out where he was working in the special prosecutor's office, called, found out he was in that day, got in my car, and drove right to the office and told the secretary that I had an appointment with Tom.

I gave my last name, figuring he would know that I was Ronnie's brother and would see me. I introduced myself, and since I was Ronnie's twin brother, he was at ease with me. I told him about my firm and that I needed an experienced trial lawyer and asked him if he would mind telling me what he was making. He told me. I offered him a 30 percent increase immediately over what he was making and told him the type of practice I had. He already knew as Ronnie had spoken to him over the years about me and my practice. He accepted immediately.

Right away, I liked him. I like people who are decisive and can make quick decisions, especially as a trial lawyer. If you didn't have the ability to make quick decisions, you would be, in my judgment, at a disadvantage. He said, "I'll give my two weeks' notice today and will start in a couple of weeks. That was it. Fast-forward, Tom has been with me for over a year and has tried several cases and won them all."

Tom now settles in with me and Clarence and Richie, who were sitting in on our conference room. I ask Clarence to start from the beginning and tell me what happened. The story he related to us is as follows: I got up on a Tuesday morning two weeks ago and had a pain in my right side. I thought it would go away, but it didn't and basically started getting worse. By twelve o'clock, while I was at work, it got really bad, and so I went to the hospital.

In the emergency room, they examined me and told me that they had to do a scope or something and go through my mouth down into my stomach since they didn't think it was my appendix. I said, okay. I just wanted the pain to go away. They never asked me if I had a bridge or anything, I guess because I'm young, I'm only twenty-six years old.

Tom said, "Are you sure they didn't ask?"

He said, "Yes, I'm sure. I was so nervous I never even thought about it. I've had the bridge for over three years, and it has become part of my mouth. I don't even think about it, but yes, I'm sure they never asked.

"I was frightened and nervous. They said they would give me a sedative, and before you know it, I was out. When I woke up, my throat was bandaged. I could hardly speak. My throat was so sore and, in a whisper, I asked the nurse who was there when I woke up, 'What happened?'

"She said the doctor would be in and explain everything. In the meantime, my side still hurt, although not as much. The doctor came in and said that when they inserted the instrument down my throat to go into my stomach to look around, they accidentally loosened the bridge of teeth I have in my mouth and pushed it down my throat. When they realized what they had done, they couldn't extract the teeth from my throat and therefore opened up my throat to get the bridge out."

I asked, "Did they actually take the bridge out through your throat or did they cut your throat partially in order to remove it through your mouth?"

He said he didn't know.

I'm in shock. I asked once more, "Are you sure they didn't ask you if you had false teeth or a bridge?"

He said, "No, they didn't."

I said, "How are you feeling now?"

He had a turtleneck on and he said, "Okay."

I said, "Before we go any further, can I see your scar, please?"

He lowers his turtleneck, and there is an ugly scar about an inch and a half long, and it looks like it's not entirely closed, although he doesn't have a bandage on it.

Tom and I get up, and we are both examining the scar when he says, "The worst thing about it is, when I smoke, the smoke comes out my neck."

I said, "Clarence, what are you talking about?"

He says, "I'll show you." And he lights up a cigarette and inhales, and some smoke starts to come out of the scar. I know this is hard to believe, but I witnessed it. I am looking at him, not knowing whether to laugh or cry, but Tom, for some reason, finds this hysterical and starts laughing so hard he literally crawls out of the room so as not to embarrass himself further.

I don't know what to say. I'm looking at Clarence and Scott. Scott is laughing, and Clarence kind of smiles and says, "A lot of people I show it to start to laugh."

I said, "Why the hell are you smoking?"

He says, "Mr. A, I almost quit smoking. I only smoke maybe one or two cigarettes after dinner, I swear."

I said, trying to be serious, "This is no laughing matter, Clarence." I use all of my might not to break up. I said, "Clarence, you have to go back to the hospital to tell them."

And he said, "I'm not going back to that hospital. I'm going to another hospital later today."

I say, "Hold on one moment, Clarence, be right back."

And I go get Tom who has finally gotten control of himself. I said, "Tom, are you crazy? You can't do that in front of a client."

He says, "I know, Bobby. I'm really sorry. I'll apologize to the client." I said, "Okay, come back, but can you control yourself?"

He says, "Yeah, I'm okay now."

To make a long story short, we represented Clarence and got him quite a handsome award. They settled the case just before we picked a jury, and by the way, Clarence had his neck repaired properly by a plastic surgeon, and you could hardly see the scar. When he came to my office, I gave him a check which was substantial. He thanked me profusely and said he was going to buy a condo with some of the money. He gave me a hug, thanked me again, and then said,

"By the way, Mr. A, nobody can figure it out, but I still have that pain in my side."

I called Richie after he left and told him I had finally given Clarence the settlement money. He was very happy with it, and I just wanted to thank Richie again and invite him out to dinner. Richie was special.

I think the time now has come to conclude my story. As you can see, so far, I've been pretty lucky. I've made my share of mistakes and have been wrong lots of times. I had an Uncle Vincent who was very bright who I was once arguing with, and it got a little heated, and I finally said, "Uncle Vin, you're wrong, you're wrong."

He looked at me and said, "I've been wrong so many times, what's one more time?"

I never forgot that. Nobody gets it right all the time.

Every time I tell you about a client, a case, a friend, or an incident, I think of several others and could go on and on, and that's why I think I'll stop here. Maybe those additional thoughts and memories are for another time.

The End-For Now

About the Author

FRANK R ALIAZZO, ESQ. (BOBBY) grew up in Ozone Park, New York. He and his twin brother, Ron, attended John Adams High School but were asked to leave for frequent truancy. They were quickly sent by their parents to Mount Assumption High School in Plattsburgh, New York, a Catholic boarding school near the Canadian border. It was here that the twins finally learned new lessons as the Brothers of Mount Assumption instilled in them the values of hard work and discipline. These later years changed the trajectory of the twins' lives and contrasted with the values learned on the streets of New York. They went on to graduate from St. Michael's College in Winooski Park, Vermont, and New York Law School.

After law school, Bobby returned to Ozone Park to join his older brother, Vinnie, in his law practice while Ron joined the district attorney's office. Bobby grew his brother Vinnie's practice into one of the largest law practices in Queens County, and Ronnie became a homicide prosecutor in the Queens County District Attorney's Office. The twins' early Ozone Park childhood upbringing, combined with their later years at boarding school and law school, uniquely shaped their characters. More importantly, it also deeply affected their own unique sense of justice and the lengths one must sometimes resort to, to see it served.

Twinnie chronicles a range of Bobby's professional and personal experiences and escapades. The true-life stories and characters seen in each chapter capture the duality of Bobby's sometimes baffling upbringing and never fail to reflect and reinforce the proverbial saying, "You can take the kid out of Queens, but you can't take Queens out of the kid."

Milton Keynes UK
Ingram Content Group UK Ltd.
UKHW042113111124
451073UK00019B/382/J